# SpringerBriefs in Computer Science

More information about this series at http://www.springer.com/series/10028

Hui-Ming Wang · Tong-Xing Zheng

# Physical Layer Security in Random Cellular Networks

Springer

Hui-Ming Wang
Department of Information
and Communications Engineering
Xi'an Jiaotong University
Xi'an, Shaanxi
China

Tong-Xing Zheng
Department of Information
and Communications Engineering
Xi'an Jiaotong University
Xi'an, Shaanxi
China

ISSN 2191-5768 ISSN 2191-5776 (electronic)
SpringerBriefs in Computer Science
ISBN 978-981-10-1574-8 ISBN 978-981-10-1575-5 (eBook)
DOI 10.1007/978-981-10-1575-5

Library of Congress Control Number: 2016949607



Printed on acid-free paper

This Springer imprint is published by Springer Nature
The registered company is Springer Nature Singapore Pte Ltd.
The registered company address is: 152 Beach Road, #22-06/08 Gateway East, Singapore 189721, Singapore

*To our families and Xi'an Jiaotong University*

# Preface

The main objective of this book is to investigate the wireless physical layer security in random cellular networks. Security is a fundamental issue in data communications. In wireless communications, security becomes more challenging due to the openness of wireless medium and its inherent vulnerability to eavesdropping. Recently, physical layer security has become an emerging research front which provides promising confidentiality for wireless transmissions. The theoretical basis of physical layer security approaches is dated back to information theory, which takes full consideration of the characteristic of wireless channels. Compared to conventional cryptographic encryption and decryption technologies to guarantee secrecy, physical layer security approaches bypass the secret key generation and distribution issues, thereby resulting in significantly lower complexity and more savings in computational resources, which makes it very competitive in many wireless applications.

Although there already have been great advances in the topic of physical layer security, most of the researches focus on the point-to-point secrecy communications. In a wireless cellular network there are a large amount of concurrent transmissions between different base station-user pairs sharing a same frequency band, which causes ubiquitous interference in the whole network. The most significant difference in a wireless cellular network is that the transmission is highly interference-limited. Basically for any receiver, the signals for the other receivers are interferences. The aggregated interference can greatly influence the secrecy performance of a wireless link. There are significantly different levels of interference that will be caused due to different path loss, shadowing, and fading, and all these effects depend heavily on the spatial locations of the terminals. Therefore, the network geometry and spatial distribution of interferers become the primary factor to impact the secrecy performance of a wireless transmission.

In this book, we will focus on the networks under the framework of stochastic geometry, which is used to model the random distributions of legitimate users/eavesdroppers and the random deployment of base stations/access points. In the first two chapters, we introduce the basic ideas of physical layer security and primary knowledge of stochastic geometry theory, especially several useful properties of Poisson point process. In Chap. 3, we introduce the physical layer security in a single-cell cellular under time division multiple access (TDMA) when the eavesdroppers are randomly located as a Poisson point process. Moreover, in Chap. 4, we elaborate the network-wide physical layer security in a multi-tier heterogeneous network, where all the locations of users, eavesdroppers and deployment of base stations are modeled as Poisson point processes. Chapter 5 includes the impact of the full-duplex transceivers on security performance of random ad hoc network, which could be considered as a special case of uplink transmissions in a random cellular network. Lastly, Chap. 6 concludes the book and discusses the possible future research directions. This book will present the readers a timely report of state-of-the-art techniques about physical layer security under the framework of stochastic geometry, and provide an explicit snapshot of this emerging topic.

Xi'an, China
July 2016

Hui-Ming Wang
Tong-Xing Zheng

# Acknowledgments

The authors would like to express our sincere gratitude to Prof. Don Towsley at the University of Massachusetts Amherst and Prof. Jinhong Yuan at the University of New South Wales, for their contributions in the presented research works.

The authors would also like to thank Prof. Zhu Han at the University of Houston and Dr. Nan Yang at the Australian National University, for their constructive comments on the draft of the book.

We would like to acknowledge all our colleagues, students, and friends in Ministry of Education Key Laboratory for Intelligent Networks and Network Security, Xi'an Jiaotong University, who encouraged us and supported us during the writing of this book. The first author also would like to thank the National Natural Science Foundation of China under Grant No. 61671364 for the financial support to carry out the research on this topic.

# Contents

# Acronyms

| | |
|---|---|
| AES | Advanced encryption standard |
| AN | Artificial noise |
| AP | Access point |
| ARSP | Average received signal power |
| AWGN | Additive white Gaussian noise |
| BPP | Binomial point process |
| BS | Base station |
| CCDF | Complementary cumulative distribution function |
| CDF | Cumulate distribution function |
| CDI | Channel distribution information |
| CRN | Cognitive radio network |
| CSI | Channel state information |
| DMC | Discrete memoryless channel |
| DPTS | Dynamic parameter transmission scheme |
| FAP | Femto access point |
| FD | Full duplex |
| HCN | Heterogeneous cellular network |
| HCPP | Hard core point process |
| HD | Half duplex |
| ICSI | Instantaneous channel state information |
| MAC | Multiple access control |
| MIMO | Multiple-input multiple-output |
| MISO | Multiple-input single-output |
| MMSE | Minimum mean square error |
| MRC | Maximal ratio combining |
| PCP | Poisson cluster process |
| PDF | Probability density function |
| PGFL | Probability-generating functional |
| PP | Point process |
| PPP | Poisson point process |

| | |
|---|---|
| QoS | Quality of service |
| RSA | Rivest–Shamir–Adleman |
| SCSI | Statistical channel state information |
| SI | Self-interference |
| SIC | Successive interference cancellation |
| SIMO | Single-input multiple-output |
| SINR | Signal-to-interference-plus-noise ratio |
| SIR | Signal-to-interference ratio |
| SNR | Signal-to-noise ratio |
| SOP | Secrecy outage probability |
| SPTS | Static parameter transmission scheme |
| TDMA | Time division multiple access |
| UE | User equipment |
| ZF | Zero forcing |

# Notations

| | |
|---|---|
| $\mathbb{C}^d$ | $d$-dimensional field of complex numbers |
| $\mathbb{R}^d$ | $d$-dimensional field of real numbers |
| $\mathbb{R}^+$ | Positive field of real numbers |
| $\mathbb{N}$ | Set of natural numbers |
| $H(X)$ | Shannon entropy of discrete random variable $X$ |
| $H(X\|Y)$ | Conditional entropy of $X$ given $Y$ |
| $I(X;Y)$ | Mutual information between random variables $X$ and $Y$ |
| $\mathbb{P}\{A\}$ | Probability that event $A$ takes place |
| $\mathbb{E}_X$ | Expected value over random variable $X$ |
| $\mathbb{I}(A)$ | Indicator function, $\mathbb{I}(A) = 1$ when $A$ is true; otherwise, $\mathbb{I}(A) = 0$ |
| $\|\mathscr{W}\|$ | Cardinality of set $\mathscr{W}$ |
| $\log_n(\cdot)$ | Base-$n$ logarithm |
| $\ln(\cdot)$ | Natural logarithm |
| $[x]^+$ | Positive part of $x$, that is $[x]^+ = \max(x, 0)$ |
| $(\cdot)^{-1}$ | Inverse |
| $(\cdot)^{\dagger}$ | Conjugate |
| $(\cdot)^{\mathrm{T}}$ | Transpose |
| $(\cdot)^{\mathrm{H}}$ | Hermitian transpose |
| $\|\cdot\|$ | Absolute value |
| $\\|\cdot\\|$ | Euclidean norm |
| $CN(\mu, \sigma^2)$ | Complex Gaussian distribution with mean $\mu$ and variance $\sigma^2$ |
| $\mathrm{Exp}(\lambda)$ | Exponential distribution with rate parameter $\lambda$ |
| $\Gamma(\alpha, \beta)$ | Gamma distribution with shape parameter $\alpha$ and scale parameter $\beta$ |
| $f_X(\cdot)$ | Probability density function of random variable $X$ |
| $F_X(\cdot)$ | Cumulate distribution function of $X$ |
| $\bar{F}_X(\cdot)$ | Complementary cumulative distribution function of $X$ |
| $F_X^{-1}(\cdot)$ | Inverse function of $F_X(\cdot)$ |
| $\mathscr{B}(o, r)$ | A disk with center $o$ and radius $r$ |
| $\frac{d^m f(\cdot)}{dx^m}$ | $m$-order derivative of function $f(\cdot)$ on variable $x$ |

| | |
|---|---|
| $\frac{\partial f(\cdot)}{\partial x}$ | Partial derivative of function $f(\cdot)$ on variable $x$ |
| $f^{(m)}(x)$ | $m$-order derivative of function $f(x)$ on variable $x$ |
| $\mathscr{L}_I(s)$ | Laplace transform of variable $I$ at $s$, that is, $\mathscr{L}_I(s) = \mathbb{E}_I[e^{-sI}]$ |
| $\boldsymbol{h}$ | Column vector |
| $\boldsymbol{H}$ | Matrix |
| $Tr(\boldsymbol{H})$ | Trace of matrix $\boldsymbol{H}$ |
| $\det(\boldsymbol{H})$ | Determinant of matrix $\boldsymbol{H}$ |
| $C_{\alpha,N}$ | $C_{\alpha,N} \triangleq \frac{\pi\Gamma(N-1+2/\alpha)\Gamma(1-2/\alpha)}{\Gamma(N-1)}, \forall N \geq 2$ |
| $\mathrm{Ei}(-x)$ | $\mathrm{Ei}(-x) \triangleq -\int_x^{\infty} \frac{e^{-t}}{t} dt, \forall x > 0$ |

# Chapter 1
# Wireless Physical Layer Security

**Abstract** In this chapter, the context and the fundamental concepts of physical layer security are well introduced. It starts at Shannon's definition of information-theoretic security, Wyner's wiretap model, and secrecy conditions. Then the secrecy metrics are described, including secrecy capacity/rate, ergodic secrecy capacity/rate, secrecy outage, and secrecy throughput. At the end of this chapter, we provide a brief survey on the recent research advances on wireless physical layer security.

## 1.1 Information-Theoretic Security

Ensuring secrecy, or privacy, is a fundamental issue in any modern information systems. For a data communications system, how to achieve confidential information transmission, i.e., to guarantee the conveyed information not to be intercepted and eavesdropped by any adversary during the data transmission, is a critical task of information security. As the rapid development of today's wireless transmission technologies, various wireless communications systems emerge, such as 4G-LTE, WLAN, Bluetooth, Zigbee, etc. On the other hand, the wide popularization of smart phones and smart terminal equipments make wireless communications become an indispensable part of daily life. Multitudinous information and data have been conveyed through the electromagnetic wave to their destinations, including personal private information, financial data, business information, and even data relevant to national security, etc. These diversified applications greatly strengthen the criticality of the secrecy of wireless communications. However, due to the openness of the physical propagation channel and the broadcast nature of the radio transmission medium, protecting confidentiality of wireless communications is believed to be more challenging compared to its wireline counterpart. Any receiver located in the covered range of the transmitter can intercept the transmitted signal, putting the conveyed information under the risk of being decoded by the adversarial users.



H.-M. Wang and T.-X. Zheng, *Physical Layer Security in Random Cellular Networks*, SpringerBriefs in Computer Science,
DOI 10.1007/978-981-10-1575-5_1

### 1.1.1 Encryption

Traditionally, cryptographic encryption and decryption technologies are exploited to protect the confidentiality of information and data. They are usually deployed in the upper layers of the protocol stack of the layered networking architecture, such as network or application layer, to achieve information secrecy, which are irrespective to the physical layer transmission medium. The basic idea of cryptographic encryption is based on a secret key, which is shared secretly by both parties of a communication. The transmitter uses the secret key to encrypt source information, i.e., plaintext, to convert it into ciphertext. The intended receiver extracts the original plaintext from the ciphertext using a corresponding key. If the ciphertext is intercepted by an eavesdropper, it cannot be extracted without the corresponding decryption key.

Basically, there are two types of encryption algorithms: secret-key based and public-key based. In a secret-key encryption system, the transmitter and the intended receiver share a common secret key, while for a public key system, they hold different keys for encryption and decryption. A public key, which can be known by all the users, possibly an eavesdropper, is used for encryption at the transmitter. A private key is maintained at the intended receiver, with which the intended receiver can extract the information encrypted by the public key. For any eavesdropper who does not know the private key, it is almost computationally impossible (usually based on certain one-way functions that are hard to invert) to obtain the source information. These methods have been shown the efficient ones in many applications. For example, the combination of the state-of-the-art algorithms like Rivest-Shamir-Adleman (RSA) and the Advanced Encryption Standard (AES) is deemed secure for a large number of applications. However, applying cryptographic encryption technologies in wireless communications is still facing the following two challenges:

1. For the secret-key encryption systems, the secret key distribution and management is very vulnerable in wireless networks. Due to the open nature of the wireless medium, it is more convenient for any eavesdropper to wiretap the transmission of secret keys. Once the secret keys are revealed, the secret-key encryption system will be compromised. Furthermore, the lack of infrastructure in decentralized wireless networks and the dynamic topology of mobile wireless networks will both make the key distribution and management difficult and expensive.
2. On the other hand, the security of a public key system relies on the unproved conjecture that certain one-way functions are impossible to invert from a mathematical calculation point of view. However, as the computing power increases very fast today, the risk of being compromised by attacks such as brute-force searching is growing. Moreover, theoretically, it is difficult to precisely quantify and compare the strengths of different encryption algorithms. Lastly, although public key algorithms are simple in terms of key management, they require considerable computational resources, which is sometimes rigorous for mobile terminals.

### 1.1.2 Physical Layer Security

To continually address the challenges, a new approach achieving secure communication for wireless networking has attracted increasing attention recently, i.e., information-theoretic security. Different from the cryptographic encryption technologies, whose secrecy mechanism is from a mathematical calculation point of view, the theoretical basis of information-theoretic security is information theory.

As early in 1949, Claude Shannon proposed the idea of "Information-theoretic perfect secrecy" in the seminal paper "communication theory of secrecy systems" [1]. This concept initially provides the definition of information secrecy using the fundamental building block of information theory, i.e., entropy. Information-theoretic perfect secrecy is defined as follows: A transmitter sends a signal $X$ conveying some confidential message $W$ to its intended receiver, and an eavesdropper also receives a copy of the signal, then if the conditional entropy of the confidential message $W$ given the observation of the signal $X$ is equal to the original entropy of $W$, we call it perfect secrecy.

Based on Shannon's new definition of information-theoretic secrecy, Wyner in his seminal work [2] in 1975 established the so-called "degraded wiretap channel model" and demonstrated that confidential messages can be transmitted securely without using an encryption key. He proposed a new notion to measure the maximal capability of secret and reliable information transmission of a communication system, i.e., secrecy capacity, which characterizes the fundamental communication limit of a system under information-theoretic secrecy constraints. The idea was later generalized to nondegraded wiretap channel by Csiszar and Korner [3], and a more general expression of secrecy capacity was established. In [4], Cheong and Hellman studied the Gaussian degraded wiretap channel model and derived its secrecy capacity. These researches revealed a fundamental idea, that is, securely transmitting confidential messages to a legitimate receiver without using an encryption key is possible by utilizing the inherent randomness of the physical transmission medium, including noise and channel fading. Through signal design and secrecy coding, the difference between the physical channel to a legitimate receiver and the channel to an eavesdropper can be exploited to achieve information-theoretic security. Since both channels and signal design/secrecy coding are in the physical layer of a communication system, we also call it physical layer security.

Compared to cryptographic encryption and decryption technologies to guarantee secrecy, physical layer security approaches have the following prominent features:

1. The theoretical basis of physical layer security approaches is strictly based on information theory. These approaches achieve provable security regardless of the unlimited computational power the eavesdroppers may possess. Precise measurements can be performed about the information that is successfully transformed to the legitimate destination and leaked to the eavesdropper.
2. Physical layer security approaches take full consideration of the characteristic of wireless channels. Using the intrinsic randomness shared by legitimate terminals,

the information-theoretic security approaches are more robust to the man-in-the-middle attack.

3. Physical layer security approaches eliminate the key generation and distribution issues, thereby resulting in significantly lower complexity and savings in computational resources, which makes it very applicable in decentralized wireless networks that lacks of infrastructure support and mobile wireless networks with dynamic topologies.

One coin has its two sides. Similarly, we have to admit that physical layer security approaches also have some disadvantages. First, physical layer security approaches should take advantage of the communication channel difference between the legitimate receiver and the potential eavesdroppers, which relies on some prior information assumptions on their channels. These assumptions sometimes might not be accurate in practice, especially for that of the eavesdroppers. To guarantee security, we can only make very conservative assumptions about the channels, which is likely to result in low secrecy capacities.

Fortunately, physical layer security approaches fit to build a layered security hierarchy system, and provide an additional layer of security that can coexist with those already deployed security schemes in upper layers, such as cryptographic encryption and decryption technologies. All these means are able to work together, each with a specific goal in the system, to protect the confidentiality of wireless communications.

## 1.2 Fundamentals of Information-Theoretic Security

In this section we introduce the initiative ideas of physical layer security, including the new definition of the information-theoretic security and the basic models of secrecy transmission.

### *1.2.1 Shannon's Perfect Secrecy*

As mentioned in Sect. 1.1, the theoretical basis for physical layer security approach is the concept of *information-theoretic perfect secrecy*, which was first introduced in Shannon's seminal work in 1949 [1]. In Shannon's original model, a source message $W$ is first encoded to a codeword $X$ then sent from a transmitter (Alice) and a legitimate receiver (Bob). One eavesdropper (Eve) also has the access to $X$ and attempts to acquire the message $W$; see Fig. 1.1a. Messages and codewords are treated as random variables. The system is defined as *perfectly secure* if for the eavesdropper, the *a posteriori* probability of $W$ given $X$ is equal to the *a priori* probabilities of $W$ for all $X$, i.e.,

$$H(W|X) = H(W), \ or, \ I(W; X) = 0. \tag{1.1}$$

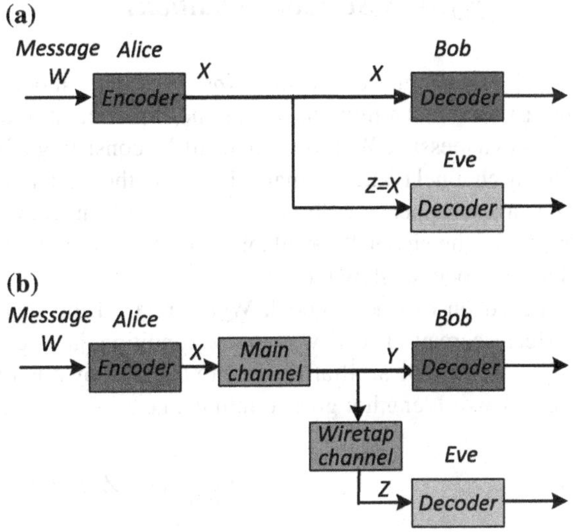


**Fig. 1.1** **a** Shannon's model of a secrecy system, and **b** Wyner's degraded wiretap channel model

$H(W|X)$ can be viewed as Eve's uncertainty about $W$ when he observed $X$, which is named *equivocation* by Shannon. Equation (1.1) means that the codeword $X$ is statistically independent of the message $W$, which implies that the eavesdropper cannot extract any new knowledge about $W$ even when it gets $X$, i.e., perfect secrecy is achieved. From this definition we can see that secrecy is in the sense of information theory and is irrespective of the computing power of Eve.

Shannon shows that perfect secrecy can be achieved through a so-called "one-time pad" approach, the basic idea of which is to generate a secret-key, independent of the message and uniformly distributed on the message alphabet $\mathscr{W}$. The secret-key is known to both Alice and Bob but unknown to Eve [1]. Alice encodes her message using the secret-key and Bob do the corresponding decoding. If at least one secret-key bit is generated for each message bit, there exists coding schemes that achieve perfect secrecy. In fact, a modulo-$|\mathscr{W}|$ addition operation between the message and secret-key is a possible coding scheme, and Bob can decode the message without error by taking a modulo-$|\mathscr{W}|$ subtraction operation between the secret-key and the received codeword, where $|\cdot|$ is the module operation. On the contrary, Eve gets nothing about $W$.

Obviously, this approach is very expensive to implement. A one-time pad requires to generate a new key bit for each message bit, which results in a great overhead. Second, secure communication becomes another secret-key distribution problem. Nevertheless, secrecy has been defined for the first time from a perspective of information theory, which is significantly distinguished to the computation-based security. Furthermore, secrecy is now quantified and can be measured and analyzed by using different algorithms.

### *1.2.2 Wyner's Secrecy Conditions*

In [2], Wyner introduced the *wiretap channel* model, where noises at both Bob and Eve are taken into consideration. In particular, the legitimate transmitter Alice encodes a message $W$ into a codeword $X^n$ consisting of $n$ symbols, which is sent over a noisy channel (called as main channel in the model) to the legitimate receiver Bob. The eavesdropper Eve observes a noisy version from the wiretap channel, denoted by $Z^n$, of the signal $Y^n$ available at Bob. This model is named "degraded" wiretap channel model as shown in Fig. 1.1b.

Based on this new model, Wyner relaxed the secrecy definition of Shannon's perfect secrecy. The new secrecy condition just requires the *equivocation rate* $\frac{1}{n}H(W|Z^n)$ to be arbitrarily close to the entropy rate of the message $\frac{1}{n}H(W)$ when the codeword length $n$ goes to infinity, i.e.,

$$\lim_{n\to\infty} \frac{1}{n} I(W; Z^n) = 0. \tag{1.2}$$

This is called the *weak* secrecy condition. Intuitively, this condition requires only the *rate* of information leaked to the eavesdropper to vanish for sufficiently large codeword length $n$. The definition can be further strengthened to the *strong* secrecy condition, which requires the amount of information leaked to the eavesdropper to vanish, i.e.,

$$\lim_{n\to\infty} I(W; Z^n) = 0. \tag{1.3}$$

Obviously, both the strong and weak secrecy conditions are relaxed to an asymptotic sense, compared to Shannon's perfect secrecy. Furthermore, the weak secrecy condition only requires that the increase of equivocation is sub-linear as the codeword length $n$ increases. It is possible to construct examples of coding schemes that satisfy the weak secrecy condition but fail to protect security. Therefore the weak secrecy condition sometimes is likely not appropriate. Fortunately, both strong and weak secrecy constraints result in the same secrecy capacity.

## 1.3 Secrecy Metrics

In this section we discuss the secrecy metrics to evaluate the level of secrecy in physical layer security.

### *1.3.1 Secrecy Capacity/Rate*

*Secrecy capacity* is the core metric in physical layer security to evaluate the efficiency of the secrecy transmission against eavesdropping. This concept was initiated by Wyner in his degraded wiretap channel model [2] and was generalized to broadcast

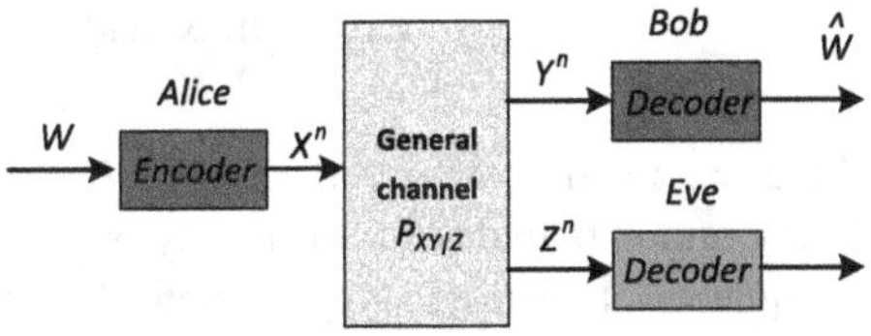


**Fig. 1.2** General DMC broadcast wiretap channel model

wiretap channel, not necessarily degraded, by Csiszár and Körner in [3]. Loosely speaking, secrecy capacity is the supremum of communication rates to the legitimate receiver at which reliability (decoding error goes to zero) and secrecy (weak/strong secrecy condition is satisfied) can be concurrently guaranteed, i.e., transmission with a rate below the secrecy capacity and appropriate secrecy coding can guarantee the reliability and the secrecy simultaneously, weak or strong secrecy condition holds. To be more precisely, we consider the general discrete memoryless channel (DMC) broadcast wiretap channel depicted in Fig. 1.2 and give the definition of secrecy capacity.

In Fig. 1.2, if a transmitter Alice wishes to send a confidential message $W$, which is randomly and uniformly distributed over a message set $\mathscr{W}$, to a legitimate receiver Bob, and an eavesdropper Eve want to intercept it. Before transmission, a encoder $f : \mathscr{W} \to \mathscr{X}^n$ maps each message $w \in \mathscr{W}$ to a codeword $x^n \in \mathscr{X}^n$ with length $n$. Then the codeword $x^n$ is transmitted over a DMC with transition probability $P_{YZ|X}(\cdot|\cdot)$, and both Bob and Eve observe the output $y^n \in \mathscr{Y}^n$ and $z^n \in \mathscr{Z}^n$, respectively. Bob uses a decoder $g : \mathscr{Y}^n \to \mathscr{W}$ to map the received $y^n$ to an estimate $\hat{w} \in \mathscr{W}$ of the transmitted message $w$. If there exists a sequence of message sets $\mathscr{W}_n, n = 1, 2, \ldots$ with $|\mathscr{W}_n| = 2^{nR}$ and encoder–decoder pairs $\{f_n, g_n\}_n$ such that the following *reliability* and *security* conditions holds, i.e.,

- Reliability: the average block probability of error for a length $n$ code approaches zero as $n$ goes to infinity, i.e.,

$$P_e^{(n)} = \mathbb{P}\left\{\hat{W} \neq W\right\} = \frac{1}{|\mathscr{W}_n|}\sum_{w=1}^{|\mathscr{W}_n|} \mathbb{P}\{\hat{w} \neq w\} \to 0. \tag{1.4}$$

- Security: the weak (strong) secrecy condition holds, or, equivalently, the equivocation rate $R_e^{(n)} = \frac{1}{n}H(W|Z^n)$ satisfies

$$\lim_{n\to\infty} \inf R_e^{(n)} \geq R, \ (\textit{weak secrecy}) \tag{1.5}$$
$$\lim_{n\to\infty} n \inf R_e^{(n)} \geq nR. \ (\textit{strong secrecy}) \tag{1.6}$$

Then, we say that a *secrecy rate* $R$ is achievable. We further defined the *secrecy capacity*, $C_s$, as the largest secrecy rate that is achievable satisfying both the reliability and security conditions, simultaneously.

With these definitions, Csiszár and Körner reported that the secrecy capacity of the DMC broadcast wiretap channel can be precisely expressed as [3]

$$C_s = \max_{P_{UX} P_{YZ|X}} \{I(U;Y) - I(U;Z)\}, \tag{1.7}$$

where the auxiliary random variable $U$ satisfies the Markov chain: $U \to X \to (Y, Z)$, and is bounded in cardinality by $|\mathcal{U}| \leq |\mathcal{X}| + 1$, respectively.

Equation (1.7) provides a complete characterization of secrecy capacity, where the auxiliary random variable $U$ is related to the additional randomization in the encoder. Unfortunately, the application and optimization of this general secrecy capacity is very difficult because there is no systematic method to optimize over the introduced auxiliary variable. To this end, some simpler forms have been investigated for some special classes of channels. And Wyner's degraded wiretap channel is of a special case.

If the channel transition distribution function satisfies $P_{YZ|X}(\cdot|\cdot) = P_{Y|X}(\cdot|\cdot) P_{Z|Y}(\cdot|\cdot)$, i.e., $X$ and $Z$ are conditionally independent given $Y$, or in other words, $X$, $Y$ and $Z$ form a Markov chain $X \to Y \to Z$, the channel is physically degraded wiretap channel, which was just investigated in Wyner's seminal work [2]. It is shown by Wyner that if the wiretap channel is degraded, the secrecy capacity is mathematically expressed as

$$C_s = \max_{p(X)} \{I(X;Y) - I(X;Z)\}. \tag{1.8}$$

We can see that in this case, the auxiliary random variable $U$ disappears. This expression provides more intuitions about the secrecy transmission at the physical layer.

1. Secrecy capacity is the supremum of rate (mutual information) difference to Bob and to Eve, optimizing over the input probability distribution $p(X)$. If we want a positive secrecy capacity, the rate from Alice to Bob should be larger than the rate from Alice to Eve, which implies the legitimate channel (from Alice to Bob) should be more "advantage" than the wiretap channel (from Alice to Eve). Otherwise, the secrecy capacity is zero and the secrecy communication is impossible. Therefore, physical layer channel qualities play a critical role in secrecy communications. This is the fundamental stand point of the physical layer security approaches.
2. Secrecy capacity can be achieved with stochastic encoding schemes. Since Bob has better channel than Eve, he can resolve the information rate up to $I(X;Y)$ while Eve could only obtain rate $I(X;Z)$, the rest of which is kept secret to Eve.
3. To reach the secrecy capacity we have to solve an optimization problem. However, since both $I(X;Y)$ and $I(X;Z)$ are convex functions over $p(X)$, the difference of two convex functions is generally not convex, which makes the problem hard to solve.

A special example of the degraded wiretap channel with *closed form* secrecy capacity is the additive white Gaussian noise (AWGN) degraded wiretap channel, where both the legitimate and wiretap channels are AWGN channels with noise covariances $\sigma_B^2$ and $\sigma_E^2$, respectively. Due to the degraded condition, we have $\sigma_B^2 < \sigma_E^2$. The secrecy capacity can be exactly expressed as

$$C_s^{Deg\text{-}AWGN} = C_B - C_E = \frac{1}{2}\log_2\left(1+\frac{P}{\sigma_B^2}\right) - \frac{1}{2}\log_2\left(1+\frac{P}{\sigma_E^2}\right), \tag{1.9}$$

where $C_B$ and $C_E$ are the capacities of the legitimate and wiretap channels, respectively, and $P$ is the signal power. This capacity is achieved when signal $X$ obeys Gaussian distribution. In fact, a general AWGN wiretap channel, not necessarily degraded, has the secrecy capacity

$$C_s^{AWGN} = [C_B - C_E]^+. \tag{1.10}$$

It is more clear that a positive secrecy capacity is only achievable when the legitimate channel has a better signal-to-noise ratio (SNR) than that of the eavesdropper.

Secrecy capacity is usually obtained by solving a non-convex optimization problem given in Eq. (1.8) over all possible distributions $p(X)$. To evaluate the secrecy more conveniently and computationally affordable, sometimes we simply use the Gaussian signal for $X$ and evaluate the *achievable secrecy rate*, which is defined as

$$R_s = [R_B - R_E]^+, \tag{1.11}$$

where $R_B$ and $R_E$ are the achievable rates to Bob and Eve with Gaussian codebook. Then we can maximize it via signal design and optimization. Obviously, this maximized achievable secrecy rate is a lower bound of the secrecy capacity, i.e., $\max R_s \leq C_s$. However, due to its computational convenience, a vast of works have taken this secrecy rate as the performance metric.

### 1.3.2 Ergodic Secrecy Capacity/Rate

Secrecy capacity/rate is defined for fixed channels, ignoring the *fading* of the wireless medium. To analyze the time-varying feature of the wireless channels, one of the metrics to evaluate the average secrecy transmission capability is the *ergodic secrecy capacity/rate*. Under many delay-tolerant applications, secrecy messages can be coded across a sufficiently large number of varying channel states, so ergodic secrecy capacity/rate reflects the average secrecy rate over the wireless fading channels [5].

Considering a single-input single-output (SISO) fading channel wiretapped by a single antenna eavesdropper corrupted by AWGN, the received signals at Bob and Eve are

$$y_B = h_B x + n_B,$$
$$y_E = h_E x + n_E,$$

where $h_B$ and $h_E$ are channel coefficients, and $n_B$ and $n_E$ are AWGNs with covariances $\sigma_B^2$ and $\sigma_E^2$. The ergodic secrecy capacity has two different definitions, depending on how much channel state information (CSI) the transmitter has [5].

1. The full CSI case. The transmitter has the access to both the instantaneous channel coefficients $h_B$ of the legitimate receiver and $h_E$ of the eavesdropper. In this case, Gaussian signal can achieve the ergodic secrecy capacity, which is

$$R_s^{Full-CSI} = \max_{\mathbb{E}(P(h_B,h_E))\leq P} \mathbb{E}\left[C_B - C_E\right]^+, \tag{1.12}$$

   where $C_B(h_B, h_E) = \log_2(1 + \gamma_B(h_B, h_E))$, and $C_E(h_B, h_E) = \log_2(1 + \gamma_E(h_B, h_E))$ are the channel capacities of the legitimate channel and wiretap channel with SNRs $\gamma_B(h_B, h_E) = \frac{|h_B|^2 P(h_B,h_E)}{\sigma_B^2}$, and $\gamma_E(h_B, h_E) = \frac{|h_E|^2 P(h_B,h_E))}{\sigma_E^2}$, respectively; $f(h_B)$ and $f(h_E)$ are the probability density functions (PDFs) of $h_B$ and $h_E$, respectively. The maximization is performed by optimizing the transmit power allocation according to both the instantaneous CSIs of the legitimate receiver and eavesdropper, under the average power constraint $\mathbb{E}\left(P(h_B, h_E)\right) \leq P$. We can see that the ergodic secrecy capacity is achieved by performing adaptive rate and power optimizations according to the instantaneous CSIs.
2. The legitimate CSI case. Only the instantaneous CSI of the legitimate receiver and the channel distribution information (CDI) of the eavesdropper are known at the transmitter. In this case, the ergodic secrecy capacity is

$$R_s^{Legi\text{-}CSI} = \max_{\mathbb{E}(P(h_B))\leq P} \mathbb{E}\left[C_B - C_E\right]^+, \tag{1.13}$$

   where $C_B(h_B) = \log_2(1 + \gamma_B(h_B))$, $C_E(h_B) = \log_2(1 + \gamma_E(h_B))$, $\gamma_B(h_B) = \frac{|h_B|^2 P(h_B)}{\sigma_B^2}$, and $\gamma_E(h_B) = \frac{|h_E|^2 P(h_B)}{\sigma_E^2}$, respectively. Compared with the full CSI case Eq. (1.12), case Eq. (1.13) has a similar form, but the power adaption could only be done according to the legitimate CSI,

An important observation on Eqs. (1.12) and (1.13) is that a positive ergodic secrecy rate can be achieved even when the wiretap channel is, on average, better than the legitimate channel. Intuitively, this is achieved by opportunistically exploiting those channels when the legitimate receiver experiences a better channel states than those of the wiretap channels.

For a general fading channel, the optimal transmission scheme achieving secrecy capacity is very difficult to obtain, since usually we have to handle a non-convex optimization problem. Therefore, *achievable ergodic secrecy rate* is usually used to evaluate the secrecy performance. With Gaussian codebook, a frequently used achievable ergodic secrecy rate is defined as

$$R_s = \left[\mathbb{E}(R_B) - \mathbb{E}(R_E)\right]^+, \tag{1.14}$$

where $\mathbb{E}(R_B)$ and $\mathbb{E}(R_E)$ are now ergodic rates of the legitimate and wiretap channels, respectively. This achievable ergodic secrecy rate is strictly smaller than the secrecy capacity. Nevertheless, in most cases it is more computationally efficient, which is usually taken as the optimization objective function, being a lower bound of the ergodic secrecy capacity.

### 1.3.3 Secrecy Outage/Throughput

When the channel undergoes quasi-static fading, encoding over multiple channel states may not be acceptable for delay-limited applications. In this case, one should consider the secrecy outage probability (SOP) or outage secrecy capacity as the performance measure [6, 7].

With the instantaneous CSI of Bob and the only CDI of Eve, a secrecy outage happens when the instantaneous secrecy capacity $C_s$ is less than a target secrecy rate $R_s$. The physical interpretation is as follows: when Alice transmits the secrecy information with a constant rate $R_s$, as long as $R_s < C_s$, wiretap channel is worse than the Alice's estimation, and secrecy can be guaranteed. Once $R_s > C_s$, the secrecy rate is too high to reach by the current channel state and the information security is compromised. The secrecy outage probability is defined as $\mathscr{P}_{so}(R_s) = \mathbb{P}\{C_s < R_s\}$. Therefore, without the instantaneous CSI of Eve, perfect secrecy can only be guaranteed by a probability $1 - \mathscr{P}_{so}$ under the quasi-static fading.

Since in many applications Alice may have the instantaneous CSI of legitimate channel via training, feedback, etc., in fact she may not have to fix her secrecy rate $R_s$. Obviously, when the legitimate channel is too poor to support a reliable transmission under rate $R_s$, i.e., $C_B < R_s$, she would certainly reduce $R_s$ to avoid such an outage [8]. Therefore, $R_s$ can be adjusted adaptively to maintain a required SOP according to the instantaneous CSI of legitimate channel, instead of transmitting with a fixed rate. In this case, *secrecy throughput* should be adopted to evaluate the average secrecy rate, which is defined as the average achievable secrecy rate over all channel realizations, subjected to a required SOP. Secrecy throughput has been taken as the optimization objective function for signal design under a certain acceptable SOP constraint in slow fading channels.

All of the above secrecy metrics would be possibly adopted to evaluate the secrecy level of the physical layer transmission in different scenarios/applications. Roughly speaking, how large the secrecy metric is depends heavily on the superiority of the legitimate channel to the wiretap channel. However, this superiority cannot be always guaranteed in wireless propagation environment. Fortunately, although the physical channels can not be controlled, by appropriate signal design and optimization, we can construct *equivalent channels*, which guarantees or enhances such superiority of the equivalent legitimate channel to the equivalent wiretap channel. Along with this line, various physical layer secrecy transmission schemes have been developed, which will be detailed in Sect. 1.4.

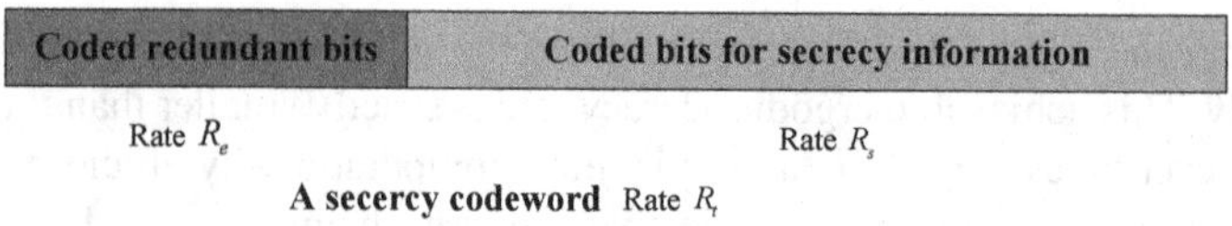


**Fig. 1.3** A Wyner's wiretap codeword

### *1.3.4 Wyner's Wiretap Code*

To achieve secrecy transmission, secrecy coding should be applied to encode the secrecy information bits. Instead of investigating any special kind of secrecy coding scheme, in this book we adopt the Wyner's wiretap encoding scheme [2]. A synopsis of the state-of-the-art secrecy encoding approaches can be found in [9].

Two rates in a Wyner's encoding scheme should be designed, namely, the rate of transmitted codewords $R_t$ and the rate of embedded secrecy information bits $R_s$. Redundant information is intentionally introduced to provide secrecy against eavesdropping, the rate of which is called the rate redundancy $R_e \triangleq R_t - R_s$, as depicted in Fig. 1.3. We can see that to protect the secrecy message, additional randomization should be added at the transmitter end to confuse eavesdropper. In the following chapters, we will see that optimizing these two rates $R_t$ and $R_s$ (or $R_e$) plays an important role in a secrecy transmission.

## 1.4 Existing Techniques in Physical Layer Security

In this section, we provide a brief survey of recent research advances on physical layer security.

### *1.4.1 MIMO*

Multiple-input multiple-output (MIMO) technique is a promising approach to greatly improve the secrecy capacity/secrecy rate. Due to the extra spatial degrees of freedom provided by multiple antennas, MIMO provides great possibilities to construct a better equivalent legitimate channel [10].

The secrecy capacity of an MIMO wiretap channel has been extensively investigated in [11–16], where an MIMO communication is wiretapped by an eavesdropper with multiple antennas. Under the constraint of the transmitter's sum power, it is proved that Gaussian signaling can achieve the secrecy capacity of an MIMO wiretap channel, which is expressed as

$$C_s^{MIMO} = \max_{\boldsymbol{K_X} \succ \boldsymbol{0}, Tr(\boldsymbol{K_X}) \leq P} \left[ \log_2 \det \left( \boldsymbol{I} + \boldsymbol{H_B K_X H_B^H} \right) - \log_2 \det \left( \boldsymbol{I} + \boldsymbol{H_E K_X H_E^H} \right) \right]^+, \tag{1.15}$$

where $\boldsymbol{H_B}$ and $\boldsymbol{H_E}$ are the MIMO legitimate channel and wiretap channel matrices, respectively, and $\boldsymbol{K_X}$ is the covariance matrix of the transmit signal under the constraint of the sum power $P$. We can see, again, to obtain the secrecy capacity requires to solve a non-convex optimization problem given in Eq. (1.15), which is very complicated [11, 12]. In the high SNR regime, it has been shown in [12] that a transmission scheme based on the generalized singular value decomposition of the legitimate and wiretap channel matrices can achieve the secrecy capacity, which has a closed-form expression, and the optimal power allocation of this scheme has been addressed in [13]. In [14], the authors have derived some rank properties of the optimal solution. In [15, 16], numerical optimization algorithms have been proposed to find a Karush–Kuhn–Tucker solution and the global optimal solution, respectively.

As a special case, multiple-input single-output (MISO) wiretap channel, where an MISO communication is wiretapped by a multiple-antenna eavesdropper, is proved to have a closed-form expression of secrecy capacity as [17]

$$C_s = \left( \log_2 \lambda_{\max} \left( \boldsymbol{I} + P \boldsymbol{h_B h_B^H}, \boldsymbol{I} + P \boldsymbol{H_E H_E^H} \right) \right)^+, \tag{1.16}$$

where $\lambda_{\max}(\boldsymbol{A}, \boldsymbol{B})$ is the maximum generalized eigenvalue of matrices pair $(\boldsymbol{A}, \boldsymbol{B})$. The capacity is achieved via beamforming along the direction of the generalized eigenvector corresponding to the maximum generalized eigenvalue $\lambda_{\max}(\boldsymbol{A}, \boldsymbol{B})$.

When considering the fading of wireless channels, the ergodic secrecy capacity/rate of MISO wiretap channel has been investigated in [18–20]. In [18], ergodic secrecy capacity has been derived when the transmitter only has the CDIs of both legitimate receiver and eavesdropper. In [19, 20], some achievable ergodic secrecy rates of Rayleigh and Rician MISO wiretap channels have been provided. On the other hand, SOP has also been investigated. For example, in [21], secrecy outage performance of an MISO wiretap channel, where the transmitter has the instantaneous legitimate CSI but the partial CSI of the eavesdropper, has been comprehensively investigated. When there are multiple eavesdroppers, the authors of [22] have optimized the outage secrecy rate with the only partial CSI of the eavesdropper.

When eavesdropper' CSI is totally unavailable, neither the secrecy capacity/rate nor the optimal signal design is known. In this case, a so-called *artificial noise* (AN) scheme is proposed in [23, 24], where no-information-bearing interference signal is transmitted along with confidential information signal to confuse the potential eavesdropper. The AN signal should be carefully designed such that the intended user will not be degraded. Interestingly, it is shown in [17] that the AN scheme in MISO wiretap channel is asymptotically near-optimal in the high SNR regime in the sense that even without the eavesdropper's CSI, the achievable secrecy rate of this scheme only has a *fixed* loss compared to the secrecy capacity when eavesdropper's CSI is available.

Since the application of AN scheme does not require eavesdroppers's CSI, it has been extensively investigated [25–31]. In [25, 26], the optimal AN design and power allocation for maximizing the ergodic secrecy rate and secrecy throughput for multiple antenna transmission have been proposed for fast fading and slow fading channels, respectively. In [27], the target is to minimize the SOP. Very recently, the scheme has been generalized to co-located MIMO system in [29, 30] and distributed multiple antenna system in [31].

### *1.4.2 Node Cooperation*

Node cooperation, which is originally proposed to provide diversity gain to combat fading for single antenna wireless communications system, has become another effective technique to enhance physical layer security. In this scheme, one/multiple cooperative nodes help the source (legitimate transmitter) to deliver confidential signals to the destination (legitimate receiver) against one/multiple eavesdroppers. In [32, 33], information-theoretically strict deviations have shown that cooperative helpers provide great potential to secure wireless transmissions, which has triggered significant research interest on this topic [34–52].

Roughly speaking, cooperation is able to improve the quality of the legitimate channel and/or degrade that of the wiretap channel, so as to establish and enhance the superiority of the equivalent legitimate channel to the equivalent wiretap channel, and to enhance the secrecy. Good surveys on physical layer security assisted by node cooperation can be found in [34, 35]. Generally, the roles of the cooperative nodes securing the legitimate transmissions can be divided into two categories: *cooperative relaying* and *cooperative jamming* [36].

Cooperative relaying is a scheme where cooperative nodes help the source to relay the confidential signals to the destination. Generally, multiple relay nodes employ amplify-and-forward (AF) or decode-and-forward (DF) [41] protocol to forward the confidential information in a collaborative manner. One of the cooperative relaying techniques is cooperative beamforming, where forward signals will be designed to superimpose constructive at the destination and destructively or even be null out at the eavesdroppers [37–40]. Another popular scheme is the relay selection technique, which is to just select a single relay out of a bunch of relay nodes to forward the confidential signal [42–44]. It sacrifices the secrecy performance to a lower complexity compared with the cooperative beamforming scheme.

Alternatively, the cooperative nodes can also transmit jamming signals collaboratively to prevent any efficient interception of eavesdroppers when source is transmitting. The jamming signal is in fact AN conveying no confidential information, thus this scheme can be considered as a distributed version of AN scheme in MIMO transmissions. By careful designing, cooperative jamming will effectively interfere with the potential eavesdroppers to harm their interception ability. Similarly, there are also two kinds of cooperative jamming schemes, i.e., coordinated jamming and jammer selection. In coordinated jamming, jamming signals should be designed coordinately to focus on the wiretap channels while bypass the legitimate channels [45–47]. Jammer selection is a low complexity alternative to coordinated jamming, where only one node is selected as jammer [48].

Relaying is to improve the quality of the main channel, and jamming is to degrade that of the wiretap channel, both of which will enhance the secrecy metrics mentioned above. Furthermore, some joint/hybrid relaying–jamming schemes have been proposed, which combine both advantages of the relaying and jamming strategies to enhance the secrecy capacity further. Specially, multiple cooperative nodes are divided into two groups: relay group and jammer group. The nodes in the relay group help to relay the signals while those in the jammer group adopt cooperative jamming to confuse the eavesdropper. In [48, 49], joint relay and jammer selection have been studied. In [50–52], hybrid cooperative beamforming and cooperative jamming schemes have been proposed to secure both one-way and two-way networks, respectively.

### *1.4.3 Full-Duplex Transceiver*

Full-duplex (FD) transceiver technology is a new research trend in wireless communications. An FD transceiver is able to transmit and receive signals simultaneously in the same frequency band, which will roughly double the bandwidth efficiency. A big challenge to realize FD transceiver is to efficiently eliminate the so called self-interference caused by the power leakage from the transmit channel to the receive channel during their simultaneously working. Recently, great progress has been achieved on in-band self-interference cancelation, e.g., self-interference being efficiently mitigated in the analog circuit domain [53], digital circuit domain [54], and spatial domain [55], respectively, thus making an FD transceiver able to work effectively [56].

When the transmitter only has a single antenna and meanwhile there is no friendly jammer, information transfer is vulnerable to eavesdropping. Fortunately, FD transceiver technology shows great possibilities to enhance the physical layer security. More degrees of freedom can be gained to protect information delivery by using a powerful FD receiver, e.g., radiating jamming signals to degrade eavesdroppers while receiving desired signals *simultaneously*. In particular, when the FD receiver is equipped with multiple antennas, it provides us with potential benefits not only in alleviating self-interference but also in designing jamming signals.

The idea of using FD receiver jamming to improve physical layer security has already been reported by [57–62] for point-to-point transmission scenarios. Specifically, the authors of [57, 58] have considered a single-input multiple-output (SIMO) channel and suggested the receiver using single and multiple antenna jamming, respectively. The authors of [59] have considered an MIMO channel and suggested both the transmitter and the receiver generating artificial noise. These works are further extended in two-way transmissions [60] and cooperative communications

[61, 62]. Recently, the authors of [63, 64] have studied the design of secrecy beamforming for an FD base station in a cellular network. All these endeavors are shown to gain a remarkable secrecy rate enhancement.

## 1.5 Summary

In this chapter, we introduce the fundamental ideas of physical layer security, including the basic model of the secrecy transmission and three secrecy performance metrics. We also provide a brief survey of recent advances in this field. A more thorough reference work in the fundamental theory of physical layer security can be found in [65–67].

## References


1. C.E. Shannon, Communication theory of secrecy systems. Bell Syst. Tech. J. **28**, 656–715 (1949)
2. A.D. Wyner, The wire-tap channel. Bell Syst. Tech. J. **54**(8), 1355–1387 (1975)
3. I. Csiszár, J. Körner, Broadcast channels with confidential messages. IEEE Trans. Inf. Theory **24**(3), 339–348 (1978)
4. S.L.Y. Cheong, M. Hellman, The Gaussian wire-tap channel. IEEE Trans. Inf. Theory **24**(4), 451–456 (1978)
5. P. Gopala, L. Lai, H. El Gamal, On the secrecy capacity of fading channels. IEEE Trans. Inf. Theory **54**(10), 4687–4698 (2008)
6. J. Barros, M.R.D. Rodrigues, Secrecy capacity of wireless channels, in *Proceedings of IEEE International Symposium on Information Theory, Seattle, WA* (2006)
7. M. Bloch, J. Barros, M.R.D. Rodrigues, S. McLaughlin, Wireless information-theoretic security. IEEE Trans. Inf. Theory **54**(6), 2515–2534 (2008)
8. X. Zhou, M.R. McKay, B. Maham, A. Hjørungnes, Rethinking the secrecy outage formulation: a secure transmission design perspective. IEEE Commun. Lett. **15**(3), 302–304 (2011)
9. W.K. Harrison, J. Almeida, M.R. Bloch, S.W. McLaughlin, J. Barros, Coding for secrecy: an overview of error-control coding techniques for physical-layer security. IEEE Signal Process Mag. **30**(5), 41–50 (2013)
10. Y.-W.P. Hong, P.-C. Lan, C.-C.J. Kuo, Enhancing physical layer secrecy in multiantenna wireless systems: an overview of signal processing approaches. IEEE Signal Process. Mag. **30**(5), 29–40 (2013)
11. F. Oggier, B. Hassibi, The secrecy capacity of the MIMO wiretap channel, in *Proceedings of IEEE International Symposium on Information Theory, Toronto, ON, Canada* (2008), pp. 524–528
12. A. Khisti, G.W. Wornell, Secure transmission with multiple antennas—Part II: the MIMOME wiretap channel. IEEE Trans. Inf. Theory **56**(11), 5515–5532 (2010)
13. S.A.A. Fakoorian, A.L. Swindlehurst, Optimal power allocation for GSVD-based beamforming in the MIMO Gaussian wiretap channel, in *Proceedings of International Symposium on Information Theory, Cambridge, MA* (2012)
14. S.A.A. Fakoorian, A.L. Swindlehurst, Full rank solutions for the MIMO Gaussian wiretap channel with an average power constraint. IEEE Trans. Signal Process. **61**(10), 2620–2631 (2013)

15. Q. Li, M. Hong, H.-T. Wai, Y.-F. Liu, W.-K. Ma, Z.-Q. Luo, Transmit solutions for MIMO wiretap channels using alternting optimizaiton. IEEE. J. Sel. Area Commun. **31**(9), 1714–1726 (2013)
16. S. Loyka, C.D. Charalambous, An algorithm for global maximization of secrecy rates in Gaussian MIMO wiretap channels. IEEE Trans. Commun. **63**(6), 2288–2299 (2015)
17. A. Khisti, G. Wornell, Secure transmission with multiple antennas I: The MISOME wiretap channel. IEEE Trans. Inf. Theory **56**(7), 3088–3104 (2010)
18. S.-C. Lin, P.-H. Lin, On secrecy capacity of fast fading multiple input wiretap channels with statistical CSIT. IEEE Trans. Inf. Forensics Secur. **8**(2), 414–419 (2013)
19. J. Li, A.P. Petropulu, On ergodic secrecy rate for Gaussian MISO wiretap channels. IEEE Trans. Wirel. Commun. **10**(4), 1176–1187 (2011)
20. J. Li, A.P. Petropulu, Ergodic secrecy rate for multiple-antenna wiretap channels with Rician fading. IEEE Trans. Inf. Forensics Secur. **6**(3), 861–867 (2011)
21. S. Gerbracht, C. Scheunert, E.A. Jorswieck, Secrecy outage in MISO systems with partial channel information. IEEE Trans. Inf. Forensics Secur. **7**(2), 704–716 (2012)
22. Q. Li, W.-K. Ma, A.M.-C. So, A safe approximation approach to secrecy outage design for MIMO wiretap channels. IEEE Signal Process. Lett. **21**(1), 118–121 (2014)
23. R. Negi, S. Goel, Secret communication using artificial noise, in *Proceedings of IEEE Vehicular Technology Conference, Dallas* vol 3 (2005), pp. 1906–1910
24. S. Goel, R. Negi, Guaranteeing secrecy using artificial noise. IEEE Trans. Wirel. Commun. **7**(6), 2180–2189 (2008)
25. X. Zhou, M.R. McKay, Secure transmission with artificial noise over fading channels: achievable rate and optimal power allocation. IEEE Trans. Veh. Technol. **59**(8), 3831–3842 (2010)
26. X. Zhang, X. Zhou, M.R. McKay, On the design of artificial-noise-aided secure multi-antenna transmission in slow fading channels. IEEE Trans. Veh. Technol. **62**(5), 2170–2181 (2013)
27. J. Xiong, K.-K. Wong, D. Ma, J. Wei, A closed-form power allocation for minimizing secrecy outage probability for MISO wiretap channels via masked beamforming. IEEE Commum. Lett. **16**(9), 1496–1499 (2012)
28. H.-M. Wang, T. Zheng, X.-G. Xia, Secure MISO wiretap channels with multi-antenna passive eavesdropper: artificial noise vs. artificial fast fading. IEEE Trans. Wirel. Commun. **14**(1), 94–106 (2015)
29. S.-H. Tsai, H.V. Poor, Power allocation for artificial-noise secure MIMO precoding systems. IEEE Trans. Signal Process. **62**(13), 3479–3493 (2014)
30. H.-M. Wang, C. Wang, D.W.K. Ng, Artificial noise assisted secure transmission under training and feedback. IEEE Trans. Signal Process. **63**(23), 6285–6298 (2015)
31. H.-M. Wang, C. Wang, D.W.K. Ng, M.H. Lee, J. Xiao, Artificial noise assisted secure transmission for distributed antenna systems. IEEE Trans. Signal Process. **64**(15), 4050–4064 (2016)
32. E. Tekin, A. Yener, The general Gaussian multiple access and two-way wire-tap channels: achievable rates and cooperative jamming. IEEE Trans. Inf. Theory **54**(6), 2735–2751 (2008)
33. L. Lai, H.E. Gamal, The relay-eavesdropper channel: cooperation for secrecy. IEEE Trans. Inf. Theory **54**(9), 4005–4019 (2008)
34. R. Bassily, E. Ekrem, X. He, E. Tekin, J. Xie, M.R. Bloch, S. Ulukus, A. Yener, Cooperative security at the physical layer: a summary of recent advances. IEEE Signal Process. Mag. **30**(5), 16–28 (2013)
35. H.-M. Wang, X.-G. Xia, Enhancing wireless secrecy via cooperation: signal design and optimization. IEEE Commun. Mag. **53**(12), 47–53 (2015)
36. H. Deng, H.-M. Wang, W. Guo, W. Wang, Secrecy transmission with a helper: to relay or to jam. IEEE Trans. Inf. Forensics Secur. **10**(2), 293–307 (2015)
37. L. Dong, Z. Han, A.P. Petropulu, H.V. Poor, Improving wireless physical layer security via cooperating relays. IEEE Trans. Signal Process. **58**(3), 1875–1888 (2010)
38. J. Li, A. Petropulu, S. Weber, On cooperative relaying schemes for wireless physical layer security. IEEE Trans. Signal Process. **59**(10), 4985–4997 (2011)
39. Z. Ding, K.K. Leung, D.L. Goeckel, D. Towsley, On the application of cooperative transmission to secrecy communications. IEEE J. Sel. Areas Commun. **30**(2), 359–368 (2012)

40. H.-M. Wang, Q. Yin, X.-G. Xia, Distributed beamforming for physical-layer security of two-way relay networks. IEEE Trans. Signal Process. **60**(7), 3532–3545 (2012)
41. T.-X. Zheng, H.-M. Wang, F. Liu, M.H. Lee, Outage constrained secrecy throughput maximization for DF relay networks. IEEE Trans. Commun. **63**(5), 1741–1755 (2015)
42. I. Krikidis, Opportunistic relay selection for cooperative networks with secrecy constraints. IET. Commun. **4**(15), 1787–1791 (2010)
43. Y. Zou, X. Wang, W. Shen, Optimal relay selection for physical-layer security in cooperative wireless networks. IEEE J. Sel. Areas Commun. **31**(10), 2099–2111 (2013)
44. V.N.Q. Bao, N.L. Trung, M. Debbah, Relay selection schemes for dual-hop networks under security constraints with multiple eavesdroppers. IEEE Trans. Wireless Commun. **12**(12), 6076–6085 (2013)
45. G. Zheng, L.-C. Choo, K.-K. Wong, Optimal cooperative jamming to enhance physical layer security using relays. IEEE Trans. Signal Process. **59**(3), 1317–1322 (2011)
46. J. Huang, A.L. Swindlehurst, Cooperative jamming for secure communications in MIMO relay networks. IEEE Trans. Signal Process. **59**(10), 4871–4885 (2011)
47. C. Wang, H.-M. Wang, Robust joint beamforming and jamming for secure AF networks: low complexity design. IEEE Trans. Veh. Technol. **64**(5), 2192–2198 (2015)
48. I. Krikidis, J. Thompson, S. Mclaughlin, Relay selection for secure cooperative networks with jamming. IEEE Trans. Wireless Commun. **8**(10), 5003–5011 (2009)
49. J.C. Chen, R.Q. Zhang, L.Y. Song, Z. Han, B.L. Jiao, Joint relay and jammer selection for secure two-way relay networks. IEEE Trans. Inf. Forensics Secur. **7**(1), 310–320 (2012)
50. H.-M. Wang, M. Luo, X.-G. Xia, Q. Yin, Joint cooperative beamforming and jamming to secure AF relay systems with individual power constraint and no eavesdropper's ICSI. IEEE Signal Process. Lett. **20**(1), 39–42 (2013)
51. H.-M. Wang, M. Luo, Q. Yin, Hybrid cooperative beamforming and jamming for physical-layer security of two-way relay networks. IEEE Trans. Inf. Forensics Secur. **8**(12), 2007–2020 (2013)
52. C. Wang, H.-M. Wang, X.-G. Xia, Hybrid opportunistic relaying and jamming with power allocation for secure cooperative networks. IEEE Trans. Wireless Commun. **14**(2), 589–605 (2015)
53. M. Duarte, C. Dick, A. Sabharwal, Experiment-driven characterization of full-duplex wireless systems. IEEE Trans. Wirel. Commun. **11**(12), 4296–4307 (2012)
54. D.W.K. Ng, E.S. Lo, R. Schober, Dynamic resource allocation in MIMO-OFDMA systems with full-duplex and hybrid relaying. IEEE Trans. Commun. **60**(5), 1291–1304 (2012)
55. T. Riihonen, S. Werner, R. Wichman, Mitigation of loopback selfinterference in full-duplex MIMO relays. IEEE Trans. Signal Process. **59**(12), 5983–5993 (2011)
56. A. Sabharwal et al., In-band full-duplex wireless: Challenges and opportunities. IEEE J. Sel. Areas Commun. **32**(9), 1637–1652 (2014)
57. W. Li, M. Ghogho, B. Chen, C. Xiong, Secure communication via sending artificial noise by the receiver: Outage secrecy capacity/region analysis. IEEE Commun. Lett. **16**(10), 1628–1631 (2012)
58. G. Zheng, I. Krikidis, J. Li, A. Petropulu, B. Ottersten, Improving physical tier secrecy using full-duplex jamming receivers. IEEE Trans. Signal Process. **61**(20), 4962–4974 (2013)
59. Y. Zhou, Z. Xiang, Y. Zhu, Z. Xue, Application of full-duplex wireless technique into secure MIMO communication: achievable secrecy rate based optimization. IEEE Signal Process. Lett. **21**(7), 804–808 (2014)
60. Ö. Cepheli, S. Tedik, G.K. Kurt, A high data rate wireless communication system with improved secrecy: full duplex beamforming. IEEE Commun. Lett. **18**(6), 1075–1078 (2014)
61. G. Chen, Y. Gong, P. Xiao, J.A. Chambers, Physical layer network security in the full-duplex relay system. IEEE Trans. Inf. Forensics Secur. **10**(3), 574–583 (2015)
62. S. Parsaeefard, T. Le-Ngoc, Improving wireless secrecy rate via full-duplex relay-assisted protocols. IEEE Trans. Inf. Forensics Secur. **10**(10), 2095–2107 (2015)
63. F. Zhu, F. Gao, M. Yao, H. Zou, Joint information- and jamming-beamforming for physical layer security With full duplex base station. IEEE Trans. Signal Process. **62**(24), 6391–6401 (2014)

64. F. Zhu, F. Gao, T. Zhang, K. Sun, M. Yao, Physical-layer security for full duplex communications with self-interference mitigation. IEEE Trans. Wirel. Commun. **15**(1), 329–340 (2016)
65. A. Mukherjee, S. Fakoorian, J. Huang, A. Swindlehurst, Principles of physical layer security in multiuser wireless networks: a survey. IEEE Commun. Surv. Tutor. **16**(3), 1550–1573 (2014)
66. Y. Liang, H. Poor, S. Shamai, Information theoretic security. Found. Trends Commun. Inf. Theory **5**(4–5), 355–580 (2009)
67. M. Bloch, J. Barros, *Physical Layer Security: From Information Theory to Security Engineering* (Cambridge Univ. Press, New York, 2011)

# Chapter 2
# Random Cellular Networks and Stochastic Geometry

**Abstract** In this chapter, we discuss the physical layer security in stochastic geometric networks. We first present the randomness of cellular networks deployment, and summarize the challenges to solve the physical layer security issue. We then introduce some primary knowledge of stochastic geometry theory, especially some useful properties of Poisson point process, which will be extensively used in the following chapters. It is concluded that various random wireless networks can be modeled and analyzed using the framework of stochastic geometry. Moreover, we introduce the network security performance metrics to evaluate the physical layer security. Finally, we provide a brief survey of recent researches on physical layer security in wireless networks, and introduce three open problems in this field which we are going to deal with in the following chapters.

## 2.1 Deployment of Cellular Networks

With the rapidly increasing demand of big traffic and high data rate, emerging wireless networks, such as heterogeneous cellular networks (HCNs), cognitive radio networks (CRNs), wireless ad hoc networks, etc., have drawn significant research interests in both academia and industry over the last decade. To protect the confidentiality of the data and information transmitted through wireless links in these networks, physical layer security approach is a very competitive solution due to its low complexity and flexibility.

In Chap. 1 we have reviewed some techniques for enhancing the physical layer security of wireless transmissions. We note that all those techniques are initially developed for a *point-to-point* communication system, i.e., there is only one source destination pair under consideration. However, a wireless communication network can be viewed as a collection of transceivers located in an area, For example, a cellular network consists of a mass of base stations (BSs) and mobile user equipments (UEs) distributed in a city. Compared with a point-to-point communication system, the most significant difference in a wireless cellular network is that the transmission is highly *interference-limited*. In a cellular network, there are a large amount of concurrent transmissions between different BS-UE pairs sharing a same frequency band, which



H.-M. Wang and T.-X. Zheng, *Physical Layer Security in Random Cellular Networks*, SpringerBriefs in Computer Science,
DOI 10.1007/978-981-10-1575-5_2

causes ubiquitous interference in the whole network. For any receiver, the signals intended for the other receivers are treated as interferences.

The aggregated interference will result in a great impact on the secrecy performance of a wireless link. As can be seen from the fact that secrecy performance depends heavily on the achievable rates at the legitimate destination and the potential eavesdroppers in Chap. 1, the ubiquitous interference will bring in two effects. On the one hand, the legitimate link rate $R_B$ will be reduced. On the other hand, the leakage rate $R_E$ will be degraded as well since any potential eavesdroppers also receive interferences. Therefore, the secrecy performance, which is a function of $R_B - R_E$, should be carefully reevaluated.

In a wireless channel, all path loss, shadowing, and fading will bring impairments to the received signal strength, and all these effects depend heavily on the spatial locations of the terminals. In a wireless cellular network, concurrent transmissions located at different spatial positions cause significantly different levels of interference strength to the same receiver. It is not uncommon for the signal-to-interference-plus-noise ratios (SINRs) to vary over different receivers by up to a hundred dBs due to differences in path loss, shadowing and fading. Since all these effects depend heavily on the spatial locations of the terminals, the network geometry and spatial distribution of interferers become the primary factors in determining a receiver's SINR and hence the achievable rate. Therefore, it is eagerly needed to develop a tractable tool to model the network geometry and analyze the secrecy performance.

### *2.1.1 Modeling and Analyzing Random Cellular Networks*

Traditionally, a tractable cellular deployment model commonly used by information theorists is the Wyner model [1, 2], which is typically one-dimensional. This model assumes a unit gain from each BS to the active user and an equal gain that is less than one to the two users in the two neighboring cells. This is obviously an overly simple and highly inaccurate model unless there is a very large amount of interference averaging over space, which greatly limits its application. On the other hand, a more realistic two-dimensional network of BS is usually modeled on a regular hexagonal lattice, or slightly more simply, a square lattice [3, 4]. However, tractable expressions for the SINR are unavailable in general for a random user location in the cell. More general results that provide guidance into typical SINR or the probability of outage/coverage over the entire cell only can be obtained by complex time-consuming Monte Carlo simulations.

It is also important to realize that although widely accepted, grid-based models are themselves highly idealized and may be increasingly inaccurate for the heterogeneous and ad hoc deployments common in urban and suburban areas, where cell size varies considerably due to differences in transmission power, tower height, and user density. Nowadays, a common characteristic of these wireless networks is the random network topology, for example, a femtocell access point (AP) in an HCN may access and quit dynamically; nodes in an ad hoc network are randomly distributed and are connected with each other in a self-organizing manner; a cognitive user may opportunistically access the idle channel in a CRN; and so on.

The randomness of cellular network geometric topology has brought the following two fundamental challenges to network modeling and secrecy performance analysis.

- *How to model network geometry?* Secrecy performance of a wireless transmission in a cellular network is closely related to network geometry. As we know, information exchange between arbitrary transmitter and receiver depends heavily on the spatial positions of themselves and of other interfering nodes in the network, and also the interplay between them. The increase of transmit power at an arbitrary transmitter will in turn introduce greater interference to those undesired receivers. In addition, cellular networks are more and more heterogeneous and the node distribution are becoming more and more irregular, with the node density differing significantly for different areas. Thus, neither the position-independent Wyner model [1, 2] nor the regular lattice model can be used to describe today's cellular networks. Network designers are crying out for a network model that is tailored to characterize node distribution accurately and meanwhile is tractable.
- *How to analyze the randomness?* The number of uncertainties in a cellular network has far exceeded that in a point-to-point scenario: not only the received power is random because of the randomness inherent to wireless channels and the mobility of the desired user, but also the interference power is governed by a series of stochastic processes including nodes' spatial distribution, shadowing, and fading. It is impossible for a node to know or to forecast the spatial positions and the channel knowledge related to all the other nodes. In other words, transmitter is not able to configure transmission parameters for a concrete space realization. In order to efficiently assess or predict network performance, a sound stochastic process is required to capture the randomness of the cellular network, including both the positions of BSs and UEs, just as a fading distribution is used for modeling a variety of possible propagation environments.

### *2.1.2 Stochastic Geometry Approach*

Fortunately, stochastic geometry has provided a new opportunity to deal with the aforementioned challenges. Using powerful tools from stochastic geometry, the randomness of a cellular network can be conveniently modeled with a sufficient accuracy, and we are able to study the average behavior of a wireless cellular network over many spatial realizations by modeling network nodes according to some probability distribution [5]. During recent years, stochastic geometry has also inspired a large number of researchers to perform security performance analysis and network parameter optimization for random cellular networks. In the following sections, we provide a brief introduction of some fundamentals of stochastic geometry. A more thorough reference work can be found in [6].

## 2.2 Fundamentals of Stochastic Geometry

Stochastic geometry is a rich branch of applied probability which is used to study random phenomena on the plane or in higher dimensions [6]. It has been widely applied in the areas of biology, astronomy and material sciences, etc. Nowadays, its application has also infiltrated into image analysis and communication networks.

### 2.2.1 Point Process

Stochastic geometry is intrinsically related to the theory of stochastic point process (PP) [6]. PP is the most basic research object studied in stochastic geometry. Here we just provide a basic introduction. A more rigorous definition can be found in [6].

Simply speaking, a PP $\Phi \triangleq \{x_i, i \in \mathbb{N}\}$ is a random collection of points residing a measure space $E$, e.g., for wireless networks, $E$ is the $d$-dimensional Euclidean space $\mathbb{R}^d$. $\Phi$ can be interpreted in terms of the so called *random set formalism*, where $\Phi = \{x_i\} \subset \mathbb{R}^d$ is a *countable* random set with each element $x_i$ being a random variable. A more convenient way to describe the PP is to count the number of points falling in any Borel set $A \subset \mathbb{R}^d$, i.e.,

$$\Phi(A) = \sum_{x_i \in \Phi} \mathbb{I}(x_i \in A). \tag{2.1}$$

Note that, $\Phi(A)$ is a random variable whose distribution depends on $\Phi$.

So far, there are four categories of PPs that have been widely studied to model the wireless network, namely, Poisson PP (PPP), binomial PP (BPP), Poisson cluster process (PCP) and Matérn hard core PP (HCPP). The strict definitions of these PPs can be found in [7]. Figure 2.1 depicts PPP, PCP and HCPP, respectively. PPP provides the baseline model (i.e., parent PP) for the other PPs, or, PPP can be converted into the other PPs [8]. Specifically,

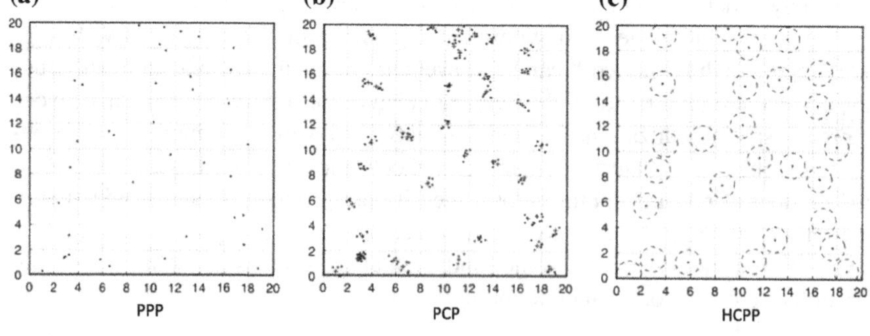


**Fig. 2.1** Three typical PPs

(1) A PPP is used to abstract a network in which a possibly infinite number of nodes randomly and independently coexist in a finite or infinite region, e.g., users in a cellular network and nodes in a wireless ad hoc network;

(2) When given the number of nodes in a finite region, a PPP becomes a BPP;

(3) When nodes are clustered according to the Multiple Access Control (MAC) protocol, a PPP evolves into a PCP, e.g., users gathered around Wi-Fi hot spots;

(4) Due to geographical constrains, network planning, or MAC protocols, a minimum distance is required to separate any two nodes, then a PPP transforms into a repulsive PP, i.e., Matérn HCPP.

Among these four categories of PPs, PPP has provided a convenient mathematical framework for random wireless network. For the self-organized ad hoc network, closed-form expressions of performance metrics like the SINR and outage probability can be easily obtained. Using PPP we can also derive tight bound results for performance metrics in those infrastructure-based networks (e.g., cellular networks) and coordinated spectrum access networks (e.g., CRNs). Thanks to these advantages, PPP has become the most popular, tractable, and important PP.

### 2.2.2 *Poisson Point Process*

This subsection introduces the PPP basic and PPP's key properties.

#### 2.2.2.1 Definitions

In the following, we define the PPP and the homogeneous PPP.

**Definition 2.1** (*PPP*) A PP $\Phi \triangleq \{x_i\} \in \mathbb{R}^d$ is a PPP if and only if

- For an arbitrary set $A \in \mathbb{R}^d$, $\Phi(A)$ is a Poisson random variable;
- For any two disjoint subsets $A_i$, $A_j \in \mathbb{R}^d$, $\Phi(A_i)$ and $\Phi(A_j)$ are independent.

**Definition 2.2** (*Homogeneous PPP*) If the intensity measure $\Lambda$[1] of a PPP $\Phi$ satisfies $\Lambda(A) = \lambda|A|$, i.e., the product of a constant value $\lambda$ and Lebesgue measure $|A|$,[2] then $\Phi$ is a homogeneous PPP with intensity $\lambda$.

Homogeneous PPP is a simple, isotropy, and stationary PP. By simple, we mean there are no two points at the same location; by isotropy and stationary, we mean that the law of a PP is invariant by rotation and translation, respectively [5]. Using homogeneous PPP will greatly simplify the mathematical analysis, which helps to reveal explicitly the influence of network parameters on network performance. Unless otherwise specified, the PPP in the following refers solely to the homogeneous one on a two-dimensional plane $\mathbb{R}^2$.

---

[1] For any Borel set $A$, its intensity measure $\Lambda$ is defined by $\Lambda(A) = \mathbb{E}[\Phi(A)]$.

[2] $|A|$ denotes the area of $A$ for a plane, and denotes the volume of $A$ for a three-dimensional space.

#### 2.2.2.2 Key Properties on PPP

Six properties are presented in the following. Knowledge regarding detailed derivations can be found in [7, 9].

**Property 2.1** *For a PPP $\Phi \subset \mathbb{R}^2$ and an arbitrary finite region $A$, $\Phi(A)$ is a Poisson random variable with mean $\lambda|A|$, i.e.,*

$$\mathbb{P}\{\Phi(A) = n\} = e^{-\lambda|A|}\frac{(\lambda|A|)^n}{n!}. \tag{2.2}$$

**Property 2.2** *For a PPP $\Phi \subset \mathbb{R}^2$ and conditionally on the fact that $\Phi(A) = n$, these $n$ points are independently and uniformly distributed in $A$, i.e., forming a BPP in $A$.*

From Property 2.2, we are able to obtain two very useful formulas, namely, Campbell's formula and probability generating functional (PGFL), respectively.

**Lemma 2.1** (Campbell's formula) *For a PPP $\Phi$ with density $\lambda$ and an arbitrary real function $f(x) : \mathbb{R}^2 \to \mathbb{R}^+$, we have*

$$\mathbb{E}_\Phi\left[\sum_{x\in\Phi} f(x)\right] = \lambda \int_{\mathbb{R}^2} f(x)dx. \tag{2.3}$$

Campbell's formula simplifies the calculation of the mean and variance of the aggregate interference power in a network.

*Example 2.1* Consider a PPP $\Phi \subset \mathbb{R}^2$with density $\lambda$, the aggregate interference power of the node at location $y \in \mathbb{R}^2$ is given by $I(y) = \sum_{x\in\Phi} \ell(x-y)$, where $\ell(x-y)$ denotes the path loss function from $x$ to $y$. The mean and variance of $I(y)$, i.e., $\mathbb{E}[I(y)]$ and $\mathbb{V}[I(y)]$ can be computed by using the Campbell's formula, given below

$$\mathbb{E}[I(y)] = \lambda \int_{\mathbb{R}^2} \ell(x)dx, \qquad \mathbb{V}[I(y)] = \lambda \int_{\mathbb{R}^2} \ell(x)^2 dx. \tag{2.4}$$

**Lemma 2.2** (PGFL) *For a PPP $\Phi \subset \mathbb{R}^2$ with density $\lambda$ and an arbitrary real function $f(x) : \mathbb{R}^2 \to [0, 1]$*

$$\mathbb{E}_\Phi\left[\prod_{x\in\Phi} f(x)\right] = \exp\left(-\lambda \int_{\mathbb{R}^2} (1 - f(x))\,dx\right). \tag{2.5}$$

An important application of PGFL is the Laplace transform of interference $I(y)$.

*Example 2.2* (Laplace transform) Recalling the aggregate interference power $I(y) = \sum_{x\in\Phi} \ell(x-y)$ given in Example 2.1, the Laplace transform of $I(y)$ is given by

$$\mathcal{L}_{I(y)}(s) = \mathbb{E}_{\Phi}\left[e^{-sI(y)}\right] = \exp\left(-\lambda \int_{\mathbb{R}^2} \left(1 - e^{-s\ell(x)}\right) dx\right). \tag{2.6}$$

If we execute operations, including superposition, thinning and displacement on a PPP, we can obtain the following invariant laws.

**Property 2.3** (Superposition) *The superposition of multiple independent PPP with density $\lambda_k$ is still a PPP with new density $\sum_k \lambda_k$.*

Property 2.3 can be used to analyze the interference in a network consisting of multiple independent tiers. For example, the aggregate interference power of a random user in a $K$-tier heterogeneous cellular network can be expressed as $I = \sum_{k=1}^{K} \sum_{x \in \Phi_k} \ell_k(x)$, where $\Phi_k$ models the locations of the interfering BSs in the $k$th tier with density $\lambda_k$, then the Laplace transform of $I$ can be calculated as

$$\mathcal{L}_I(s) = \prod_{k=1}^{K} \mathbb{E}_{\Phi_k}\left[e^{-s\sum_{x \in \Phi_k} \ell_k(x)}\right] = \exp\left(-\sum_{k=1}^{K} \lambda_k \int_{\mathbb{R}^2} \left(1 - e^{-s\ell_k(x)}\right) dx\right). \tag{2.7}$$

**Property 2.4** (Thinning) *The thinning of a PPP of density $\lambda$ with retention probability $p$ is still a PPP of new density $p\lambda$.*

Property 2.4 can be used to analyze the performance of a network in which the interfering nodes opportunistically transmit at a certain activation probability. For example, each BS in a cellular network of density $\lambda$ is activated at a probability $p$, then the aggregate interference power of a random user can by given by $I = \sum_{x \in \Phi_A} \ell(x)$, where $\Phi_A$ denotes the set of the locations of those active BSs. Accordingly, the Laplace transform of $I$ can be calculated as

$$\mathcal{L}_I(s) = \mathbb{E}_{\Phi}\left[e^{-s\sum_{x \in \Phi_A} \ell(x)}\right] = \exp\left(-p\lambda \int_{\mathbb{R}^2} \left(1 - e^{-s\ell(x)}\right) dx\right). \tag{2.8}$$

**Property 2.5** (Displacement) *The displacement of a PPP of density $\lambda$ by a Markov kernel $\rho(x, y)$ from $x$ to $y$ is still a of density $\lambda$.*

Property 2.5 can be used to model mobile wireless networks. For example, consider a mobile ad hoc network where the locations of nodes in the current time slot are modeled as a PPP $\Phi \triangleq \{x_i\} \subset \mathbb{R}^2$ of density $\lambda$, if each node moves from $x_i$ to a new location $y_i$ independently in the next time slot, then the new locations set $\Phi^\circ \triangleq \{y_i\}$ is still a PPP of density $\lambda$.

**Property 2.6** (Slivnyak theorem) *Consider a PPP $\Phi$ with a point $\delta_x$ located at $x$, if we remove $\delta_x$ from $\Phi$, the distribution of the reduced PPP $\Phi - \delta_x$ is the same as that of the original PPP $\Phi$.*

Slivnyak theorem implies that the addition or removal of a user in a network does not change the distribution of the other users, hence we can always place the user of interest at the origin in coordinates as a typical user to analyze user performance in aspects like outage probability and end-user throughput.

## 2.3 Using Stochastic Geometry to Model Wireless Networks

PPP is recognized as the most random stationary process friendly presenting a wireless network with nodes randomly distributed or with substantial mobility. In addition, using PPP to model the positions of network nodes simplifies the analysis, which facilitates the investigation of the relationships between network performance and network parameters.

Based on whether there is public infrastructure or not, wireless networks can be divided into two classes, namely, infrastructure-based networks (e.g., cellular networks) and infrastructureless networks (e.g., ad hoc networks and CRNs). PPP has been widely applied in both classes. In the following, we concentrate on cellular networks and wireless ad hoc networks, and the application of PPP in CRNs can be found in [10–13].

### *2.3.1 Cellular Networks*

A cellular network is an infrastructure-based network possessing fixed BSs or APs as well as explicit MAC protocols. Traditionally, cellular network is characterized by using a regular hexagonal grid model, in which each BS covers a hexagonal cell. The biggest weakness of such a model is that it makes modeling and analyzing intercell interference extremely sophisticated. Moreover, demands of transmission capacity in downtown, uptown and rural areas, etc., differ a great deal, and therefore traditional grid planning can no longer capture the deployment of BSs nowadays. During the past few years, due to the built-out urban areas, BSs are deployed in an increasingly irregular and random way. These contribute to modeling the locations of BSs using tools from stochastic geometry.

Considering that no service provider will deploy its two BSs arbitrarily close to each other in a real cellular network, using a repulsive PP such as the Matérn HCPP to model a cellular network topology is more practical [14]. However, an HCPP-based cellular network suffers a great loss of analytical tractability and the Matérn HCPP itself is flawed, i.e., the nonexistence of the PGFL [15]. By contrast, PPP is much more appealing given the simplicity and tractability. In a PPP-base cellular network, each mobile user is associated with the nearest BS, thus forming a Poisson Voronoi diagram, just as shown in Fig. 2.2. Assuming the locations of BSs are completely uncorrelated seems a bit unrealistic, but Andrews et al. [16] has figured out that the PPP yields a tight lower bound on the coverage probability provided by an actually deployed cellular network as well as an approximation on the upper bound mean transmission rate provided by the idealized grid-based model. Such validations can be further found in [14, 17].

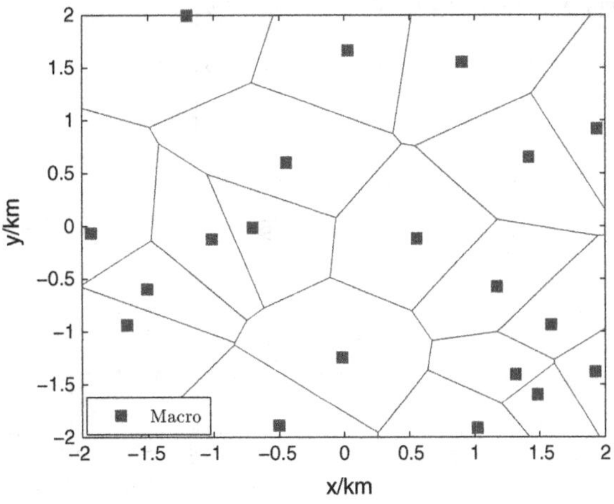


**Fig. 2.2** Single-tier cellular network

## 2.3.2 *Heterogeneous Cellular Networks*

Traditional single-tier macrocellular network has been incapable of meeting a 1000× average data rate increase in 5G networks [18], and the deployment of HCNs is an irreversible trend in future wireless networks. An HCN is generally formed by overlay a variety of low-power infrastructure on an existing macrocellular network. Figure 2.3 depicts a three-tier HCN with picocells and femtocells coexisting with macrocells. These pico/femto BSs are often low-end and in large numbers and demand-based. For example, femtocell BSs can either be installed by individuals and enterprises to enlarge household and office coverage, or be planned by network operators to increase capacity for airports, stadiums and other areas of dense demand [19]. In addition, femto APs support "plug-and-play," i.e., accessing and quitting the network may happen at any minute, and the division of service areas is much more irregular compared with conventional macrocellular networks. All these make it reasonable to use PPP to characterize the deployment of picocells and femtocells APs. In [20–22], the authors have investigated the spectrum allocation, access control and interference avoidance for both downlink and uplink communications in a two-tier HCN, where the locations of macrocell BSs are modeled as hexagonal grid and the locations of femtocell BS and of users are modeled as independent PPPs. It is shown in [23] that, even modeling all tiers of an HCN including the macrocell tier as independent PPPs, the distribution of the SINR of a typical user greatly approximates that provided by a grid-based macrocell tier case.

#### 2.3.2.1 Femto Access Control

Based on the PPP HCN, femto access control including closed access [24] and open access [23] have been discussed in [25, 26]. In closed access, femto access points

Fig. 2.3 Three-tier HCN

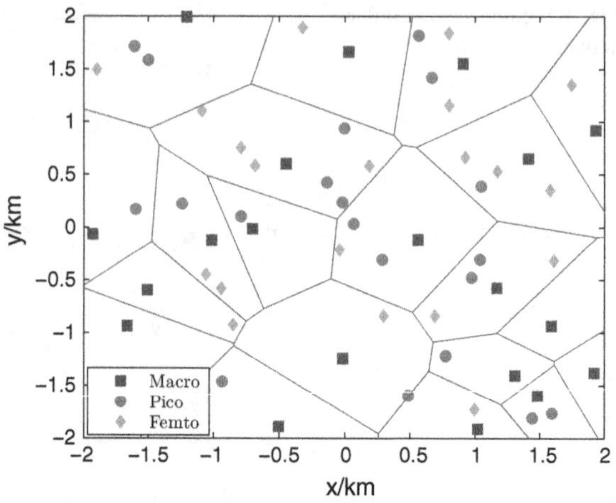


(FAPs) provide service to only specified subscribers to monopolize their own femtocell and its backhaul to ensure privacy and security; whereas in open access, arbitrary nearby users can use the femtocell. Xia et al. [26] have pointed that, compared with closed access, open access is preferred by network operators not only because it expends network capacity in an inexpensive way by leveraging third-party backhaul for free, but also because it greatly reduces cross-tier interference by allowing macrocell user to access femtocell nearby. Under different access strategies, the issues of load balancing [27, 28], coverage probability [24, 29], throughput [30, 31], etc., have been investigated.

#### 2.3.2.2 Mobile Association Policy

Mobile association, or, cell selection, is one of the core issues in designing an HCN. There are two general classes of mobile association policies: (1) average received power based (long-term results), where each mobile user connects to the BS providing the largest average received power [23, 27, 29], (2) instantaneous received power or SINR based, where each user connects to the BS providing the largest instantaneous received power or SINR [24, 28]. It is shown in [23] that, network designers prefer the average power based policy, with which the "ping-pong" effect, i.e., the unnecessary information exchange caused by shadowing and fading, can be avoided. Under such a mobile association policy, users do not connect to the nearest BSs any more due to the differences in transmit power of different tier of BSs, and thus the tessellation corresponds to a weighted Voronoi diagram instead of a standard Voronoi diagram formed in the conventional single-tier cellular network.

Figure 2.4 depicts the mobile association policy in an HCN consisting of a macrocell tier and a picocell tier. Specifically, Fig. 2.4a shows, a user connects to a macro BS instead of a much nearer pico BS since the latter provides a lower average received power for this user. Figure 2.4b shows, although the macro-BS has a high transmit

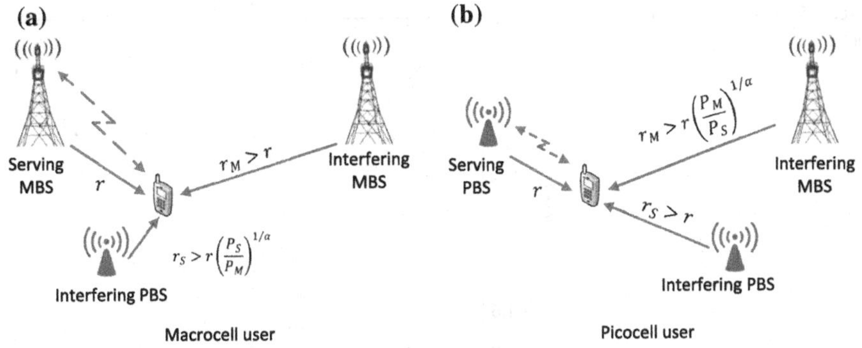


**Fig. 2.4** Mobile association policy in a two-tier macro/pico HCN

power, it actually does not provide a sufficiently large average received power for a user due to a large distance, thus making this user connect to a pico BS nearby. Visibly, the deployment of pico BSs allows macro-BSs to offload more users, and in addition setting an extra bias for pico BSs toward admitting users [32] further provides relief to the macrocell tier.

#### 2.3.2.3 Multiple-Antenna HCNs

As a natural extension, the study of downlink HCNs has been carried out in multiple-antenna scenarios recently [33–37]. Specifically, Heath et al. [33] have investigated the interference distribution of a user associated with a fixed-size cell, which is inscribed within a weighted Voronoi cell in a Poisson field of interferers. Dhillon and Gupta et al. [34, 35] have derived closed-form expressions for both coverage probability and per user rate by using tools from stochastic orders, which nevertheless are not analytically tractable. Adhikary et al. [36] have proposed interference coordination strategies through spatial blanking by exploiting the directionality in channel vectors at the massive MIMO regime. Li et al. in a very recent contribution [37] have developed a semi-closed expression for success probability in a multi-user MIMO HCN, where the tradeoff between link reliability and the area spectrum efficiency has been discussed.

### *2.3.3 Wireless Ad hoc Networks*

Wireless ad hoc networks are fully distributed, autonomous and infrastructureless networks, and have been the most important application field of PPP. In an ad hoc network, all transmitter and receiver nodes are randomly distributed, connecting with each other in any way they want; the connection relation varies all the time. In addition, transmitters make their transmission decisions in a non-coordinated fashion, but adopt slotted Aloha as the MAC protocol, i.e., each node independently decides whether transmits or not in each time slot.

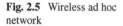

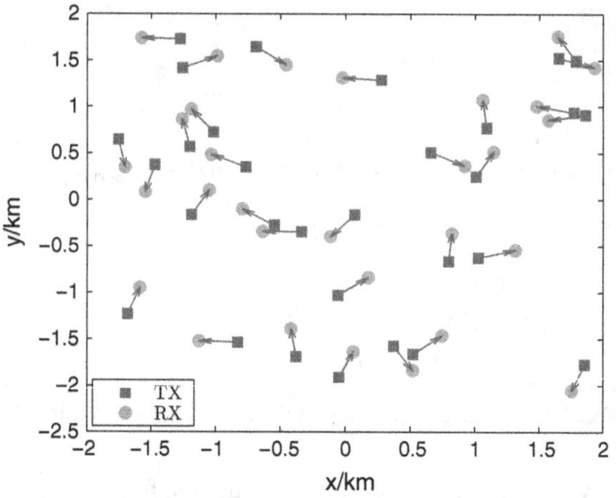


**Fig. 2.5** Wireless ad hoc network

Figure 2.5 illustrates a snapshot of a single-hop wireless ad hoc network, where the locations of all transmitters are modeled as a PPP and each of them connects to a unique receiver. It has been more than three decades that PPP has been used to model wireless ad hoc networks, and a flood of literature has studied the PPP-based ad hoc networks, providing analytically tractable expressions for metrics such as the PDF of interference [38], outage probability [39–41], scaling laws of network capacity [42–44], and more recently the area spectral efficiency [45–47], etc.

## 2.4 Interference Characterization

Equipped with the tool of stochastic geometry and its validation to model the spatial distribution of a random network, in this section we explain how to analyze the effect of the aggregate interference on a receiver in the network. We associate mathematical characterization of the SINR with a *typical user* in the network, which plays a critical role for the secrecy performance analysis in the subsequent chapters.

Given that radio signals suffer from small-scale fading (multiple-path fading and shadowing) and large-scale path loss (power law attenuation with respect to the path distance), the power gain can be characterized as

$$G_{xy} = g_{xy} r_{xy}^{-\alpha}, \tag{2.9}$$

where $x$ and $y$ denote the locations of transmitter and receiver, $g_{xy}$ denotes the small-scale fading gain, $r_{xy}$ denotes the path distance, and $\alpha$ denotes the path loss exponent.[3]

[3]In free space, $\alpha = 2$, whereas over ground with scattering and absorption, the value of $\alpha$ is usually better modeled by a value between 2.5 and 4.

Consider a random wireless network where the locations of all potential transmitters are modeled as a PPP $\Phi \in \mathbb{R}^2$ of density $\lambda$. Without loss of generality, we place a receiver of interest at the origin $o$ of the coordinate system as a typical user. According to the Slivnyak theorem provided by Property 2.6, this operation does not affect the distribution of other nodes. The SINR of the typical user is given by

$$\text{SINR} \triangleq \frac{S}{I+W}, \quad \text{with} \quad I = \sum_{z\in\Phi_t} P_z g_{zo} r_{zo}^{-\alpha}, \tag{2.10}$$

where $S$, $I$ and $W$ denote the received signal power, interference power and noise power; $P_z$ denotes the transmit power of an interfering node located at location $z$, $\Phi_t$ denotes the set of the locations of those interfering nodes transmitting concurrently, which is obviously a subset of $\Phi$. Note that the determination of $\Phi_t$ depends heavily on the network behavior and related MAC protocols (e.g., Aloha, TDMA). For example, in a wireless ad hoc network with slotted Aloha, all interfering nodes transmit independently and randomly with probability $p$, then $\Phi_t$ is a thinning of $\Phi$, i.e., a PPP of density $p\lambda$. As to a multiple-tier HCN where the mobile association policy based on the average received power is adopted [23], as depicted in Fig. 2.4, if the typical user access the $k$th tier and the distance to its serving BS is $r$, there always exists an exclusion region where no interfering BSs in the $j$th tier can be found in it. The exclusion region is centered at the typical user with radius $r_j = r\left(\frac{P_k}{P_j}\right)^{1/\alpha}$, which can be denoted as $\mathcal{B}(o, r_j)$. Then $\Phi_t$ can be given by $\Phi_t = \bigcup_j \left(\Phi\backslash\mathcal{B}(o, r_j)\right)$.

Due to the randomness of both wireless channels and network geometry, the interference term $I$ in Eq. (2.10) can be regarded as a random variable, the distribution of which can be characterized via the Laplace transform. Taking a multiple-tier HCN as an example, assuming that all interfering BSs in the $j$th tier transmit at power $P_j$ with locations obeying PPP $\Phi_j$ of density $\lambda_j$ and small-scale channel gain $g_{zo}$ is independent and identically distributed (i.i.d.) obeying Rayleigh fading, i.e., exponent distribution with unit mean. Given that the interfering BSs in the $j$th tier are outside the exclusion region $\mathcal{B}(o, r_j)$, the Laplace transform of the aggregate interference power from the $j$th tier $I_j = \sum_{z\in\Phi_j} P_j g_{zo} r_{zo}^{-\alpha}$ can be calculated as

$$\begin{aligned}
\mathcal{L}_{I_j}(s) \triangleq \mathbb{E}_{I_j}\left[e^{-sI_j}\right] &= \mathbb{E}_{\Phi_j, g}\left[\prod_{z\in\Phi_j} e^{-sP_j g_{zo} r_{zo}^{-\alpha}}\right] \\
&\overset{(a)}{=} \exp\left(-2\pi\lambda_j \int_{r_j}^{\infty} \left(1 - \mathcal{L}_g(sP_j r^{-\alpha})\right) r dr\right) \\
&\overset{(b)}{=} \exp\left(-2\pi\lambda_j \int_{r_j}^{\infty} \left(1 - \frac{1}{1+sP_j r^{-\alpha}}\right) r dr\right),
\end{aligned} \tag{2.11}$$

where $\delta \triangleq 2/\alpha$, $(a)$ follows from the PGFL in Lemma 2.2 along with the independence of $\Phi_t$ and $g$, and $(b)$ holds for exponent distribution of $g$.

As to an ad hoc network, due to the absence of an exclusion region around the receiver of interest, to which any interfering node can be arbitrarily close, and thus $r_j$ in Eq. (2.11) is set to zero. Therefore, we obtain a closed-form expression of $\mathcal{L}_{I_j}(s)$, which is

$$\mathcal{L}_{I_j}(s) = \exp\left(-\pi\lambda_j \Gamma(1+\delta)\Gamma(1-\delta)(P_j s)^{\delta}\right). \tag{2.12}$$

One can see that $\mathcal{L}_I(s)$ solely depends on the density of interfering nodes $\lambda_t$ and path loss exponent $\alpha$ (or $\delta$). Note that only if $\delta < 1$ does $\mathcal{L}_I(s)$ in Eq. (2.12) makes sense.

Kindly note that the derivations in Eqs. (2.11) and (2.12) can be applied to more general channel distributions but not limited to Rayleigh fading.

## 2.5 Physical Layer Security in Random Cellular Networks

Recently, stochastic geometry has been extensively used for physical layer security analysis in random wireless networks, where the locations of both legitimate nodes and eavesdropping nodes are modeled as independent PPPs. As discussed previously, modeling legitimate nodes as a PPP is mainly due to the mobility and the random distribution and also the tractability of PPP itself. The reasons behind PPP eavesdroppers is twofold

- On one hand, although the locations of eavesdroppers are unknown in real wiretap scenarios, modeling them as a PPP is still reasonable for the following two cases: 1) for the regular but unlicensed users in the network who are treated as potential eavesdroppers, they share the same mobility as the legitimate nodes do; 2) for the malicious eavesdroppers in the network, they need to imitate the mobility and other behaviors as legitimate nodes to hide their identities, or otherwise they can be easily detected [48].
- On the other hand, PPP is the most random stochastic process, the secure transmission techniques or schemes designed base on which have sufficiently strong robustness.

In the following, we describe several performance metrics to evaluate the physical layer security in a random cellular network, which will be used in the whole book.

### 2.5.1 *Connection Outage and Secrecy Outage*

As mentioned in Chap. 1, Wyner's wiretap encoding scheme will be discussed in this book. In such a coding scheme, two rate parameters, i.e., transmission rate $R_t$ and confidential information rate $R_s$, should be carefully designed to meet the requirements of reliable and secrecy transmissions. Usually, the performances are evaluated in terms of connection outage, secrecy outage probabilities, and network-wide secrecy throughput.

#### 2.5.1.1 Connection Outage

Connection outage probability measures the probability of a unsuccessful transmission. If a legitimate link has capacity $C_B$ and the transmission rate $R_t$ of the adopted Wyner's code satisfies $R_t < C_B$, the legitimate receiver is able to decode the secret message correctly and perfect connection is assured in this link; otherwise a connection outage occurs. The probability that this connection outage event takes place is referred to as the connection outage probability, denoted as $\mathscr{P}_{co}$.

#### 2.5.1.2 Secrecy Outage

According to the basic definition of secrecy outage in Sect. 1.3.3 and under Wyner's coding scheme, SOP is defined as the probability that the confidential information rate $R_s$ exceeds that of the secrecy capacity $C_s$, which is denoted as $\mathscr{P}_{so}$.

Since $R_e = R_t - R_s$, $R_s > C_s$ is equivalent to $R_e < C_E$ where $C_E$ is channel capacity from the transmitter to the eavesdropper. In a wireless network there are a large number of potential eavesdroppers distributed randomly. Under a reasonable assumption that these eavesdroppers do not collude with each other due to the differences in geographic positions but only decode messages individually, which corresponds to a compound wiretap channel model [49], $C_E$ is the capacity of the most detrimental eavesdropping link.

The connection outage and secrecy outage probabilities have played a key role in analyzing physical layer security in random wireless networks, and have been extensively investigated in cellular networks [50–52], wireless ad hoc networks [53, 54], CRNs [55, 56], and relay networks [57], etc.

### 2.5.2 *Secrecy Throughput*

Secrecy throughput is used to evaluate the average capability of secrecy information transmission of a wireless link. Under a predefined connection outage probability $\mathscr{P}_{co} = \sigma$ and a secrecy outage probability $\mathscr{P}_{so} = \varepsilon$, the confidential information rate $R_s$ of the Wyner's coding could be adjusted if some CSI of the wireless link is available at the transmitter. Mathematically, secrecy throughput is defined as

$$\mathscr{T}_s = \mathbb{E}(R_s(\sigma, \varepsilon)). \tag{2.13}$$

Note that secrecy rate $R_s$ is a function of $\sigma$ and $\varepsilon$, which can be expressed as $R_s(\sigma, \varepsilon) = [R_t(\sigma) - R_e(\varepsilon)]^+$, where codeword rate $R_t$ and redundant rate $R_e$ satisfy $\mathscr{P}_{co}(R_t) = \sigma$ and $\mathscr{P}_{so}(R_e) = \varepsilon$, respectively. Clearly, only under the condition $R_t(\sigma) > R_e(\varepsilon)$ can a positive secrecy rate $R_s(\sigma, \varepsilon)$ be achieved. This implies, not all selected parameters $\sigma$ and $\varepsilon$ can be simultaneously satisfied.

### 2.5.3 Network-Wide Secrecy Throughput

In a wireless network, apart from the security performance of a typical node, e.g., outage probability, achievable secrecy rate and capacity, etc., the *network-wide* security performance and the potential benefits brought by secure transmission techniques and strategies are also highly interested. In this monograph, we concern ourselves with the important metric, named network-wide secrecy throughput, to assess the efficiency of secure transmissions, which is defined as the achievable rate of successful transmission of information bits per unit area under required connection outage and secrecy outage probabilities [53, 54].

The network-wide secrecy throughput under a connection outage probability $\mathscr{P}_{co} = \sigma$ and a secrecy outage probability $\mathscr{P}_{so} = \varepsilon$ is given by

$$\mathscr{T}_s \triangleq \lambda(1-\sigma)R_s(\sigma, \varepsilon), \tag{2.14}$$

where the unit is bits/s/Hz/m$^2$. Note that here we assume all the secrecy transmission links in the wireless network adopt a common and constant confidential information rate $R_s$ rather than adjust it for each transmitter. This is a practical assumption to make the network-wide performance analysis more tractable.

Through investigating outage probabilities and network-wide secrecy throughput, we can gain a better understanding of the significance of physical layer security in random wireless networks, and provide a more explicit guideline for secure transmission techniques and schemes tailored for future wireless networks.

### 2.5.4 A Brief Survey on Physical Layer Security in Wireless Networks

Physical layer security in wireless networks has become an emerging topic very recently, and there have been already some advances reported in the last five years. Here we provide a brief survey where the works are not limited to the cellular network but a general random wireless network.

Early studies on wireless network security from an information-theoretic viewpoint have mainly characterized the secure connectivity of large-scale wireless networks utilizing the concept of secrecy random graph. For example, the statistical characteristic of in-degree and out-degree of network connectivity under security constraints are investigated by Haenggi [58], Pinto et al. [59], and Goel et al. [60]. The existence of a secrecy graph is analyzed in [58, 60] using tools from percolation theory. The authors in [61] show that using directional antenna elements and eigen-beamforming efficiently improves secure connectivity. Scaling laws for secrecy capacity/rate in large wireless networks have been investigated in [62, 63], which are characterized as the order-of-growth of the secrecy capacity/rate as the node number increases. Although scaling laws can provide insights into the secrecy capacity of large-scale networks, they can not reflect the impact of key system parameters and transmission protocols, since most of these factors affect network throughput but not the scaling laws [5].

Research on physical layer security has been further extended to cellular networks [51, 52, 64–66] and ad hoc networks [53, 54, 57, 67], where placement of both legitimate and wiretapping nodes are modeled as PPPs. Specifically, the authors in [51] evaluate the secrecy rate of a cellular network considering cell association as well as information exchange between BSs, under different assumptions on eavesdroppers' location information. This work is extended by [64–66] with both small-scale fading and intercell interference taken into account, and a regularized channel inversion linear precoding is proposed to improve the average secrecy rate. In [53, 54], the authors measure the secrecy transmission capacity with single and multiple-antenna transmitters in ad hoc networks, and provide a tradeoff analysis between connectivity and secrecy. In [57], the authors consider a secure transmission via randomize-and-forward relays in a wireless ad hoc network and discuss the problem that when relay transmission gives a more secure connection. In [67], the authors investigate the issue of secure routing using decode-and-forward relays in a multiple-hop ad hoc network. In [68], the authors investigate physical layer security in a multiple-tier wireless sensor network, and introduce the concept of distributed network secrecy throughput to quantize the network security performance. This topic has also been carried out in emerging wireless networks, including cognitive radio networks, device-to-device networks, Internet of Things, etc., and more details can be found in [56, 69, 70].

Although many efforts have been devoted to physical layer security in random wireless networks, there are still some open problems in this field. In the following, we introduce three of them which we are going to deal with in the following three chapters, respectively.

1. How to optimally allocate the power between information-bearing signal and artificial noise for the artificial noise scheme against randomly distributed eavesdroppers? Although artificial noise scheme has been applied to confuse randomly located eavesdroppers [54, 71], there is still no explicit solution on the optimal power allocation. Providing explicit optimization solutions is of significance for practical secure transmission designs.
2. How to analyze physical layer security for an HCN? Existing literature on HCNs has mainly focused on loading balance, spectrum efficiency, energy efficiency [27, 28, 31, 37], etc.; little of it has involved security issues. It is of necessity to establish a fundamental analysis framework to evaluate the security performance of an HCN in order to protect secure transmissions in HCNs.
3. How to improve the security performance when the transmitter has only one antenna and meanwhile no friendly jammer exists? Many research works on physical layer security in random wireless networks assume that there are either multi-antenna transmitters or friendly jammers [53, 54], which sometimes might not be available due to constraints of size, hardware cost, etc. New approaches are needed to protect information security in these unfavorable scenarios.

## References

1. A.D. Wyner, Shannon-theoretic approach to a Gaussian cellular multiple-access channel. IEEE Trans. Inf. Theory **40**(11), 1713–1727 (1994)
2. S. Shamai, A.D. Wyner, Information-theoretic considerations for symmetric, cellular, multiple-access fading channels-parts I & II. IEEE Trans. Inf. Theory **43**(11), 1877–1911 (1997)
3. T.S. Rappaport, *Wireless Communications: Principles and Practice*, 2nd edn. (Prentice-Hall, Upper Saddle River, 2002)
4. A.J. Goldsmith, *Wireless Communications* (Cambridge Univ. Press, Cambridge, 2005)
5. M. Haenggi, J. Andrews, F. Baccelli, O. Dousse, M. Franceschetti, Stochastic geometry and random graphs for the analysis and design of wireless networks. IEEE J. Sel. Areas Commun. **27**(7), 1029–1046 (2009)
6. D. Stoyan, W. Kendall, J. Mecke, *Stochastic Geometry and Its Applications*, 2nd edn. (Wiley, New York, 1996)
7. M. Haenggi, *Stochastic Geometry for Wireless Networks* (Cambridge University Press, Cambridge, 2012)
8. H. ElSawy, E. Hossain, M. Haenggi, Stochastic geometry for modeling, analysis, and design of multi-tier and cognitive cellular wireless networks: a survey. IEEE Commun. Surv. Tutor. **15**(3), 996–1019 (2013)
9. F. Baccelli, B. Blaszczyszyn, *Stochastic Geometry and Wireless Networks in Foundations and Trends in Networking*, vol. 1 (Now Publishers, Breda, 2009)
10. S. Cheng, S. Lien, F. Hu, K. Chen, On exploiting cognitive radio to mitigate interference in macro/femto heterogeneous networks. IEEE Wirel. Commun. **18**(3), 40–47 (2011)
11. A. Ghasemi, E. Sousa, Interference aggregation in spectrum sensing cognitive wireless networks. IEEE J. Sel. Topics Signal Process. **2**(1), 41–56 (2008)
12. C.-H. Lee, M. Haenggi, Interference and outage in Poisson cognitive networks. IEEE Trans. Wirel. Commun. **11**(4), 1392–1401 (2012)
13. A. Rabbachin, T.Q.S. Quek, H. Shin, M.Z. Win, Cognitive network interference. IEEE J. Sel. Areas Commun. **29**(2), 480–493 (2011)
14. A. Guo, M. Haenggi, Spatial stochastic models and metrics for the structure of base stations in cellular networks. IEEE Trans. Wirel. Commun. **12**(11), 5800–5812 (2013)
15. M. Haenggi, Mean interference in hard-core wireless networks. IEEE Commun. Lett. **15**(8), 792–794 (2011)
16. J.G. Andrews, F. Baccelli, R.K. Ganti, A tractable approach to coverage and rate in cellular networks. IEEE Trans. Commun. **59**(11), 3122–3134 (2011)
17. B. Blaszczyszyn, M.K. Karray, H.-P. Keeler, Using Poisson processes to model lattice cellular networks, in *Proceedings of 32th Annual IEEE International Conference on Computer Communications (INFOCOM'13), Turin, Italy* (2013), pp. 14-19
18. J.G. Andrews, S. Buzzi, W. Choi, S.V. Hanly, A. Lozano, A.C.K. Soong, J.C. Zhang, What will 5G be? IEEE J. Sel. Areas Commun. **32**(6), 1065–1082 (2014)
19. V. Chandrasekhar, J.G. Andrews, A. Gatherer, Femtocell networks: a survey. IEEE Commun. Mag. **46**(9), 59–67 (2008)
20. V. Chandrasekhar, J. Andrews, Spectrum allocation in tiered cellular networks. IEEE Trans. Commun. **57**(10), 3059–3068 (2009)
21. W. Cheung, T. Quek, M. Kountouris, Throughput optimization, spectrum allocation, and access control in two-tier femtocell networks. IEEE J. Sel. Areas Commun. **30**(3), 561–574 (2012)
22. V. Chandrasekhar, J. Andrews, Uplink capacity and interference avoidance for two-tier femtocell networks. IEEE Trans. Wirel. Commun. **8**(7), 3498–3509 (2009)
23. H.-S. Jo, Y.J. Sang, P. Xia, J.G. Andrews, Heterogeneous cellular networks with flexible cell association: a comprehensive downlink SINR analysis. IEEE Trans. Wirel. Commun. **11**(10), 3484–3495 (2012)
24. H.S. Dhillon, R.K. Ganti, F. Baccelli, J.G. Andrews, Modeling and analysis of K-tier downlink heterogeneous cellular networks. IEEE J. Sel. Areas Commun. **30**(3), 550–560 (2012)

25. G. de la Roche, A. Valcarce, D. López-Pérez, J. Zhang, Access control mechanisms for femtocells. IEEE Commun. Mag. **48**(1), 33–39 (2010)
26. P. Xia, V. Chandrasekhar, J.G. Andrews, Open vs. closed access femtocells in the uplink. IEEE Trans. Wirel. Commun. **9**(12), 3798–3809 (2010)
27. S. Singh, H.S. Dhillon, J.G. Andrews, Offloading in heterogeneous networks: modeling, analysis, and design insights. IEEE Trans. Wirel. Commun. **12**(5), 2484–2497 (2013)
28. H.S. Dhillon, R.K. Ganti, J.G. Andrews, load-aware modeling and analysis of heterogeneous cellular networks. IEEE Trans. Wirel. Commun. **12**(4), 1666–1677 (2013)
29. S. Mukherjee, Distribution of downlink SINR in heterogeneous cellular networks. IEEE J. Sel. Areas Commun. **30**(3), 575–585 (2012)
30. M.D. Renzo, A. Guidotti, G.E. Corazza, Average rate of downlink heterogeneous cellular networks over generalized fading channels: A stochastic geometry approach. IEEE Trans. Commun. **61**(7), 3050–3071 (2013)
31. H.S. Dhillon, J.G. Andrews, Downlink rate distribution in heterogeneous cellular networks under generalized cell selection. IEEE Wirel. Commun. Lett. **3**(1), 42–45 (2014)
32. S. Parkvall, A. Furuskar, E. Dahlman, Evolution of LTE toward IMT-advanced. IEEE Commun. Mag. **49**(2), 84–91 (2011)
33. R.W. Heath, M. Kountouris, T. Bai, Modeling heterogeneous network interference using Poisson Point Processes. IEEE Trans. Signal Process. **61**(16), 4114–4126 (2013)
34. H.S. Dhillon, M. Kountouris, J.G. Andrews, Downlink MIMO HetNets: modeling, ordering results and performance analysis. IEEE Trans. Wirel. Commun. **12**(10), 5208–5222 (2013)
35. A.K. Gupta, H.S. Dhillon, S. Vishwanath, J.G. Andrews, Downlink multi-antenna heterogeneous cellular network with load balancing. IEEE Trans. Commun. **62**(11), 4052–4067 (2014)
36. A. Adhikary, H.S. Dhillon, G. Caire, Massive-MIMO meets HetNet: interference coordination through spatial blanking. IEEE J. Sel. Areas Commun. **33**(6), 1171–1186 (2015)
37. C. Li, J. Zhang, J.G. Andrews, K.B. Letaief, Success probability and area spectral efficiency in multiuser MIMO HetNets. IEEE Trans. Commun. **64**(4), 1544–1556 (2016)
38. E.S. Sousa, Optimum transmission range in a direct-sequence spread spectrum multihop packet radio network. IEEE J. Sel. Areas Commun. **8**(5), 762–771 (1990)
39. R. Mathar, J. Mattfeldt, On the distribution of cumulated interference power in Rayleigh fading channels. Wirel. Netw. **1**(1), 31–36 (1995)
40. M. Souryal, B. Vojcic, R. Pickholtz, Ad hoc, multihop CDMA networks with route diversity in a Rayleigh fading channel, in *Proceedings of IEEE Military Communication Conference (MILCOM'01)* (2001), pp. 1003–1007
41. S. Weber, J.G. Andrews, N. Jindal, An overview of the transmission capacity of wireless networks. IEEE Trans. Commun. **58**(12), 3593–3604 (2010)
42. O. Lévêque, I.E. Teletar, Information-theoretic upper bounds on the capacity of large extended ad hoc wireless networks. IEEE Trans. Inf. Theory, 858–865 (2005)
43. M. Franceschetti, A note on Lévêque and Telatar's upper bound on the capacity of wireless ad hoc networks. IEEE Trans. Inf. Theory **53**(9), 3207–3211 (2007)
44. A. Özgür, O. Lévêque, D. Tse, Hierarchical cooperation achieves optimal capacity scaling in ad hoc networks. IEEE Trans. Inf. Theory **53**(10), 3549–3572 (2007)
45. S. Weber, X. Yang, J.G. Andrews, G. de Veciana, Transmission capacity of wireless ad hoc networks with outage constraints. IEEE Trans. Inf. Theory **51**(12), 4091–4102 (2005)
46. K. Huang, V.K.N. Lau, Y. Chen, Spectrum sharing between cellular and mobile ad hoc networks: transmission-capacity trade-off. IEEE J. Sel. Areas Commun. **27**(7), 1256–1267 (2009)
47. V. Mordachev, S. Loyka, On node density-outage probability tradeoff in wireless networks. IEEE J. Sel. Areas Commun. **27**(7), 1120–1131 (2009)
48. Y. Liang, H.V. Poor, L. Ying, Secrecy throughput of MANETs with malicious nodes, in *Proceedings of IEEE ISIT Seoul, Korea* (2009), pp. 1189–1193
49. Y. Liang, G. Kramer, H.V. Poor, S. Shamai, Compound wiretap channels. EURASIP J. Wirel. Commun. Netw. (2009)
50. T.-X. Zheng, H.-M. Wang, Q. Yin, On transmission secrecy outage of a multi-antenna system with randomly located eavesdroppers. IEEE Commun. Lett. **18**(8), 1299–1302 (2014)

51. H. Wang, X. Zhou, M.C. Reed, Physical layer security in cellular networks: a stochastic geometry approach. IEEE Trans. Wirel. Commun. **12**(6), 2776–2787 (2013)
52. H.-M. Wang, T.-X. Zheng, J. Yuan, D. Towsley, M.H. Lee, Physical layer security in heterogeneous cellular networks. IEEE Trans. Commun. **64**(3), 1204–1219 (2016)
53. X. Zhou, R. Ganti, J. Andrews, A. Hjørungnes, On the throughput cost of physical layer security in decentralized wireless networks. IEEE Trans. Wirel. Commun. **10**(8), 2764–2775 (2011)
54. X. Zhang, X. Zhou, M.R. McKay, Enhancing secrecy with multi-antenna transmission in wireless ad hoc networks. IEEE Trans. Inf. Forensics Secur. **8**(11), 1802–1814 (2013)
55. Y. Deng, L. Wang, S.A.R. Zaidi, J. Yuan, M. Elkashlan, Artificial-noise aided secure transmission in large scale spectrum sharing networks. IEEE Trans. Commun. **64**(5), 2116–2129 (2016)
56. X.M. Xu, B. He, W.W. Yang, X. Zhou, Secure transmission design for cognitive radio networks with Poisson distributed eavesdroppers. IEEE Trans. Inf. Forensics Secur. **11**(2), 373–387 (2016)
57. C. Cai, Y. Cai, X. Zhou, W. Yang, W. Yang, When does relay transmission give a more secure connection in wireless ad hoc networks? IEEE Trans. Inf. Forensics Secur. **9**(4), 624–632 (2014)
58. M. Haenggi, The secrecy graph and some of its properties, in *Proceedings of IEEE ISIT, Toronto, Canada*, (2008), pp. 539–543
59. P.C. Pinto, M.Z. Win, Percolation and connectivity in the intrinsically secure communications graph. IEEE Trans. Inf. Theory **58**(3), 1716–1730 (2010)
60. S. Goel, V. Aggarwal, A. Yener, A.R. Calderbank, Modeling location uncertainty for eavesdroppers: a secrecy graph approach, in *Proceedings of IEEE ISIT, Austin, USA* (2010), pp. 2627–2631
61. P.C. Pinto, J. Barros, M.Z. Win, Secure communication in stochastic wireless networks Part I: Connectivity. IEEE Trans. Inf. Forensics Secur. **7**(1), 125–138 (2012)
62. O.O. Koyluoglu, C.E. Koksal, H.E. Gamal, On secrecy capacity scaling in wireless networks. IEEE Trans. Inf. Theory **58**(5), 3000–3015 (2012)
63. C. Capar, D. Goeckel, B. Liu, D. Towsley, Secret communication in large wireless networks without eavesdropper location information, in *Proceedings of IEEE INFOCOM, Orlando, USA* (2012), pp. 1152–1160
64. G. Geraci, R. Couillet, J. Yuan, M. Debbah, I.B. Collings, Large system analysis of linear precoding in MISO broadcast channels with confidential messages. IEEE J. Sel. Areas Commun. **31**(9), 1660–1671 (2013)
65. G. Geraci, S. Singh, J.G. Andrews, J. Yuan, I.B. Collings, Secrecy rates in broadcast channels with confidential messages and external eavesdroppers. IEEE Trans. Wirel. Commun. **13**(5), 2931–2943 (2014)
66. G. Geraci, H.S. Dhillon, J.G. Andrews, J. Yuan, I.B. Collings, Physical layer security in downlink multi-antenna cellular networks. IEEE Trans. Commun. **62**(6), 2006–2021 (2014)
67. J. Yao, S. Feng, X. Zhou, Y. Liu, Secure routing in multihop wireless ad-hoc networks with decode-and-forward relaying. IEEE Trans. Commun. **64**(2), 753–764 (2016)
68. J. Lee, A. Conti, A. Rabbachin, M.Z. Win, Distributed network secrecy. IEEE J. Sel. Areas Commun. **31**(9), 1889–1900 (2013)
69. D. Wu, J. Wang, R.Q. Hu, Y. Cai, Energy-efficient resource sharing for mobile device-to-device multimedia communications. IEEE Trans. Veh. Technol. **63**(5), 2093–2103 (2014)
70. A. Mukherjee, Physical-layer security in the Internet of Things: sensing and communication confidentiality under resource constraints. Proc. IEEE **103**(10), 1747–1761 (2015)
71. M. Ghogho, A. Swami, Physical-layer secrecy of MIMO communications in the presence of a Poisson random field of eavesdroppers, in *Proceedings of IEEE ICC Workshops* (2011), pp. 1–5

# Chapter 3
# Physical Layer Security in Cellular Networks Under TDMA

**Abstract** In this chapter, we discuss the physical layer secrecy transmission in a downlink cellular network under TDMA, coexisting with randomly located eavesdroppers. We adopt and investigate a secure multi-antenna transmission scheme in which artificial noise is injected into the null space of the legitimate channel to confuse eavesdroppers, and provide a comprehensive secrecy performance analysis and system design/optimization under the stochastic geometry framework. We first analyze the optimal power allocation to minimize the SOP. Subject to an SOP constraint, we then propose a dynamic parameter transmission scheme (DPTS) and a static parameter transmission scheme (SPTS) to maximize secrecy throughput. Our results give new insight into secure transmission designs in a random cellular network. Numerical results are demonstrated to validate our theoretical analysis.

## 3.1 Introduction

In this chapter, we focus on the physical layer security performance of a single-user downlink transmission, where a BS with multiple antennas transmits confidential information to a user with a single antenna, coexisting with PPP distributed eavesdroppers. This scenario happens in a TDMA cellular network with light frequency reuse between cells, where in each time slot only one user accesses the BS so the intercell interference is ignorable. This is perhaps the simplest case for secrecy performance evaluation. The more sophisticated scenarios will be discussed in the following chapters.

Under this scenario, we adopt an AN-aided secrecy signaling for the BS, where no-information-bearing AN is broadcasted together with the confidential signal to confuse the eavesdroppers. Since the BS is able to obtain the instantaneous channel state information (ICSI) of the user, we propose a so-called *on-off* secrecy scheme, where the transmission is "on" when the channel is sufficiently good; otherwise, it is "off." In such a manner, there will be no transmission when the main channel is bad so the secrecy performance will be improved.



H.-M. Wang and T.-X. Zheng, *Physical Layer Security in Random Cellular Networks*, SpringerBriefs in Computer Science,
DOI 10.1007/978-981-10-1575-5_3

In the following sections, we will provide a comprehensive secrecy performance analysis and system design/optimization under the stochastic geometry framework. Specifically, we will first analyze the SOP of the secure transmission and optimize the power allocation between the information signal and the artificial noise to minimize the SOP; we will then propose a dynamic parameter transmission scheme (DPTS) and a static parameter transmission scheme (SPTS) to maximize secrecy throughput under a SOP constraint, and provide insights into secure transmission designs.

## 3.2 System Model

This section presents the details of system model and the underlying optimization problem related to our performance metrics.

Consider a downlink cellular network under TDMA where a BS (Alice) deliveries a message to a user (Bob) in a certain time slot but should keep this message secret to the other users, and thus all the other users are naturally treated as potential eavesdroppers (Eves). Alice has $M$ antennas while Bob and Eves are all equipped with single antenna. Without loss of generality, we place Alice at the origin and Bob at a deterministic position with a distance $r_b$ from Alice. Eves are placed according to a homogeneous PPP $\Phi_e$ of density $\lambda_e$ on the two-dimensional plane with the $k$th Eve a distance $r_k$ from Alice.

Both the main (Alice to Bob) and wiretap channels (Alice to Eves) are assumed to undergo flat Rayleigh fading together with a large-scale path loss governed by exponent $\alpha$. The channel vector related to node $i$ is expressed as $\boldsymbol{h}_i r_i^{-\frac{\alpha}{2}}$, where $\boldsymbol{h}_i \in \mathbb{C}^{M\times 1}$ is the fading coefficient vector, with independent and identically distributed (i.i.d.) entries $h_{i,j} \sim \mathcal{CN}(0,1)$. We assume that the ICSI of Bob and the statistic CSIs (SCSIs) of Eves are known to Alice.

### 3.2.1 AN-Aided Secrecy Signaling

To confuse Eves while providing a reliable link to Bob, Alice adopts an AN-aided transmission signal, which is originally proposed in [1] and also have been introduced in Sect. 1.4.1. In this scheme, the transmitted signal $\boldsymbol{x}$ is in the form of

$$\boldsymbol{x} = \sqrt{\phi P}\boldsymbol{w}s + \sqrt{(1-\phi)P}\boldsymbol{W}\boldsymbol{v}, \tag{3.1}$$

where $s$ is the secret information-bearing signal with $\mathbb{E}[|s|^2] = 1$, $\boldsymbol{v} \in \mathbb{C}^{M-1\times 1}$ is an AN vector with i.i.d. entries $v_i \sim \mathcal{CN}(0, \frac{1}{M-1})$, and $\phi$ represents the power allocation ratio of the information signal power to the total transmit power $P$. $\boldsymbol{w} = \frac{\boldsymbol{h}_b^\dagger}{\|\boldsymbol{h}_b\|}$, $\boldsymbol{W} \in \mathbb{C}^{M\times M-1}$ is the projection matrix onto the null space of vector $\boldsymbol{h}_b^\dagger$, i.e., $\boldsymbol{h}_b^{\mathrm{T}}\boldsymbol{W} = \boldsymbol{0}$, and the columns of $[\boldsymbol{w}\ \boldsymbol{W}]$ constitute an orthogonal basis.

The SINRs of Bob and the $k$th Eve are

$$\eta_b = \phi P \|\boldsymbol{h}_b\|^2 r_b^{-\alpha}, \tag{3.2}$$

$$\eta_k = \frac{\phi P |\boldsymbol{h}_k^{\mathrm{T}} \boldsymbol{w}|^2 r_k^{-\alpha}}{(1-\phi) P \|\boldsymbol{h}_k^{\mathrm{T}} \boldsymbol{W}\|^2 r_k^{-\alpha}/(M-1)+1}. \tag{3.3}$$

Throughout the chapter, for ease of notation, we define $\rho \triangleq \frac{P}{r_b^{\alpha}}$ as the normalized transmit power, $\gamma \triangleq \|\boldsymbol{h}_b\|^2$ as the power gain of the main channel, and $\delta \triangleq \frac{2}{\alpha}$.

### 3.2.2 On–Off Secrecy Transmission Strategy

As mentioned in Sect. 2.5.1.2, in a non-colluding wiretap scenario the capacity of the wiretap channel is $C_E = \log_2(1+\eta_e)$ with $\eta_e \triangleq \max_{e_k \in \Phi_e} \eta_k$ the equivalent SINR of the most detrimental Eve. Since the ICSI of Bob is known by Alice, the capacity of main channel $C_B = \log_2(1+\eta_b)$ can also be obtained before transmission. To avoid an undesired capacity outage ($R_t > C_B$) or an intolerably high possibility of secrecy outage ($R_e < C_E$), we adopt the *on-off* transmission strategy [2] Alice transmits only when the main channel is sufficiently good, i.e., $\gamma$ is not below a predefined threshold $\mu$; otherwise she remains silent. Under this strategy, we define the SOP for a given $\gamma$ as

$$\mathcal{P}_{so}(\gamma) \triangleq \mathbb{P}\{C_E > R_t - R_s|\gamma\}, \quad \forall \gamma \geq \mu. \tag{3.4}$$

To further evaluate the average performance of the secrecy transmission, we also investigate the *secrecy throughput* [3], which is introduced in Sect. 2.5.2 and is expressed as

$$\Omega \triangleq \mathbb{E}_{\gamma}[R_s(\gamma)]. \tag{3.5}$$

Note that $R_s$ can be designed according to the gain of the main channel, $\gamma$.

In Sects. 3.3 and 3.4, we minimize $P_{so}(\gamma)$ under a target $R_s$ and maximize $\Omega$ subject to an SOP constraint $\mathcal{P}_{so}(\gamma) \leq \varepsilon \in [0, 1]$, respectively.

## 3.3 Secrecy Outage Probability Minimization

In this section, we adaptively adjust the optimal power allocation $\phi$ under each $\gamma$ to minimize the SOP $\mathcal{P}_{so}(\gamma)$. Before proceeding, we first give the CDF of the equivalent SINR $\eta_e$ of the wiretap channels.

**Lemma 3.1** *Let $\beta \triangleq \pi\delta\Gamma(\delta)$ and $\xi \triangleq \frac{\phi^{-1}-1}{M-1}$. The CDF of $\eta_e$ for a given $\phi$ is*

$$F_{\eta_e}(x) = \exp\left(-\beta\lambda_e(\phi P)^{\delta} x^{-\delta}(1+\xi x)^{1-M}\right). \tag{3.6}$$

*Proof* Define $u = |\boldsymbol{h}_k^{\mathrm{T}}\boldsymbol{w}|^2$ and $v = \|\boldsymbol{h}_k^{\mathrm{T}}\boldsymbol{W}\|^2$. We know that $u \sim \mathrm{Exp}(1)$, and $v \sim \Gamma(M-1, 1)$. Due to the orthogonality between $\boldsymbol{w}$ and $\boldsymbol{W}$, $u$ and $v$ are independent of each other. From Eq. (3.3), the CDF of $\eta_k$ can be given by

$$F_{\eta_k}(x) = \mathbb{P}\left\{\frac{\phi P u}{\phi \xi P v + r_k^{\alpha}} < x\right\} = \mathbb{P}\left\{u < \frac{\phi \xi P v + r_k^{\alpha}}{\phi P} x\right\} = 1 - e^{-\frac{r_k^{\alpha} x}{\phi P}} (1 + \xi x)^{1-M}.$$

The CDF of $\eta_e$, which is defined as $F_{\eta_e}(x) = \mathbb{P}\left\{\max_{e_k \in \Phi_e} \eta_k < x\right\}$, can be calculated as

$$F_{\eta_e}(x) = \mathbb{E}_{\Phi_e}\left[\prod_{e_k \in \Phi_e} \mathbb{P}\{\eta_k < x\}\right] \overset{(a)}{=} \exp\left(-\frac{\pi \lambda_e \int_0^{\infty} e^{-\frac{r^{\alpha/2} x}{\phi P}} dr}{(1 + \xi x)^{M-1}}\right), \tag{3.7}$$

where Eq. $(a)$ holds for the PGFL [4]. Calculating Eq. (3.7) with Eq. [5, (3.326.1)] yields Eq. (3.6). ■

With the knowledge of $\gamma$, Alice sets $R_t$ arbitrarily close to $C_B$, whereas $R_s$ should not exceed $C_B$ in order to guarantee secrecy against Eves. We obtain from Eq. (3.2) that $R_s \le C_B \Rightarrow \phi \ge \phi_{\min} \triangleq \frac{T-1}{\rho\gamma}$. Clearly, $\gamma < \frac{T-1}{\rho}$ yields $\phi \ge \phi_{\min} > 1$, which violates the constraint $\phi \le 1$, and there is no feasible $\phi$ for transmissions. In other words, $\gamma \ge \frac{T-1}{\rho}$ must be promised, and thereby we set the transmission threshold $\mu \triangleq \frac{T-1}{\rho}$.

If $\gamma \ge \frac{T-1}{\rho}$ holds, i.e., $\phi_{\min} \le 1$, then given an arbitrary $\phi \in [\phi_{\min}, 1]$, we have

$$\mathscr{P}_{so}(\gamma) = \mathbb{P}\left\{\eta_e > (1 + \eta_b - T)/T \middle| \gamma\right\} = 1 - e^{-\beta \lambda_e P^{\delta}\left((1-T^{-1})\right)^{-\delta} J(\phi)}, \tag{3.8}$$

where $J(\phi) \triangleq \Delta\phi^{-\delta}(1 + \Psi(\phi))^{1-M}$, with $\Delta\phi \triangleq \frac{1}{\phi_{\min}} - \frac{1}{\phi}$ and $\Psi(\phi) \triangleq \frac{\Delta\phi(T-1)(1-\phi)}{T(M-1)}$. The problem of minimizing $\mathscr{P}_{so}(\gamma)$ is formulated as

$$\min_{\phi} \mathscr{P}_{so}(\gamma), \quad \text{s.t.} \quad \phi_{\min} \le \phi \le 1. \tag{3.9}$$

Clearly, the problem given in Eq. (3.9) is equivalent to minimizing $J(\phi)$. Due to the continuity and differentiability of $J(\phi)$ w.r.t. $\phi$, the minimum $J(\phi)$ can only be obtained either at the zero-crossing point of the first-order derivative $\frac{dJ(\phi)}{d\phi}$ within the feasible set or at the boundary $\phi_{\min}$ or 1. The first-order derivative $\frac{dJ(\phi)}{d\phi}$ can be given by

$$\frac{dJ(\phi)}{d\phi} = \frac{(T-1)\left(\phi^3 + a\phi^2 + b\phi + c\right)}{T\phi_{\min}^2 \Delta\phi^{1+\delta}(1 + \Psi(\phi))^M \phi^3}, \tag{3.10}$$

with $a = \frac{2\phi_{\min}}{\alpha(M-1)} - \phi_{\min}$, $b = -\frac{2(T-1)\phi_{\min}^2}{\alpha T} - \frac{2(1+\phi_{\min})\phi_{\min}}{\alpha(M-1)} - \phi_{\min}$, and $c = \frac{2\phi_{\min}^2}{\alpha(M-1)} + \phi_{\min}^2$. Obviously, the sign of $\frac{dJ(\phi)}{d\phi}$ follows that of $\phi^3 + a\phi^2 + b\phi + c$. We establish the cubic equation $\phi^3 + a\phi^2 + b\phi + c = 0$, and obtain three possible roots

$$\begin{cases} \phi_1 = w_1 + w_2 - \frac{a}{3}, \\ \phi_2 = \frac{-1+\sqrt{3}j}{2} w_1 + \frac{-1-\sqrt{3}j}{2} w_2 - \frac{a}{3}, \\ \phi_3 = \frac{-1-\sqrt{3}j}{2} w_1 + \frac{-1+\sqrt{3}j}{2} w_2 - \frac{a}{3}, \end{cases} \tag{3.11}$$

where $j = \sqrt{-1}$, $w_1 = \sqrt[3]{-\frac{q}{2} + \sqrt{\frac{p^3}{27} + \frac{q^2}{4}}}$, and $w_2 = \sqrt[3]{-\frac{q}{2} - \sqrt{\frac{p^3}{27} + \frac{q^2}{4}}}$ with $p = b - \frac{a^2}{3}$, $q = c - \frac{ab}{3} + \frac{2a^3}{27}$. We denote the real roots of Eq. (3.11) within $[\phi_{\min}, 1]$ as $\mathscr{R}$, then the optimal $\phi$ that minimizes $J(\phi)$ or $\mathscr{P}_{so}(\gamma)$ can be given as

$$\phi^* = \arg \min_{\phi \in \mathscr{R} \bigcup \{\phi_{\min}, 1\}} J(\phi). \tag{3.12}$$

## 3.4 Secrecy Throughput Maximization

This section maximizes secrecy throughput. We consider two transmission strategies, i.e., a DPTS and a SPTS, respectively. The difference lies in whether the transmission parameters can adjust. In DPTS, transmission parameters are adaptively adjusted to the ICSI of Bob, and the optimization procedure is performed online. In SPTS, these parameters are designed off-line based on the SCSI of Bob, and remain fixed during transmissions.

### *3.4.1 Dynamic Parameter Transmission Scheme*

In the DPTS, we maximize secrecy throughput $\Omega_{\mathrm{D}}$ by dynamically adjusting transmission parameters according to the ICSI of the main channel. It is easy to observe from Eq. (3.5) that if we maximize $R_s$ under each $\gamma$, $\Omega_{\mathrm{D}}$ is naturally maximized, i.e.,

$$\max \Omega_{\mathrm{D}} \Leftrightarrow \max(R_s(\gamma)). \tag{3.13}$$

Therefore, we focus on the problem of maximizing $R_s(\gamma)$, which we formulate as

$$\max_{\mu, \phi(\gamma), R_t(\gamma)} \quad R_s(\gamma) \tag{3.14a}$$

$$\text{s.t.} \quad 0 < R_s(\gamma) \le R_t(\gamma) \le C_B, \tag{3.14b}$$

$$\mathscr{P}_{so}(\gamma) \le \varepsilon, \tag{3.14c}$$

$$0 \le \phi(\gamma) \le 1,\ 0 < \mu, \tag{3.14d}$$

where Eqs. (3.14b)–(3.14d) represent the constraints for reliable transmission, secrecy outage, power allocation, and transmission threshold, respectively. *For ease of notation, we omit $\gamma$ from $R_s(\gamma)$, $R_t(\gamma)$ and $\phi(\gamma)$, and treat them as functions of $\gamma$ by default in DPTS.* The SOP can be obtained form Eq. (3.4) as $\mathcal{P}_{so}(\gamma) = 1 - F_{\eta_e}\left(2^{R_t - R_s} - 1\right)$. Before proceeding, we transform the SOP constraint (3.14c) into a more explicit form. Due to the monotonicity of CDF $F_{\eta_e}(x)$, we obtain

$$1 - F_{\eta_e}\left(2^{R_t - R_s} - 1\right) \le \varepsilon \Leftrightarrow 2^{R_t - R_s} - 1 \ge F_{\eta_e}^{-1}(1-\varepsilon). \tag{3.15}$$

Define $\chi(\phi) \triangleq \frac{F_{\eta_e}^{-1}(1-\varepsilon)}{\phi}$, then Eq. (3.14c) can be reformed as

$$R_s \le R_t - \log_2\left(1 + \phi\chi(\phi)\right). \tag{3.16}$$

Obviously, from Eqs. (3.14b) and (3.16), to obtain a larger $R_s$, we should set $R_t$ to its maximum value, which is $R_t^{\max} = \log_2(1 + \phi\rho\gamma)$ from Eq. (3.14b); and thus

$$R_s = \left[\log_2 \frac{1 + \phi\rho\gamma}{1 + \phi\chi(\phi)}\right]^+. \tag{3.17}$$

To achieve a positive $R_s$, we should guarantee $\chi(\phi) < \rho\gamma$. Although $\chi(\phi)$ is an implicit function of $\phi$ due to the complicated transcendental equation $F_{\eta_e}(x) = \varepsilon$ (see Eq. (3.6)), we reveal the relationship between $\chi(\phi)$ and $\phi$ in the following lemma:

**Lemma 3.2** *$\chi(\phi)$ is a monotonically increasing and convex function of $\phi \in [0, 1]$.*

*Proof* Combining $F_{\eta_e}(\phi\chi) = 1 - \varepsilon$ with Eq. (3.6) yields

$$\Xi(\phi, \chi) - C = 0, \tag{3.18}$$

where $\Xi(\phi, \chi) \triangleq \chi^{\delta}\left(1 + \chi\frac{1-\phi}{M-1}\right)^{M-1}$, and $C \triangleq \frac{\beta\lambda_e P^{\delta}}{-\ln(1-\varepsilon)}$. Using the derivative rule for implicit functions in Eq. (3.18), the first- and second-order derivatives of $\chi$ on $\phi$ are

$$\frac{d\chi}{d\phi} = -\frac{\partial\Xi(\phi,\chi)/\partial\phi}{\partial\Xi(\phi,\chi)/\partial\chi} = \frac{\chi(\phi)^2}{\delta + D(1-\phi)\chi(\phi)}, \tag{3.19}$$

$$\frac{d^2\chi}{d\phi^2} = \frac{2}{\chi}\left(\frac{d\chi}{d\phi}\right)^2 + \frac{D\chi^2\left(\chi - (1-\phi)\frac{d\chi}{d\phi}\right)}{(\delta + D(1-\phi)\chi)^2}, \tag{3.20}$$

where $D = 1+\frac{\delta}{M-1}$. Obviously, $\frac{d\chi}{d\phi} > 0$ always holds. Substituting $\frac{d\chi}{d\phi}$ into Eq. (3.20) yields $\chi - (1-\phi)\frac{d\chi}{d\phi} = \frac{\delta\chi+(D-1)(1-\phi)\chi^2}{\delta+D(1-\phi)\chi} > 0$, where the inequality holds due to the fact $\delta > 0$ and $D > 1$. Resorting to the above inequality, we obtain

$$\frac{d^2\chi}{d\phi^2} > \frac{2}{\chi}\left(\frac{d\chi}{d\phi}\right)^2 > 0. \tag{3.21}$$

With $\frac{d\chi}{d\phi} > 0$ and $\frac{d^2\chi}{d\phi^2} > 0$, we complete the proof. ■

Lemma 3.2 shows that the maximum $\chi(\phi)$ is obtained at $\phi = 1$, which is $\chi_1 \triangleq \chi(1) = C^{\frac{\alpha}{2}}$ from Eq. (3.18). Given an arbitrary $\phi$, we see that the auxiliary function $Z(\chi) \triangleq \Xi(\phi, \chi) - C$ monotonically increases with $\chi$. Moreover, we have $Z(0) = -C < 0$ and $Z(\chi_1) \geq \chi_1^{2/\alpha} - C = 0$. Therefore, we can numerically calculate the unique root $\chi(\phi)$ of $Z(\chi) = 0$ using the bisection method in the range $[0, \chi_1]$.

*Remark 3.1* $\chi(\phi)$ can be considered as a metric that measures the difficulty of achieving secrecy against eavesdropping. For instance, to resist more eavesdroppers (a larger $\lambda_e$) or to meet a stronger SOP constraint (a smaller $\varepsilon$), $\chi(\phi)$ increases, which means it is harder to achieve a higher secrecy rate.

Next, we formulate the problem of maximizing $R_s$. To achieve a positive $R_s$ in Eq. (3.17), $\chi(\phi) < \rho\gamma$ should be satisfied. Since $\chi(\phi)$ monotonically increases with $\phi$, we easily see that if the minimum $\chi(\phi)$, denoted by $\chi_0 \triangleq \chi(0)$, is not below $\rho\gamma$, i.e., $\chi_0 \geq \rho\gamma \Rightarrow \gamma \leq \frac{\chi_0}{\rho}$, the inequality $\chi(\phi) < \rho\gamma$ is violated, i.e., there is no feasible $\phi$ to support a positive $R_s$ in Eq. (3.17). Therefore, $\gamma > \frac{\chi_0}{\rho}$ must be guaranteed, and as a consequence we set $\mu^* = \frac{\chi_0}{\rho}$, which corresponds to an on-off transmission.

When $\chi(\phi) < \rho\gamma$, problem (3.14a) can be simplified as

$$\max_{\phi} \ R_s = \log_2 \frac{1+\phi\rho}{1+\phi\chi(\phi)} \quad \text{s.t.} \ \ \chi(\phi) < \rho\gamma,\ 0 \leq \phi \leq 1. \tag{3.22}$$

**Theorem 3.1** *$R_s$ in Eq. (3.22) is concave on $\phi$. The optimal $\phi$ that maximizes $R_s$ is*

$$\phi^* = \begin{cases} 1, & \gamma > \frac{\delta\chi_1+\chi_1^2}{\rho(\delta-\chi_1^2)} \ \textit{and} \ \lambda_e < \frac{-\ln(1-\varepsilon)\delta^{1/\alpha}}{\beta P^{\delta}} \\ \phi^\star, & \textit{otherwise} \end{cases} \tag{3.23}$$

*where $\phi^\star$ is the unique root of the equation $\frac{dR_s}{d\phi} = 0$ with*

$$\frac{dR_s}{d\phi} = \frac{1}{\ln 2}\left(\frac{\rho\gamma}{1+\phi\rho\gamma} - \frac{\chi(\phi)+\phi\frac{d\chi(\phi)}{d\phi}}{1+\phi\chi(\phi)}\right). \tag{3.24}$$

*Proof* Please see Appendix A.1. ■

Note that, the condition $\phi^* = 1$ actually implies that, when the quality of the main channel is good enough while the density of Eves is small, the beamforming scheme without AN provides a higher secrecy rate than the AN scheme does. Otherwise, a fraction of power should be allocated to the AN to enhance secrecy performance.

Due to the concavity of $R_s$ w.r.t. $\phi$, we can efficiently calculate the optimal $\phi^\star$ that satisfies $\frac{dR_s}{d\phi} = 0$ using the bisection method.

**Corollary 3.1** *The optimal $\phi^\star$ increases in $\gamma$ and $\varepsilon$, while decreases in $\lambda_e$.*

*Proof* Please see Appendix A.2. ■

Corollary 3.1 indicates that, in order to enhance the secrecy rate $R_s$, more power should be (1) allocated to the information signal under a better quality of the main channel (a larger $\gamma$), (2) allocated to the AN under a stronger SOP constraint (a smaller $\varepsilon$) or in a denser eavesdropper scenario (a larger $\lambda_e$).

Having obtained the optimal $\phi^*$, we can derive the maximum $R_s^*(\gamma)$ from Eq. (3.17). The maximum $\Omega_{\rm D}$ can be calculated as

$$\Omega_{\rm D}^* = \int_{\chi_0/\rho}^{\infty} R_s^*(\gamma) f_\gamma(x) dx. \tag{3.25}$$

The following theorem provides a closed-form approximation, denoted as $\Omega_{\rm D}^\circ$, at the high-SNR regime:

**Theorem 3.2** *At the high-SNR regime as $P \to \infty$, the maximum secrecy throughput $\Omega_{\rm D}^\circ$ is given by*

$$\Omega_{\rm D}^\circ = \frac{e^{-\frac{\chi^\circ}{\rho}}}{\ln 2\Gamma(M)} \sum_{k=0}^{M-1} \binom{M-1}{k} \left(\frac{\chi^\circ}{\rho}\right)^{M-1-k} \sum_{m=0}^{k} \frac{k!}{(k-m)!} \left( \sum_{n=1}^{k-m} (n-1)! \times \left(-\frac{1+\phi^\circ\chi^\circ}{\rho\phi^\circ}\right)^{k-m-n} - e^{\frac{1+\phi^\circ\chi^\circ}{\rho\phi^\circ}} \left(-\frac{1+\phi^\circ\chi^\circ}{\rho\phi^\circ}\right)^{k-m} \mathrm{Ei}\left[-\left(\frac{1+\phi^\circ\chi^\circ}{\rho\phi^\circ}\right)\right]\right),$$

*where $\chi^\circ \triangleq \chi(\phi^\circ)$ with $\phi^\circ$ the unique root of $\phi^2 \frac{d\chi(\phi)}{d\phi} = 1$ and independent of $\gamma$.*

*Proof* At the high-SNR regime as $P \to \infty$, we have $\frac{dR_s}{d\phi} = 0 \Rightarrow \phi^2 \frac{d\chi}{d\phi} = 1$ from Eq. (3.24). Clearly, the optimal $\phi$ that satisfies $\frac{dR_s}{d\phi} = 0$, denoted as $\phi^\circ$, is irrespective to $\gamma$. Substitute $\phi^\circ$ and $\chi^\circ \triangleq \chi(\phi^\circ)$ into Eq. (3.17) and calculating Eq. (3.25) yield

$$\begin{aligned}\Omega^\circ &= \int_{\chi^\circ/\rho}^{\infty} \log_2 \frac{1+\phi^\circ\rho x}{1+\phi^\circ\chi^\circ} f_\gamma(x) dx \overset{(b)}{=} \frac{\int_0^\infty \ln\left(1+\frac{\phi^\circ\rho y}{1+\phi^\circ\chi^\circ}\right)\left(y+\frac{\chi^\circ}{\rho}\right)^{M-1} e^{-y-\frac{\chi^\circ}{\rho}} dy}{\ln 2\Gamma(M)} \\ &= \frac{e^{-\frac{\chi^\circ}{\rho}}}{\Gamma(M)} \sum_{k=0}^{M-1} \binom{M-1}{k} \left(\frac{\chi^\circ}{\rho}\right)^k \int_0^\infty \log_2\left(1+\frac{\phi^\circ\rho}{1+\phi^\circ\chi^\circ} y\right) y^{M-1-k} e^{-y} dy,\end{aligned} \tag{3.26}$$

where Eq. (*b*) holds for the transformation $y = x - \frac{\chi^\circ}{\rho}$. Expending the integral term inside Eq. (3.26) according to Eq. [5, (4.337.5)] completes the proof. ■

*Remark 3.2* High-SNR secrecy rate $R_s^\circ(\gamma)$ can be obtained by substituting $\phi^\circ$ into Eq. (3.22). As $P \to \infty$, rate redundancy $R_e^\circ = R_t^\circ - R_s^\circ$ converges to $\log_2(1+\phi^\circ\chi^\circ)$, which is independent of $\gamma$. This conclusion is quite similar to Eq. [3, (32)].

### 3.4.2 Static Parameter Transmission Scheme

In DPTS, code rates are adjusted in real time, resulting in a high-complexity system implementation. To reduce the complexity, we propose an SPTS, in which transmission parameters are designed based on the SCSI of the main channel (i.e., independent of $\gamma$) and remain fixed during transmissions.

Since $R_s$ is irrelevant to $\gamma$, the secrecy throughput can be rewritten in SPTS as

$$\Omega_S = R_s \mathscr{P}_t(R_s), \tag{3.27}$$

where $\mathscr{P}_t(R_s) = \mathbb{P}\{\gamma \geq \mu\}$ represents the transmission probability for a target $R_s$. To guarantee a reliable transmission, the following inequality should be satisfied:

$$0 < R_s \leq R_t \leq \log_2(1 + \rho\phi\mu) \leq C_B. \tag{3.28}$$

Note that, $\mathscr{P}_t(R_s)$ is closely related to parameters $\mu$, $\phi$, $R_t$ and $R_s$. To maximize $\Omega_S$, we carry on the following equivalent transformation according to Sect. [6, 4.1.3],

$$\max_{\mu,\phi,R_t,R_s} R_s\mathscr{P}_t(R_s) \Leftrightarrow \max_{R_s} \max_{\mu,\phi,R_t} R_s\mathscr{P}_t(R_s). \tag{3.29}$$

This equation suggests that the entire optimization procedure can be decomposed into two steps: We maximize $R_s\mathscr{P}_t(R_s)$ by first maximizing over variables $\{\phi, \mu, R_t\}$, and then maximizing over the remaining variable $R_s$.

*Step 1:* Given a $R_s$, we maximize $R_s\mathscr{P}_t(R_s)$, or $\mathscr{P}_t(R_s)$, by maximizing over $\mu$, $\phi$ and $R_t$. From Eqs. (3.16) and (3.28), this subproblem can be formulated as follows:

$$\max_{\mu,\phi,R_t} \quad \mathscr{P}_t(R_s) \tag{3.30a}$$

$$\text{s.t.} \quad R_t \leq \log_2(1 + \rho\phi\mu), \tag{3.30b}$$

$$0 < R_s \leq R_t - \log_2(1 + \phi\chi(\phi)), \tag{3.30c}$$

$$0 \leq \phi \leq 1,\ 0 < \mu. \tag{3.30d}$$

Since $\mathscr{P}_t(R_s)$ decreases w.r.t. $\mu$, problem (3.30a) is equivalent to minimizing $\mu$. We know from Eq. (3.30b) that to achieve a smaller $\mu$, $R_t$ should be set to its minimum value, which is $R_t^{\min} = R_s + \log_2(1+\phi\chi(\phi))$ according to Eq. (3.30c). Substituting $R_t^{\min}$ into Eq. (3.30b) yields the minimum $\mu$ under a given $\phi$

$$\mu(\phi) = \frac{1}{\rho}\left(T\chi(\phi) + \frac{T-1}{\phi}\right). \tag{3.31}$$

The problem of minimizing $\mu(\phi)$ can be formulated as

$$\min_{\phi} \mu(\phi) \quad \text{s.t.} \quad 0 \leq \phi \leq 1. \tag{3.32}$$

**Theorem 3.3** *$\mu(\phi)$ in Eq.* (3.31) *is convex on $\phi$. The optimal $\phi$ that minimizes $\mu(\phi)$ is*

$$\phi^* = \begin{cases} 1, & \frac{T-1}{T} \geq \frac{\alpha}{2}C^\alpha \\ \phi^\star, & \frac{T-1}{T} < \frac{\alpha}{2}C^\alpha \end{cases} \tag{3.33}$$

*where $\phi^\star$ is the unique root of the equation $\frac{d\mu(\phi)}{d\phi} = 0$, with*

$$\frac{d\mu(\phi)}{d\phi} = \frac{1}{\rho}\left(T\frac{d\chi(\phi)}{d\phi} - \frac{T-1}{\phi^2}\right). \tag{3.34}$$

*Proof* From Eq. (3.34), we obtain the second-order derivative of $\mu$ on $\phi$,

$$\frac{d^2\mu}{d\phi^2} = \frac{1}{\rho}\left(T\frac{d^2\chi}{d\phi^2} + \frac{2(T-1)}{\phi^3}\right). \tag{3.35}$$

Since $\frac{d^2\chi}{d\phi^2} > 0$ (see Eq. (3.21)) and $T > 1$, we have $\frac{d^2\mu}{d\phi^2} > 0$, i.e., $\mu$ is convex on $\phi$. The optimal $\phi$ that minimizes $\mu$ is obtained at either 0 or 1, or the zero-crossing point of $\frac{d\mu}{d\phi}$. The boundary values of $\frac{d\mu}{d\phi}$ are $\frac{d\mu}{d\phi}|_{\phi=0} = -\infty$ and $\frac{d\mu}{d\phi}|_{\phi=1} = \frac{1}{\rho}\left(\frac{\alpha}{2}T\chi_1^2 - (T-1)\right)$, respectively. Clearly, if $\frac{d\mu}{d\phi}|_{\phi=1} \leq 0$, i.e., $\frac{T-1}{T} \geq \frac{\alpha}{2}\chi_1^2$, $\mu$ monotonically decreases w.r.t. $\phi$ in the entire range [0, 1], and the minimum $\mu$ is achieved at the boundary $\phi^* = 1$, otherwise the optimal $\phi^*$ is the unique root of $\frac{d\mu}{d\phi} = 0$. ■

Theorem 3.3 indicates that, when $\frac{T-1}{T} \geq \frac{\alpha}{2}C^\alpha$, which corresponds to a small $P$ or $\lambda_e$, or a large $\varepsilon$ $\left(\text{since } C^\alpha = P^{\frac{2}{\alpha}}\left(\frac{-\beta\lambda_e}{\ln(1-\varepsilon)}\right)^{\alpha}\right)$, the beamforming scheme in which $\phi = 1$ is optimal, otherwise AN should better be injected. Due to the convexity of $\mu(\phi)$ w.r.t. $\phi$, we can efficiently calculate the optimal $\phi^\star$ that satisfies $\frac{d\mu(\phi)}{d\phi} = 0$ using the bisection method. The following corollary gives some insight into $\phi^\star$:

**Corollary 3.2** *The optimal $\phi^\star$ in Eq.* (3.33) *increases in $R_s$ and $\varepsilon$, and decreases in $\lambda_e$.*

*Proof* Please see Appendix A.3. ■

Corollary 3.2 suggests that in order to enlarge $\mathcal{P}_t(R_s)$, more power should be: (1) allocated to the information signal to meet a higher secrecy rate $R_s$, (2) allocated to the AN when $\lambda_e$ increases or $\varepsilon$ decreases.

We observe from $\frac{d\mu(\phi)}{d\phi} = 0$ that as $R_s \to \infty$, the optimal $\phi^\star$ converges to the unique root of $\phi^2 \frac{d\chi(\phi)}{d\phi} = 1$, which is independent of $R_s$. Interestingly, the converged value equals $\phi^\circ$ given in Theorem 3.2. SPTS yields an identical rate redundancy $R_e^\circ = \log_2(1 + \phi^\circ \chi^\circ)$ as the high-SNR DPTS does, regardless of $R_s$.

Having obtained the optimal $\phi^*$ into Eq. (3.31), we obtain the maximum $\mathcal{P}_t(R_s)$

$$\mathcal{P}_t^*(R_s) = \bar{\Gamma}(M, \mu_{\min}) = e^{-\mu_{\min}} \sum_{k=0}^{M-1} \frac{\mu_{\min}^k}{k!}. \tag{3.36}$$

*Step 2:* We maximize $\Omega_S = R_s \mathcal{P}_t^*(R_s)$ by maximizing over $R_s$, i.e.,

$$\max_{R_s} \; R_s \mathcal{P}_t^*(R_s), \quad \text{s.t.} \quad R_s > 0. \tag{3.37}$$

Since $\mathcal{P}_t(R_s)$ decreases with $R_s$ (see Eq. (3.31)) and reduces to 0 as $R_s \to \infty$, Eq. (3.37) indicates that $R_s$ should be neither too small nor too large for achieving a high secrecy throughput. The following theorem gives the optimal $R_s$ that maximizes $\Omega_S$:

**Theorem 3.4** *$\Omega_S$ in Eq.* (3.37) *is a quasi-concave function Sect. [6, 3.4.2] of $R_s$, and the optimal $R_s^*$ that maximizes $\Omega_S$ is the unique root of the following equation:*

$$\sum_{k=0}^{M-1} \frac{\mu_{\min}^{k+1-M}}{k!} - \frac{R_s 2^{R_s} \ln 2}{\Gamma(M)\rho} \left( \chi(\phi^*) + \frac{1}{\phi^*} \right) = 0. \tag{3.38}$$

*Proof* Please see Appendix A.4. ■

As Appendix A.4 shows, the left-hand side (LHS) of Eq. (3.38) decreases in $R_s$, and thus we can numerically calculate the optimal $R_s^*$ using the bisection method.

With the above two-step procedure, we have solved the problem given in Eq. (3.29), and the maximum $\Omega_S^*$ in SPTS can be obtained by substituting the optimal $R_s^*$ into Eq. (3.37).

## 3.5 Simulations

This section presents numerical results to validate our theoretical analysis. Through the experiments, we set $\alpha = 4$ and let $r_b$ be the unit distance.

### *3.5.1 Outage-Optimal Power Allocation*

Figure 3.1 describes the optimal power allocation ratio $\phi^*$ and the minimum SOP $\mathcal{P}_{so}(\gamma)$ versus $P$ for different values of $\gamma$. As discussed previously, Alice remains

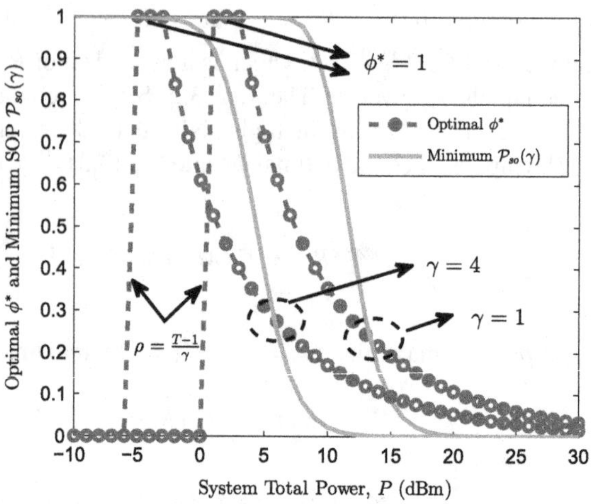


**Fig. 3.1** Optimal $\phi^*$ and minimum $\mathscr{P}_{so}(\gamma)$ versus $P$, with $M = 2$, $R_s = 1$, and $\lambda_e = 2$. @[2015] IEEE. Reprinted, with permission, from Ref. [7]

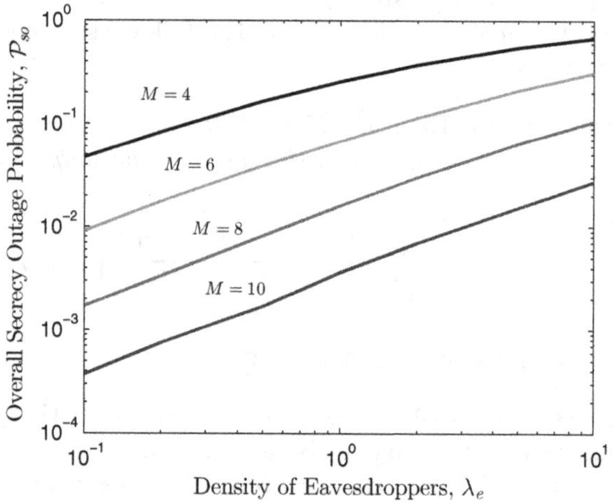


**Fig. 3.2** Overall $\mathscr{P}_{so}$ versus $\lambda_e$ for different $M$'s, with $P = 5$ dBm, and $R_s = 1$. @[2015] IEEE. Reprinted, with permission, from Ref. [7]

silent when $\rho < \frac{T-1}{\gamma}$, otherwise it transmits. After $\rho \geq \frac{T-1}{\gamma}$, $\phi^*$ is nearly one at first, and $\mathscr{P}_{so}(\gamma)$ maintains a high value. The underlying reason is that the current transmit power $P$ is not large enough to support the target $R_s$, such that almost full power should be allocated to the information signal to guarantee a reliable link to Bob. As $P$ increases further, both $\phi^*$ and $\mathscr{P}_{so}(\gamma)$ drop, which indicates that a larger fraction of power is shifted to AN in order to confuse eavesdroppers. Similarly, for a given $P$, both $\phi^*$ and $\mathscr{P}_{so}(\gamma)$ decrease as $\gamma$ increases.

Figure 3.2 plots the overall SOP $\mathscr{P}_{so}$ versus $\lambda_e$ for different values of $M$. We see that $\mathscr{P}_{so}$ significantly decreases as $M$ increases. However, in a denser eavesdropper scenario, $\mathscr{P}_{so}$ increases and converges to one under an extremely large $\lambda_e$.

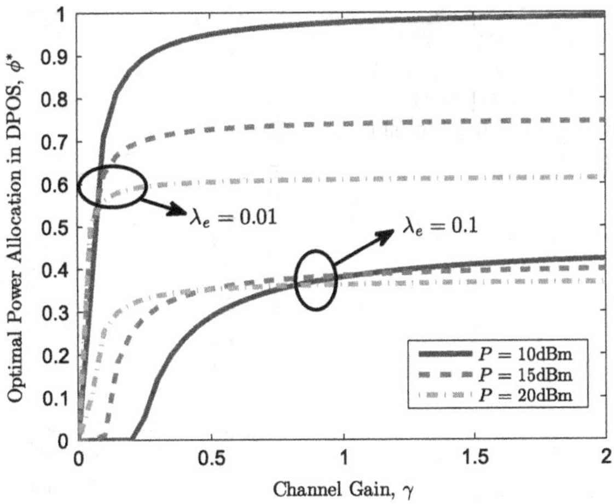


**Fig. 3.3** Optimal power allocation ratio $\phi^*$ in DPTS versus $\gamma$, with $M = 4$, and $\varepsilon = 0.1$. @[2015] IEEE. Reprinted, with permission, from Ref. [7]

### 3.5.2 Secrecy Throughput Optimization for DPTS and SPTS

Figure 3.3 illustrates the optimal $\phi^*$ as a function of $\gamma$ for different values of $\lambda_e$ and $P$ in DPTS. We find that $\phi^*$ decreases as $\gamma$ does, which implies that as the quality of the main channel decreases, secure transmissions become more vulnerable to overhearing. Hence more power should be allocated to the AN to confuse eavesdroppers, which is just opposite of the behavior in Fig. 3.1 where the minimum SOP is taken as the optimization objective. When $\gamma$ becomes sufficiently small, transmission is suspended. For a given $\gamma$, as $\lambda_e$ reduces, we can allocate more power (even full power) to the information signal to enlarge the secrecy rate. Interestingly, when $\gamma$ is small, the optimal $\phi^*$ increases as $P$ increases, which suggests that we ought to allocate more power to the information signal to achieve a higher message rate. However, things reverse when $\gamma$ is large, and the optimal $\phi^*$ decreases as $P$ increases. This occurs because the quality of the main channel is good enough to allow a larger fraction of power for the AN. In addition, as revealed in Theorem 3.2, $\phi^*$ at the high-SNR regime tends to a constant which is irrespective to $\gamma$.

Figure 3.4 depicts the maximum secrecy throughput $\Omega_{\mathrm{D}}^*$ versus $\lambda_e$ for different values of $\varepsilon$. $\Omega_{\mathrm{D}}^*$ linearly decreases with a larger $\log_{10} \lambda_e$ or a smaller $\log_{10} \varepsilon$, which implies that secrecy performance improves under a moderate SOP constraint (a large $\varepsilon$) or in a sparse eavesdropper scenario (a small $\lambda_e$).

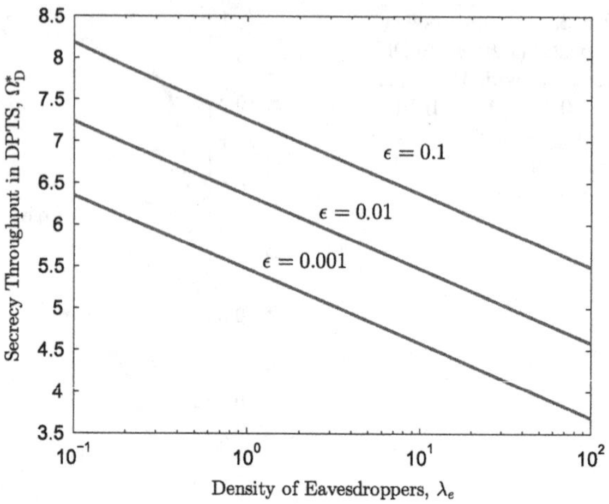


**Fig. 3.4** Maximum secrecy throughput $\Omega_D^*$ in DPTS versus $\lambda_e$, with $P = 30\,\text{dBm}$, and $M = 4$. @[2015] IEEE. Reprinted, with permission, from Ref. [7]

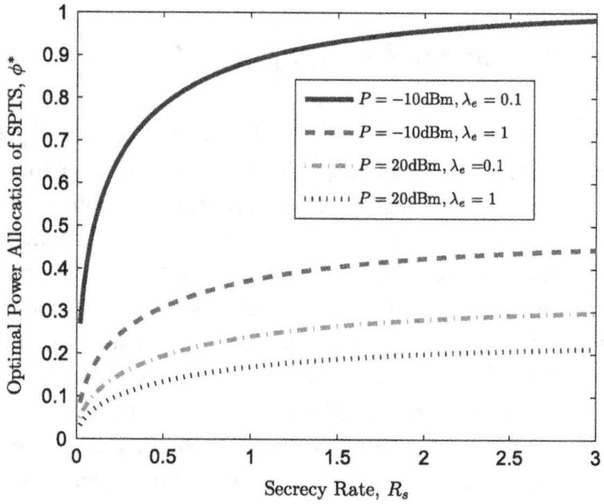


**Fig. 3.5** Optimal power allocation ratio $\phi^*$ of SPTS versus $R_s$, with $M = 4$, and $\varepsilon = 0.1$. @[2015] IEEE. Reprinted, with permission, from Ref. [7]

Figure 3.5 illustrates how the optimal $\phi^*$ varies w.r.t. $R_s$ in SPTS. We find that $\phi^*$ increases as $R_s$ increases for given $\lambda_e$ and $P$. It indicates that, to support a larger $R_s$, we should give more power to the information signal to improve the main channel. As stated in Corollary 3.2, the optimal $\phi^*$ converges to a constant when $R_s$ is extremely large. Similar to DPTS, $\phi^*$ decreases as $\lambda_e$ or $P$ increases, which means that we should increase the AN power to resist eavesdroppers.

Figure 3.6 presents the transmission probability $\mathscr{P}_t(R_s)$ as well as the secrecy throughput $\Omega_S$ versus $R_s$ for different values of $M$ in SPTS. The top figure shows that $\mathscr{P}_t(R_s)$ monotonically decreases with $R_s$, and rapidly reduces to 0 when $R_s$ becomes sufficiently large. There is a tradeoff between $\mathscr{P}_t(R_s)$ and $R_s$ to maximize $\Omega_S$. As the bottom figure indicates, $\Omega_S$ first lineally rises and then exponentially decreases as a function of $R_s$. A proper $R_s$ should be carefully designed to maximize $\Omega_S$. This

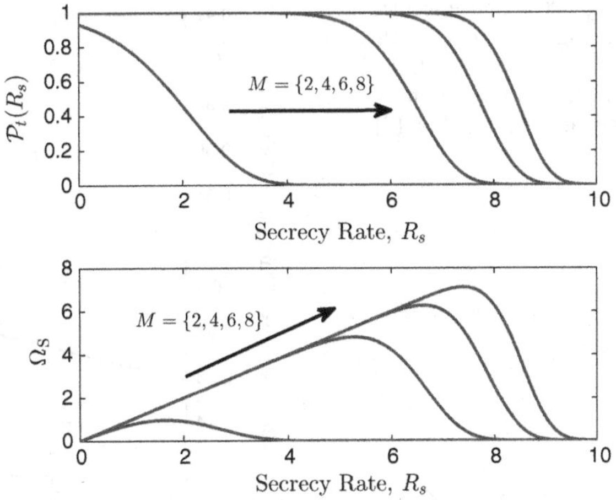


**Fig. 3.6** Transmission probability $\mathscr{P}_t(R_s)$ and secrecy throughput $\Omega_S$ in SPTS versus $R_s$, with $P = 30$ dBm, $\lambda_e = 1$, and $\varepsilon = 0.01$. @[2015] IEEE. Reprinted, with permission, from Ref. [7]

is consistent with our previous analysis. We also find that, the benefit introduced by adding transmit antennas is significant when $M$ is small, e.g., $M = 2, 4$.

### 3.5.3 *Comparison Between DPTS and SPTS*

Figure 3.7 plots the maximum $\Omega^*$ in DPTS and SPTS versus $P$ for different values of $M$. In both schemes, $\Omega^*$ becomes larger as $M$ or $P$ increases, which confirms the fact that either adding antennas or increasing transmit power is conducive to improving $\Omega^*$. As expected, due to the adaptive design, DPTS always outperforms SPTS. In addition, the high-SNR approximation $\Omega_D^\circ$ is very close to the exact $\Omega_D^*$.

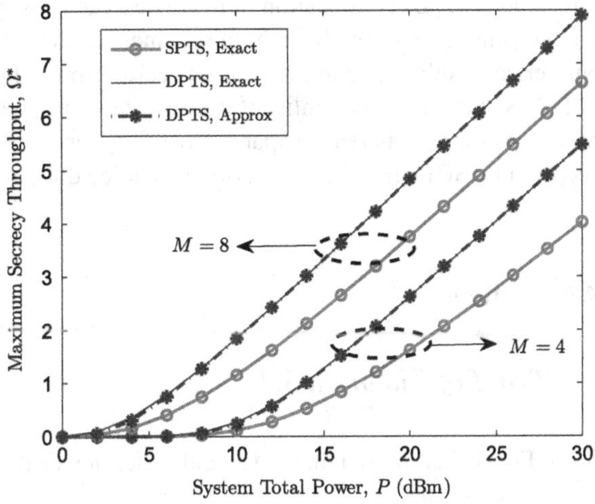


**Fig. 3.7** Maximum secrecy throughput $\Omega_D^*$ and $\Omega_S^*$ versus $P$, with $\lambda_e = 10$, and $\varepsilon = 0.01$. @[2015] IEEE. Reprinted, with permission, from Ref. [7]

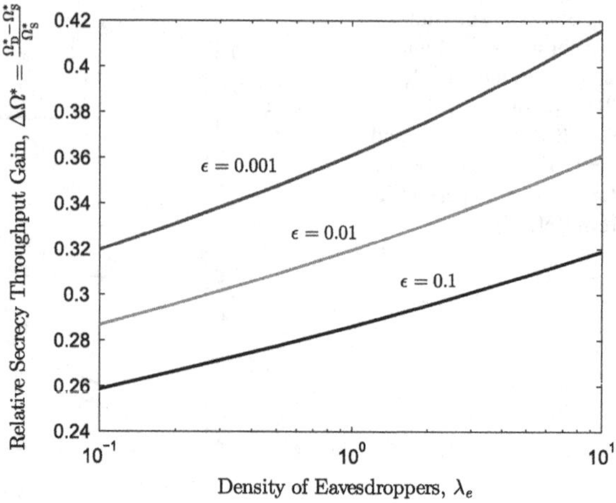


**Fig. 3.8** Relative secrecy throughput gain of DPTS over SPTS $\Delta\Omega^*$. @[2015] IEEE. Reprinted, with permission, from Ref. [7]

Figure 3.8 presents the relative secrecy throughput gain $\Delta\Omega^* = \frac{\Omega_D^*-\Omega_S^*}{\Omega_S^*}$ of DPTS over SPTS. We observe that, $\Delta\Omega^*$ increases as $\lambda_e$ increases or $\varepsilon$ decreases. It implies that the superiority of DPTS over SPTS becomes greater in denser eavesdropper scenarios or under more rigorous SOP constraints.

## 3.6 Conclusions

This chapter investigates the design of the AN-aided multi-antenna transmission in slow fading channels against PPP distributed eavesdroppers in a single-user downlink cellular network. A closed-form expression of the optimal power allocation that minimizes the SOP is first derived. To maximize secrecy throughput subject to an SOP constraint, both DPTS and SPTS are proposed, where code rates, transmission threshold, and power allocation ratio are designed based on the ICSI and SCSI of the main channel, respectively. In both schemes, explicit design solutions are provided. Numerical results and comparisons on secrecy throughput reveal that the superiority of DPTS over SPTS is significant in dense eavesdropper scenarios or under rigorous SOP constraints, whereas in sparse eavesdropper situations or under moderate SOP constraints, SPTS may be an alternative choice due to its low complexity.

## Appendices

### *A.1 Proof of Theorem 3.1*

From Eq. (3.24), we obtain the second-order derivatives of $R_s$

$$\frac{d^2R_s}{d\phi^2}=\frac{1}{\ln 2}\left(\frac{-\rho^2\gamma^2}{(1+\phi\rho\gamma)^2}-\frac{2\frac{d\chi}{d\phi}+\phi\frac{d^2\chi}{d\phi^2}}{1+\phi\chi}+\left(\frac{\chi+\phi\frac{d\chi}{d\phi}}{1+\phi\chi}\right)^2\right), \tag{3.39}$$

where $\frac{d\chi}{d\phi}$ and $\frac{d^2\chi}{d\phi^2}$ are given in Eqs. (3.19) and (3.20), respectively. Substituting Eq. (3.21) into Eq. (3.39) produces the following inequality

$$\frac{d^2R_s}{d\phi^2}<-\frac{1}{\ln 2}\left(\frac{\rho^2\gamma^2}{(1+\phi\rho\gamma)^2}-\frac{\chi^2}{(1+\phi\chi)^2}\right). \tag{3.40}$$

Since $\rho\gamma>\chi \Rightarrow \frac{\rho\gamma}{1+\phi\rho\gamma}-\frac{\chi}{1+\phi\chi}=\frac{\rho\gamma-\chi}{(1+\phi\rho\gamma)(1+\phi\chi)}>0$, we have proven $\frac{d^2R_s}{d\phi^2}<0$, i.e., $R_s$ is a concave function of $\phi$.

From Eq. (3.24), we have $\frac{dR_s}{d\phi}|_{\phi=0}=\frac{1}{\ln 2}(\rho\gamma-\chi_0)>0$, and

$$\frac{dR_s}{d\phi}|_{\phi=1}=\frac{1}{\ln 2}\left(\frac{\rho\gamma}{1+\rho\gamma}-\frac{\chi_1+\frac{d\chi}{d\phi}|_{\phi=1}}{1+\chi_1}\right), \tag{3.41}$$

where $\frac{d\chi}{d\phi}|_{\phi=1}=\frac{\alpha}{2}\chi_1^2$ is given from Eq. (3.19). Due to the concavity of $R_s$ w.r.t. $\phi$, when $\frac{dR_s}{d\phi}|_{\phi=1}>0$, the maximum $R_s$ is achieved on the boundary $\phi=1$, otherwise the optimal $\phi^*$ is the unique root of $\frac{dRs}{d\phi}=0$. The conditions for $\phi^*=1$ can be easily concluded from Eq. (3.41), which is given in Eq. (3.23).

## *A.2 Proof of Corollary 3.1*

Substituting $\frac{d\chi}{d\phi}$ into $\frac{dR_s}{d\phi}=0$ produces

$$(\rho\gamma\phi^2-D\phi+\phi+D)\chi^2+(D\rho\gamma\phi-D\rho\gamma+\delta)\chi-\delta\rho\gamma=0. \tag{3.42}$$

Denote the LHS of Eq. (3.42) as $Q_1(\phi)$, and we have $Q_1(\phi^\star)=0$.

(1) $\phi^\star\sim\gamma$: Using the derivative rule for implicit functions with $Q_1(\phi^\star)=0$ yields

$$\frac{d\phi}{d\gamma}=-\frac{\partial Q_1/\partial\gamma}{\partial Q_1/\partial\phi}=-\frac{\rho\phi^2\chi^2-\rho(\delta+D(1-\phi)\chi)}{\varpi_1(\phi,\chi)\frac{d\chi}{d\phi}+\varpi_2(\phi,\chi)}, \tag{3.43}$$

where $\varpi_1(\phi,\chi)=2(\rho\gamma\phi^2-D\phi+\phi+D)\chi+(D\rho\gamma\phi-D\rho\gamma+\delta)$, $\varpi_2(\phi,\chi)=(1+2\rho\gamma\phi)\chi^2+D(\rho\gamma-\chi)\chi$, and $\frac{d\chi}{d\phi}>0$ (see Lemma 3.2). From Eq. (3.42), we get $(\rho\gamma\phi^2+\phi+D)\chi^2+(D\rho\gamma\phi+\delta)\chi=D\phi\chi^2+D\rho\gamma\chi+\delta\rho\gamma$. Substituting this obtained equation into $\varpi_1(\phi,\chi)$ directly proves $\varpi_1(\phi,\chi)>0$. Since $\rho\gamma>\chi$, $\varpi_2(\phi,\chi)>0$ always holds. Hence, we obtain $\frac{\partial Q_1}{\partial\phi}>0$. From $\frac{dR_s}{d\phi}=0$ in Eq. (3.24), we have $\frac{\chi+\phi\frac{d\chi}{d\phi}}{1+\phi\chi} = \frac{\rho\gamma}{1+\phi\rho\gamma} < \frac{1}{\phi} \Rightarrow \phi^2\frac{d\chi}{d\phi} < 1 \Rightarrow \phi^2\chi^2 < (\delta + D(1-\phi)\chi)$ (see Eq. (3.19)), i.e., $\frac{\partial Q_1}{\partial\gamma} < 0$. By now, we have proven $\frac{d\phi}{d\gamma} > 0$.

(2) $\phi^\star \sim \lambda_e$: As done in Eq. (3.43), $\frac{d\phi}{d\lambda_e}$ is given by $\frac{d\phi}{d\lambda_e} = -\frac{\varpi_1(\phi,\chi)\frac{d\chi}{d\lambda_e}}{\partial Q_1/\partial\phi}$, where $\varpi_1(\phi,\chi) > 0$ and $\frac{\partial Q_1}{\partial\phi} > 0$ have been already verified in (1), and $\frac{d\chi}{d\lambda_e} > 0$ can be directly given from Eq. (3.18). In that case, we have proven that $\frac{d\phi}{d\lambda_e} < 0$.

(3) $\phi^\star \sim \varepsilon$: Quite similar to (2), we give $\frac{d\phi}{d\varepsilon} = -\frac{\varpi_1(\phi,\chi)\frac{d\chi}{d\varepsilon}}{\partial Q_1/\partial\phi}$, and $\frac{d\chi}{d\varepsilon} < 0$ from Eq. (3.18). Therefore, we have proven that $\frac{d\phi}{d\varepsilon} > 0$.

### A.3 Proof of Corollary 3.2

Plugging $\frac{d\chi}{d\phi}$ in Eq. (3.19) into $\frac{d\mu}{d\phi} = 0$ produces

$$T\phi^2\chi^2 - D(T-1)(1-\phi)\chi - \delta(T-1) = 0. \tag{3.44}$$

Denote the LHS of Eq. (3.44) as $Q_2(\phi)$, and we have $Q_2(\phi^\star) = 0$.

(1) $\phi^\star \sim Rs$: Using the derivative rule for implicit functions in $Q_2(\phi^\star) = 0$ yields

$$\frac{d\phi}{dT} = -\frac{\partial Q_2(\phi)/\partial T}{\partial Q_2(\phi)/\partial\phi} = -\frac{\phi^2\chi^2 - D(1-\phi)\chi - \delta}{\varpi_3(\phi,\chi)\frac{d\chi}{d\phi} + \varpi_4(\phi,\chi)}, \tag{3.45}$$

where $\varpi_3(\phi,\chi) \triangleq 2T\phi^2\chi - D(T-1)(1-\phi)$, and $\varpi_4(\phi,\chi) \triangleq 2T\phi\chi^2 + D(T-1)\chi$. From Eq. (3.44), the numerator of Eq. (3.45) satisfies $\phi^2\chi^2 - D(1-\phi)\chi - \delta = -\frac{1}{T}(\delta + D(1-\phi)\chi) < 0$. Similarly, we prove $\varpi_3(\phi,\chi), \varpi_4(\phi,\chi) > 0$. Since $\frac{d\chi}{d\phi} > 0$ (Lemma 3.2), we have $\frac{\partial Q_2(\phi)}{\partial\phi} > 0$, which produces $\frac{d\phi}{dT} > 0$.

(2) $\phi^\star \sim \lambda_e$: From Eq. (3.44), $\frac{d\phi}{d\lambda_e}$ can be given by $\frac{d\phi}{d\lambda_e} = -\frac{\varpi_3(\phi,\chi)\frac{d\chi}{d\lambda_e}}{\partial Q_2/\partial\phi}$, where $\varpi_3(\phi,\chi) > 0$ and $\frac{\partial Q_2}{\partial\phi} > 0$ have been already verified in (1), and $\frac{d\chi}{d\lambda_e} > 0$ can be directly given from Eq. (3.18). Hence, we have $\frac{d\phi}{d\lambda_e} < 0$.

(3) $\phi^\star \sim \varepsilon$: Similar to (2), we prove $\frac{d\chi}{d\varepsilon} < 0 \Rightarrow \frac{d\phi}{d\varepsilon} > 0$.

### A.4 Proof of Theorem 3.4

We give the first-order derivative of $\Omega_S$ w.r.t. $R_s$ from Eq. (3.27)

$$\frac{d\Omega_S}{dR_s} = \mathcal{P}_t + R_s\frac{d\mathcal{P}_t}{dR_s} = \mathcal{P}_t + R_s\frac{d\mathcal{P}_t}{d\mu}\frac{d\mu}{dR_s}. \tag{3.46}$$

Since $\mathscr{P}_t$ is actually the CCDF of $\gamma$, we can easily obtain

$$\frac{d\mathscr{P}_t}{d\mu} = -f_\gamma(\mu) = -\frac{\mu^{M-1}}{\Gamma(M)}e^{-\mu}. \tag{3.47}$$

Substituting Eqs. (3.36) and (3.47) into Eq. (3.46) yields

$$\frac{d\Omega_S}{dR_s} = e^{-\mu}\mu^{M-1}\left(\sum_{k=0}^{M-1}\frac{\mu^{-M+k+1}}{k!} - \frac{R_s}{\Gamma(M)}\frac{d\mu}{dR_s}\right). \tag{3.48}$$

Denote the term in the parenthesis of Eq. (3.48) as $\mathscr{L}(R_s)$. It is clear that the sign of $\frac{d\Omega_S}{dR_s}$ remains consistent with that of $\mathscr{L}(R_s)$ since $e^{-\mu}\mu^{M-1}$ is always positive. We observe that, since $\mu$ increases w.r.t. $R_s$ (see Eq. (3.31)), $\sum_{k=0}^{M-1}\frac{\mu^{-M+k+1}}{k!}$ is a strictly decreasing positive function of $R_s$. Besides, we easily have $\mathscr{L}(0) > 0$ and $\mathscr{L}(\infty) < 0$. Supposing $R_s\frac{d\mu}{dR_s}$ monotonically increases with $R_s$, there obviously exists a unique $R_s^*$ that makes $\mathscr{L}(R_s)$ first positive and then negative after $R_s$ exceeds $R_s^*$. That is, we may prove $\Omega_S$ is a first-increasing-then-decreasing function of $R_s$. Invoking the definition of single-variable quasi-concave function section [6, 3.4.2], $\Omega_S$ is a quasi-concave function of $R_s$, and the above $R_s^*$ is the optimal solution that maximizes $\Omega_S$, which is obtained when $\mathscr{L}(R_s) = 0$. Based on the above discussion, in what follows we focus on proving the monotonicity of $R_s\frac{d\mu}{dR_s}$ w.r.t. $R_s$. Since $R_s\frac{d\mu}{dR_s} = T\ln T\frac{d\mu}{dT}$, where $\frac{d\mu}{dT}$ can be given from Eq. (3.31)

$$\frac{d\mu}{dT} = \frac{1+\phi\chi(\phi)}{\rho\phi} = \frac{1}{T}\left(\mu + \frac{1}{\rho\phi}\right), \tag{3.49}$$

we introduce the following auxiliary function

$$Y(T) \triangleq T\ln T\frac{d\mu}{dT} = \ln T\left(\mu + \frac{1}{\rho\phi}\right), \tag{3.50}$$

and proving the monotonicity of $R_s\frac{d\mu}{dR_s}$ w.r.t. $R_s$ is equivalent to proving the monotonicity of $Y(T)$ w.r.t. $T$. To complete the proof, we consider the following two cases of Eq. (3.33).

(1): When $\frac{T-1}{T} \geq \frac{\alpha}{2}\chi_1^2$, we have $\phi^* = 1$, and $\mu = \frac{1}{\rho}(T\chi_1 + T - 1)$. Then $Y(T) = \frac{1+\chi_1}{\rho}T\ln T$, which is evidently a monotonically increasing function of $T$.

(2): When $\frac{T-1}{T} < \frac{\alpha}{2}\chi_1^2$, the optimal $\phi^*$ satisfies $\frac{d\mu}{d\phi} = 0$. The first-order derivative of $Y(T)$ w.r.t. $T$ is

$$\frac{dY(T)}{dT} = \frac{1}{T}\left(\mu + \frac{1}{\rho\phi}\right) + \ln T\left(\frac{d\mu}{dT} - \frac{1}{\rho\phi^2}\frac{d\phi}{dT}\right). \tag{3.51}$$

Recalling Eq. (3.34), we define $Y_1(\phi) \triangleq T\frac{d\chi}{d\phi} - \frac{T-1}{\phi^2}$. Since $\frac{d\mu}{d\phi} = 0$, i.e., $Y_1(\phi^*) = 0$, $\frac{d\phi}{dT}$ in Eq. (3.51) is given by $\frac{d\phi}{dT} = -\frac{\partial Y_1/\partial T}{\partial Y_1/\partial \phi}$, where $\frac{\partial Y_1}{\partial T} = \frac{d\chi}{d\phi} - \frac{1}{\phi^2}$, and $\frac{\partial Y_1}{\partial \phi} = T\frac{d^2\chi}{d\phi^2} + \frac{2(T-1)}{\phi^3}$. From $Y_1(\phi^*) = 0$, we have $\frac{d\chi}{d\phi} = \frac{T-1}{T\phi^2}$, and from Eq. (3.21), we know $\frac{d^2\chi}{d\phi^2} > \frac{2}{\chi}\left(\frac{d\chi}{d\phi}\right)^2$. Combine with Eq. (3.31), then we obtain

$$\frac{d\phi}{dT} < \frac{\phi\chi}{2(T-1)\rho\mu} = \frac{1}{T}\left(\frac{\phi}{2(T-1)} - \frac{1}{2\rho\mu}\right), \tag{3.52}$$

where the right-hand side (RHS) equality holds for $\frac{\chi}{\rho} = \frac{1}{T}\left(\mu - \frac{T-1}{\rho\phi}\right)$ (see Eq. (3.31)). Substituting Eq. (3.52) into Eq. (3.51) yields

$$\frac{dY(T)}{dT} > \frac{1}{T}\left((1+\ln T)\,\mu + \frac{\ln T}{2\rho^2\phi^2\mu} + \frac{Y_2(T)}{2(T-1)\rho\phi}\right) > \frac{Y_2(T)}{2(T-1)T\rho\phi}, \tag{3.53}$$

where $Y_2(T) = 2(1+\ln T)(T-1) - \ln T$. The first-order derivative of $Y_2(T)$ w.r.t. $T$ is $\frac{dY_2}{dT} = 2\ln T + 4 - \frac{3}{T} > 0$. Therefore, $Y_2$ monotonically increases w.r.t. $T$, then $Y_2(T) \geq Y_2(1) = 0$ always holds, with which we have proven $\frac{dY(T)}{dT} > 0$, i.e., $Y(T)$ monotonically increases w.r.t. $T \in [1, \infty)$. By now, we have completed the proof.

## References


1. S. Goel, R. Negi, Guaranteeing secrecy using artificial noise. IEEE Trans. Wirel. Commun. **7**(6), 2180–2189 (2008)
2. P. Gopala, L. Lai, H. El Gamal, On the secrecy capacity of fading channels. IEEE Trans. Inf. Theory **54**(10), 4687–4698 (2008)
3. X. Zhang, X. Zhou, M.R. McKay, On the design of artificial-noise-aided secure multi-antenna transmission in slow fading channels. IEEE Trans. Veh. Technol. **62**(5), 2170–2181 (2013)
4. D. Stoyan, W. Kendall, J. Mecke, *Stochastic Geometry and Its Applications*, 2nd edn. (Wiley, London, 1996)
5. I.S. Gradshteyn, I.M. Ryzhik, A. Jeffrey, D. Zwillinger, S. Technica, *Table of Integrals, Series, and Products*, 7th edn. (Academic Press, New York, 2007)
6. S. Boyd, L. Vandenberghe, *Convex Optimization* (Cambridge Univ. Press, Cambridge, 2004)
7. T.-X. Zheng, H.-M. Wang, J. Yuan, D. Towsley, M.H. Lee, Multi-antenna transmission with artificial noise against randomly distributed eavesdroppers. IEEE Trans. Commun. **63**(11), 4347–4362 (2015)

# Chapter 4
# Physical Layer Security in Heterogeneous Cellular Network

**Abstract** The heterogeneous cellular network is believed to be a promising deployment of cellular networks in 5G. This chapter comprehensively studies physical layer security in a multitier HCN where BSs, authorized users and eavesdroppers are all randomly located. We first propose a *truncated average received signal power*-based secrecy mobile association policy. Under this policy, we investigate and provide tractable expressions for the connection probability and secrecy probability of a randomly located user. We further evaluate the network-wide secrecy throughput and the minimum secrecy throughput per user under both connection and secrecy probability constraints. We prove that the proposed mobile association policy significantly enhances the secrecy throughput performance of the HCN.

## 4.1 Introduction

In this chapter, we extend physical layer security to a $K$-tier HCN where the positions of BSs, authorized users and Eves are all modeled as independent homogeneous PPPs. Due to the multitier hierarchical architecture, HCNs bring new challenges to the investigation of physical layer security compared with the conventional single-tier topology. In addition to cross-cell interference, HCNs introduce severe cross-tier interference. Both reliability and secrecy of data transmissions should be taken into account, which makes analyzing the impact of interference on both UEs and Eves much more complicated, especially when system parameters differ between different tiers. Besides, mobile terminals can access an arbitrary tier, e.g., open access, which calls for specific mobile association policies that consider both quality of service (QoS) and secrecy.

To protect the confidential signal we still propose the AN-aided multi-antenna secure transmission as in Chap. 3. We then provide a comprehensive performance analysis and optimization under the stochastic geometry framework. Note that the conventional single-tier random cellular network is a special case of the $K$-tier HCN when $K = 1$, so all the analysis in this chapter apply to the conventional random cellular network.



H.-M. Wang and T.-X. Zheng, *Physical Layer Security in Random Cellular Networks*, SpringerBriefs in Computer Science,
DOI 10.1007/978-981-10-1575-5_4

The aim of this chapter is to leverage some analytical expressions to provide tractable predictions of network performance and guidelines for future network designs. In the following sections, we will first propose a secrecy mobile association policy based on the *truncated average received signal power* (ARSP), and derive the corresponding tier association probability (the probability that a tier is associated with the typical UE) and the BS activation probability (the probability that a BS associates at least one UE); then we will analyze the connection probability and the secrecy probability of a randomly located UE, and provide some analytically tractable expressions; finally, we will investigate network-wide secrecy throughput subject to connection and secrecy probability constraints, and explain how the power allocation ratio of the artificial noise scheme and the access threshold of the mobile association policy will influence the network-wide secrecy throughput performance.

## 4.2 System Model

This section presents the details of the system secrecy model for a $K$-tier HCN.

### 4.2.1 *Cellular Deployment and Channel Model*

We consider a $K$-tier HCN where the BSs in different tiers have different operating parameters (e.g., transmit powers $P_k$ and antenna numbers $M_k$), while in the same tier they share the same parameters. Define $\mathcal{K} \triangleq \{1, 2, \cdots, K\}$. In tier $k$, the BSs are spatially distributed according to a homogeneous PPP $\Phi_k$ with density $\lambda_k$ in a two-dimensional plane $\mathbb{R}^2$. As depicted in Fig. 4.1, there coexist UEs and Eves, where the UEs are legitimate destinations while the Eves are wiretappers attempting to intercept the secret information intended for the UEs. The locations of the UEs and Eves are characterized by two independent homogeneous PPPs $\Phi_u$ and $\Phi_e$ with densities $\lambda_u$ and $\lambda_e$, respectively.

Wireless channels are supposed to undergo flat Rayleigh fading together with a large-scale path loss governed by the exponent $\alpha > 2$. Each BS in tier $k$ has $M_k$ antennas, and UEs and Eves are each equipped with a single antenna. The channel from the BS located at $z$ in tier $k$ to the receiver node (UE or Eve) located at $x$ is characterized by $\boldsymbol{h}_{zx} r_{zx}^{-\alpha/2}$, where $\boldsymbol{h}_{zx} \in \mathbb{C}^{M_k \times 1}$ denotes the small-scale fading vector with independent and identically distributed (i.i.d.) entries $h_{zx,j} \sim CN(0, 1)$, and $r_{zx}$ denotes the path distance. We assume that each BS knows the CSIs of its associated UEs. Since each Eve passively receives signals, its ICSI is unknown, whereas its SCSI is available.

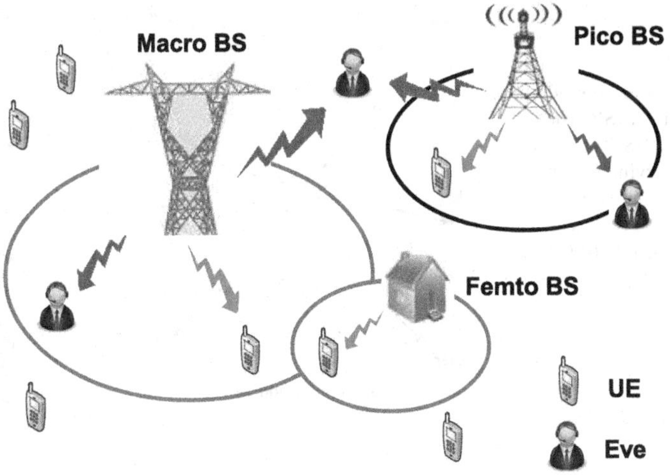


**Fig. 4.1** A three-tier macro/pico/femto HCN where authorized users coexist with eavesdroppers. @[2016] IEEE. Reprinted, with permission, from Ref. [1]

### 4.2.2 Secure Transmission Signaling

Utilizing the Wyner's wiretap encoding scheme introduced in Sect. 1.3.4, we denote $R_{t,k}$, $R_{e,k}$, and $R_{s,k} = R_{t,k} - R_{e,k}$ as the transmission rate, redundant rate, and confidential information rate related to tier $k$. Each BS employs the AN-aided transmission strategy to guarantee both reliability and secrecy. The transmitted signal of the BS located at $z$ in tier $k$ is designed as follows and more details can be found in Sect. 3.2.1,

$$\boldsymbol{x}_z = \sqrt{\phi_k P_k}\boldsymbol{w}_z s_z + \sqrt{(1-\phi_k)P_k}\boldsymbol{W}_z \boldsymbol{v}_z,\ z \in \Phi_k. \tag{4.1}$$

For convenience, we let $\delta \triangleq 2/\alpha$, $\Xi \triangleq \sum_{j\in\mathcal{K}} \lambda_j (P_j M_j)^{\delta}$, and $C_{j,k} \triangleq \frac{C_j}{C_k}$, $\forall C \in \{P, M, \lambda, \phi\}$.

### 4.2.3 Secrecy Mobile Association Policy

Consider an open-access system where each UE is allowed to access an arbitrary tier. In order to avoid access with too poor channel conditions and meanwhile to improve transmission secrecy, we propose a *truncated ARSP* based mobile association policy, as illustrated in Fig. 4.2: a UE is associated with the BS providing the maximum ARSP, but remains idle if this ARSP falls below an *access threshold* $\tau$. Mathematically, the truncated ARSP is defined as

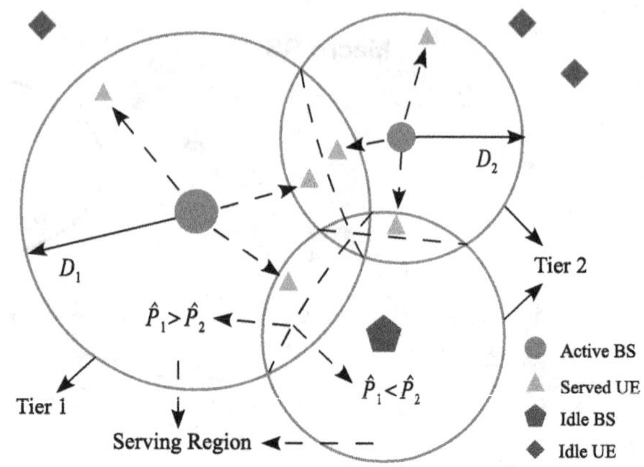


**Fig. 4.2** An illustration of our mobile association policy in a 2-tier HCN. A UE connects to the BS providing the maximum ARSP instead of the nearest BS. Those UEs outside the serving regions of BSs can not be served. A BS remains idle if it has no UE to serve. @[2016] IEEE. Reprinted, with permission, from Ref. [1]

$$\hat{P}_k = \begin{cases} P_k M_k r_k^{-\alpha}, & r_k \leq D_k, \\ 0, & r_k > D_k, \end{cases} \tag{4.2}$$

where $r_k$ denotes the distance from the UE to the nearest BS in tier $k$, and $D_k \triangleq \left(\frac{P_k M_k}{\tau}\right)^{\frac{1}{\alpha}}$ denotes the radius of the *serving region* of an arbitrary BS in tier $k$. Therefore the index of the tier to which the typical UE is associated with is

$$n^* = \arg\max_{k \in \mathcal{K}} \hat{P}_k. \tag{4.3}$$

We will see in subsequent analysis that $\tau$ plays a critical role in secrecy transmissions. With such a policy, the association probability of tier $k$ is mathematically defined as

$$S_k \triangleq \mathbb{P}\{n^* = k\} = \mathbb{P}\{\hat{P}_k > \hat{P}_j, \forall j \in \mathcal{K} \backslash k\}, \tag{4.4}$$

which has a closed-form expression provided by the following lemma.

**Lemma 4.1** *The association probability of tier k is given by*

$$S_k = \lambda_k (P_k M_k)^{\delta} \Xi^{-1} \left(1 - e^{-\pi \tau^{-\delta} \Xi}\right). \tag{4.5}$$

*Proof* From Eqs. (4.2) and (4.4), we know that a UE located at the origin $o$ is associated with tier $k$ only if $r_k \leq D_k$ and $\hat{P}_k > \hat{P}_j, \forall j \neq k$ simultaneously hold. Therefore, $S_k$ can be calculated as

$$S_k = \int_0^{D_k} \prod_{j \in \mathcal{K} \backslash k} \mathbb{P}\left\{\hat{P}_k > \hat{P}_j | r_k\right\} f_{r_k}(r) dr, \tag{4.6}$$

where $f_{r_k}(r) = 2\pi\lambda_k r e^{-\pi\lambda_k r^2}$ [2]. The term $\mathbb{P}\left\{\hat{P}_k > \hat{P}_j | r_k\right\}$ can be calculated as

$$\mathbb{P}\left\{\hat{P}_k > \hat{P}_j | r_k\right\} \overset{(a)}{=} \mathbb{P}\left\{r_j > \min\left\{D_j, \left(P_{j,k}M_{j,k}\right)^{\frac{1}{\alpha}} r_k\right\} | r_k\right\} \overset{(b)}{=} \mathbb{P}\left\{r_j > \left(P_{j,k}M_{j,k}\right)^{\frac{1}{\alpha}} r_k\right\}$$
$$= \mathbb{P}\left\{\textit{No BS in tier } j \textit{ is inside } \mathscr{B}\left(o, \left(P_{j,k}M_{j,k}\right)^{\frac{1}{\alpha}} r_k\right)\right\} \overset{(c)}{=} e^{-\pi\lambda_j \left(P_{j,k}M_{j,k}\right)^{\delta} r_k^2}, \quad (4.7)$$

where Eq. $(a)$ follows from the fact that $\hat{P}_k > \hat{P}_j$ holds if $r_j > D_j$ or $\frac{P_j M_j}{r_j^\alpha} < \frac{P_k M_k}{r_k^\alpha} \Rightarrow r_j > \left(P_{j,k}M_{j,k}\right)^{\frac{1}{\alpha}} r_k$, Eq. $(b)$ holds for $D_j = \left(\frac{P_j M_j}{\tau}\right)^{\frac{1}{\alpha}} = \left(P_{j,k}M_{j,k}\right)^{\frac{1}{\alpha}} D_k \geq \left(P_{j,k}M_{j,k}\right)^{\frac{1}{\alpha}} r_k$, and Eq. $(c)$ is obtained from the basic nature of PPP [3]. Substituting Eq. (4.7) into Eq. (4.6) and calculating the integral, we complete the proof. ■

From Lemma 4.1, we make the following two observations: (1) Tiers with large BS densities, high transmit power and more BS antennas are more likely to have UEs associated with them. (2) Due to the restriction of $\tau$, an arbitrary UE has a probability $1 - \sum_{k\in\mathscr{K}} S_k = e^{-\pi\tau^{-\delta}\Xi}$ of being idle.

We assume that a BS utilizes TDMA to efficiently eliminate intra-cell interference. Due to the overlap of serving regions among cells, a BS will remain inactive when it is associated with no UE (see the idle BS in Fig. 4.2). The *BS activation probability* of tier $k$ is defined as

$$A_k \triangleq \mathbb{P}\{\textit{A BS in tier } k \textit{ associates with at least one UE}\}, \quad (4.8)$$

which has a closed-form expression provided by the following lemma.

**Lemma 4.2** *The BS activation probability of tier k is given by*

$$A_k = 1 - \exp\left(-\lambda_u (P_k M_k)^{\delta} \Xi^{-1} \left(1 - e^{-\pi\tau^{-\delta}\Xi}\right)\right). \quad (4.9)$$

*Proof* Consider a tagged BS located at $z$ in tier $k$. Let $\Phi_u^o \triangleq \Phi_u \bigcap \mathscr{B}(z, D_k)$, and the BS idle probability of tier $k$, $\bar{A}_k \triangleq 1 - A_k$, can be calculated as follows

$$\bar{A}_k = \mathbb{E}\left[\prod_{x\in\Phi_u^o} \mathbb{P}\{\textit{a UE located at x is not associated with the tagged BS}\}\right]$$
$$= \mathbb{E}\left[\prod_{x\in\Phi_u^o} \mathbb{P}\left\{\frac{P_k M_k}{r_{zx}^\alpha} < \max_{j\in\mathscr{K}} \hat{P}_j\right\}\right] \overset{(d)}{=} \mathbb{E}_{\Phi_u}\left[\prod_{x\in\Phi_u^o} 1 - e^{-\pi\Xi(P_k M_k)^{-\delta} r_{zx}^2}\right]$$
$$\overset{(e)}{=} \exp\left(-2\pi\lambda_u \int_0^{D_k} e^{-\pi\Xi(P_k M_k)^{-\delta} r^2} r dr\right),$$

where Eq. $(d)$ is obtained from Eq. (4.7) and Eq. $(e)$ is derived by using the PGFL over PPP. Solving the integral term in $\bar{A}_k$ completes the proof. ■

From Lemmas 4.1 and 4.2, we obtain $A_k = 1 - e^{-\frac{\lambda_u}{\lambda_k} S_k}$. Obviously, BSs with higher power and more antennas have higher activation probabilities. The set of active BSs in tier $k$ is a thinning of $\Phi_k$, denoted by $\Phi_k^o$, with density $\lambda_k^o = A_k \lambda_k$.

## 4.3 Secrecy Performance Analysis

In this section, we investigate and provide tractable expressions for the connection probability and secrecy probability of a randomly located user in the HCN. We further evaluate the network-wide secrecy throughput and the minimum secrecy throughput per user under both connection and secrecy probability constraints.

### 4.3.1 *User Connection Probability*

This section investigates the connection probability of a random UE, which corresponds to the probability that a secret message is decoded by this UE. Without lose of generality, we consider a typical UE located at the origin $o$ and served by the BS located at $b$ in tier $k$. The received signal at the typical UE is given by

$$y_o = \underbrace{\frac{\sqrt{\phi_k P_k} \boldsymbol{h}_b^{\mathrm{T}} \boldsymbol{w}_b s_b}{R_k^{\alpha/2}}}_{\text{information signal}} + \underbrace{\sum_{j \in \mathcal{K}} \sum_{z \in \Phi_j^o \setminus b} \frac{\sqrt{\phi_j P_j} \boldsymbol{h}_{zo}^{\mathrm{T}} \boldsymbol{w}_z s_z + \sqrt{(1-\phi_j) P_j} \boldsymbol{h}_{zo}^{\mathrm{T}} \boldsymbol{W}_z \boldsymbol{v}_z}{r_{zo}^{\alpha/2}}}_{\text{intra- and cross-tier interference (signal and AN)}} + n_o, \tag{4.10}$$

where $R_k$ represents the distance between the typical user and the serving BS.

#### 4.3.1.1 Interference-Limited HCN

To provide a tractable analysis, we consider the interference-limited case by ignoring thermal noise. This is a reasonable assumption due to ubiquitous interference in the HCN. The connection probability of the typical UE is defined as

$$\mathcal{P}_{c,k}^{int} \triangleq \mathbb{P}\{\boldsymbol{SIR}_{o,k} \geq \beta_t\}, \tag{4.11}$$

where $\beta_t$ denotes the target signal-to-interference ratio (SIR) and $\boldsymbol{SIR}_{o,k}$ is given by

$$\boldsymbol{SIR}_{o,k} = \frac{\phi_k P_k \|\boldsymbol{h}_b\|^2 R_k^{-\alpha}}{\sum_{j \in \mathcal{K}} I_{jo}}, \tag{4.12}$$

with $I_{jo} = \sum_{z \in \Phi_j^o \setminus b} \frac{\phi_j P_j (|\boldsymbol{h}_{zo}^{\mathrm{T}} \boldsymbol{w}_z|^2 + \xi_j \|\boldsymbol{h}_{zo}^{\mathrm{T}} \boldsymbol{W}_z\|^2)}{r_{zo}^{\alpha}}$, and $\xi_j \triangleq \frac{\phi_j^{-1}-1}{M_j-1}$. Note that, there exists an exclusion region $\mathscr{B}\left(o, \left(P_{j,k} M_{j,k}\right)^{\frac{1}{\alpha}} R_k\right)$ around the typical UE for tier $j \in \mathscr{K}$, i.e., all interfering BSs in tier $j$ are located outside of it.

Let $I_o = \sum_{j \in \mathscr{K}} I_{jo}$ and $s \triangleq \frac{R_k^{\alpha} \beta_t}{\phi_k P_k}$. Plugging Eq. (4.12) into Eq. (4.11) yields

$$\begin{aligned} \mathscr{P}_{c,k}^{int} &= \mathbb{E}_{R_k} \mathbb{E}_{I_o} \left[ \mathbb{P}\left\{ \|\boldsymbol{h}_b\|^2 \geq s I_o \right\} \right] \stackrel{(f)}{=} \mathbb{E}_{R_k} \mathbb{E}_{I_o} \left[ e^{-s I_o} \sum_{m=0}^{M_k-1} \frac{s^m I_o^m}{m!} \right] \\ &\stackrel{(g)}{=} \sum_{m=0}^{M_k-1} \mathbb{E}_{R_k} \left[ \frac{(-1)^m s^m}{m!} \mathscr{L}_{I_o}^{(m)}(s) \right], \end{aligned} \tag{4.13}$$

where Eq. ($f$) holds for $\|\boldsymbol{h}_b\|^2 \sim \Gamma(M_k, 1)$, and Eq. ($g$) is obtained from [4, Theorem 1] with $\mathscr{L}_{I_o}^{(p)}(s)$ the $p$-order derivative of the Laplace transform $\mathscr{L}_{I_o}(s)$ evaluated at $s$.

**Theorem 4.1** *The connection probability of a typical UE associated with tier k is*

$$\mathscr{P}_{c,k}^{int} = \frac{\lambda_k}{S_k} \sum_{m=0}^{M_k-1} \frac{\|\boldsymbol{Q}_{M_k}^m\|_1}{\pi^m \Upsilon_k^{m+1}} \left( 1 - \sum_{l=0}^{m} \frac{\pi^l e^{-\pi \Upsilon_k D_k^2}}{l! D_k^{-2l} \Upsilon_k^{-l}} \right), \tag{4.14}$$

*where* $\|\cdot\|_1$ *is the* $L_1$ *induced matrix norm, i.e.,* $\|\boldsymbol{W}\|_1 = \max_{1 \leq j \leq N} \sum_{i=1}^{M} |W_{ij}|$ *for* $\boldsymbol{W} \in \mathbb{R}^{M \times N}$, $\Upsilon_k = \sum_{j \in \mathscr{K}} \lambda_j \left(P_{j,k} M_{j,k}\right)^{\delta} \left\{ 1 - A_j + \left(\frac{\phi_{j,k}\beta_t}{M_{j,k}}\right)^{\delta} A_j \Upsilon_{j1} + \frac{\delta M_{j,k}}{\phi_{j,k}\beta_t} A_j \Upsilon_{j2} \right\}$, *with*

$$\Upsilon_{j1} = \begin{cases} C_{\alpha, M_j+1}, & \xi_j = 1, \\ \frac{C_{\alpha,2}}{(1-\xi_j)^{M_j-1}} - \sum_{n=0}^{M_j-2} \frac{\xi_j^{1+\delta} C_{\alpha,n+2}}{(1-\xi_j)^{M_j-1-n}}, & \xi_j \neq 1, \end{cases} \tag{4.15}$$

$$\Upsilon_{j2} = \begin{cases} \left(\frac{M_{j,k}}{\phi_{j,k}\beta_t}\right)^{M_j-1} \frac{{}_2F_1\left(M_j, M_j+\delta; M_j+\delta+1; -\frac{M_{j,k}}{\phi_{j,k}\beta_t}\right)}{M_j+\delta}, & \xi_j = 1, \\ \frac{{}_2F_1\left(1, \delta+1; \delta+2; -\frac{M_{j,k}}{\phi_{j,k}\beta_t}\right)}{1+\delta(1-\xi_j)^{M_j-1}} - \sum_{n=0}^{M_j-2} \left(\frac{M_{j,k}}{\xi_j \phi_{j,k}\beta_t}\right)^n \frac{{}_2F_1\left(n+1, n+1+\delta; n+2+\delta; -\frac{M_{j,k}}{\xi_j \phi_{j,k}\beta_t}\right)}{(n+1+\delta)(1-\xi_j)^{M_j-1-n}}, & \xi_j \neq 1, \end{cases}$$

${}_2F_1(\cdot)$ *denotes the Gauss hypergeometric function.* $\boldsymbol{Q}_M^i(p,q)$ *is the row-p-column-q entry of the i-power* $\boldsymbol{Q}_M^i$*, where* $\boldsymbol{Q}_M$ *is a Toeplitz matrix*

$$\boldsymbol{Q}_M \triangleq \begin{bmatrix} 0 & & & & \\ g_1 & 0 & & & \\ g_2 & g_1 & 0 & & \\ \vdots & & & \ddots & \\ g_{M-1} & g_{M-2} & \cdots & g_1 & 0 \end{bmatrix}, \tag{4.16}$$

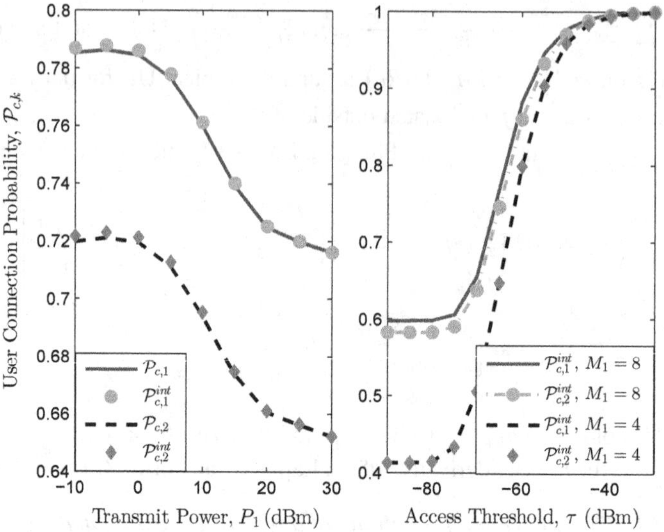


**Fig. 4.3** Connection probabilities in a 2-tier HCN, with $\{P_1, P_2\} = \{30, 10\}$ dBm, $M_2 = 4$, $\{\lambda_2, \lambda_u\} = \{4, 10\}\lambda_1$, $\beta_t = 10$, and $\{\phi_1, \phi_2\} = \{0.8, 0.8\}$. Unless otherwise specified, we set $\alpha = 4$ and $\lambda_1 = \frac{1}{\pi 400^2 \text{m}^2}$. @[2016] IEEE. Reprinted, with permission, from Ref. [1]

*with* $g_i = \frac{\pi\delta}{i-\delta}\sum_{j\in\mathcal{K}} A_j\lambda_j \left(P_{j,k}M_{j,k}\right)^{\delta}\left(\frac{\phi_{j,k}\beta_t}{M_{j,k}}\right)^i Z_{j,i}$ *and*

$$Z_{j,i} = \begin{cases} \binom{M_j+i-1}{M_j-1} {}_2F_1\left(M_j+i, i-\delta; i-\delta+1; -\frac{\phi_{j,k}\beta_t}{M_{j,k}}\right), & \xi_j = 1, \\ \dfrac{{}_2F_1\left(i+1, i-\delta; i-\delta+1; -\frac{\phi_{j,k}\beta_t}{M_{j,k}}\right) - \sum_{n=0}^{M_j-2}\binom{n+i}{n}\frac{\xi_j^{i+1}\,{}_2F_1\left(n+i+1, i-\delta; i-\delta+1; -\frac{\xi_j\phi_{j,k}\beta_t}{M_{j,k}}\right)}{(1-\xi_j)^n}}{(1-\xi_j)^{M_j-1}}, & \xi_j \neq 1, \end{cases}$$

*Proof* Please see Appendix A.1. ∎

The term $\sum_{l=0}^{m}\frac{\pi^l e^{-\pi\Upsilon_k D_k^2}}{l! D_k^{-2l}\Upsilon_k^{-l}}$ in Eq. (4.14) is a consequence of $\tau \neq 0$, which goes to zero as $\tau \to 0$, i.e., non-threshold mobile association policy.

Figure 4.3 compares the Monte Carlo simulated value $\mathcal{P}_{c,k}$ and the interference-limited value $\mathcal{P}^{int}_{c,k}$ given in Eq. (4.14). We can see that they nearly merge, which validates our analysis. In the subsequent analysis we focus on the latter for convenience.

#### 4.3.1.2 Asymptotic Analysis on $\mathcal{P}^{int}_{c,k}$

In the following, we provide some insights into the behavior of $\mathcal{P}^{int}_{c,k}$ by performing an asymptotic analysis, with the corresponding proof relegated to Appendix A.2.

**Property 4.1** *For the case that all tiers share the same number of BS antennas M and power allocation ratio* $\phi$, *and* $\lambda_u \gg \lambda_j$, $\forall j \in \mathcal{K}$, $\mathcal{P}_{c,k}^{int}$ *converges to a value that is independent of the transmit power* $P_j$, *BS density* $\lambda_j$ *and* $k \in \mathcal{K}$ *as* $\tau \to 0$.

**Property 4.2** $\mathcal{P}_{c,k}^{int} \to 1$ *as* $\tau \to \infty$ *for* $k \in \mathcal{K}$.

**Property 4.3** *When the transmit power of tier 1 is much larger than that of the other tiers,* $\mathcal{P}_{c,k}^{int}$ *increases with* $\tau$ *and* $\lambda_l$, $\forall l \neq 1$, *and decreases with* $\lambda_u$, $\forall k \in \mathcal{K}$.

**Property 4.4** *When* $P_{j,1} \ll 1$, $\forall j \neq 1$, $\mathcal{P}_{c,k}^{int}$ *decreases with* $P_1$, *and converges to a constant value as* $P_1 \to \infty$, $\forall k \in \mathcal{K}$.

Property 4.1 shows that under a loose control on mobile access ($\tau \to 0$), the connection probability becomes insensitive to transmit power and BS densities, i.e., increasing transmit power or randomly adding new infrastructure does not influence connection performance (link quality). This *insensitivity* property obtained for this special case is also observed in a single-antenna unbiased HCN [5, 6].

Property 4.2 implies that increasing $\tau$ improves the connection probability, just as explained in Sect. 4.3.1.2. Nevertheless, $\tau$ should not be set as large as possible in practice. As will be observed later in Sect. 4.3.3, $\tau$ should be properly chosen to achieve a high secrecy throughput under certain connection constraints.

Properties 4.1 and 4.2 are validated in Fig. 4.3. We find that both $\mathcal{P}_{c,1}^{int}$ and $\mathcal{P}_{c,2}^{int}$ increase with $M_1$. The reason is that, on one hand a larger $M_1$ produces a higher diversity gain, and improves the link quality for tier 1. On the other hand, a larger $M_1$ also provides a stronger bias towards admitting UEs, thus the UE originally associated with tier 2 under low link quality (e.g., at the edge of a cell in tier 2) now connects to tier 1, which as a consequence enhances the link quality of tier 2.

Property 4.3 provides some interesting counter-intuitive insights into connection performance. For instance, deploying more pico/femto BSs improves connection probabilities. This is because a larger $\lambda_l$ decreases the number of active BSs in the other tiers, which reduces the aggregate network interference especially when the transmit power of the other tiers is large. However, the connection probability decreases when more UEs are introduced, since more BSs are now activated, resulting in more severe interference. Although Property 4.3 is obtained as $P_{j,1} \to 0$, it applies to more general results, as illustrated in Fig. 4.4. We see that, a larger $\lambda_u$ decreases $\mathcal{P}_{c,k}^{int}$ for $k = 1, 2$. In addition, when $\frac{\lambda_u}{\lambda_2} \leq 50$, a larger $\lambda_2$ increases $\mathcal{P}_{c,k}^{int}$, whereas when $\frac{\lambda_u}{\lambda_2} > 50$, it decreases $\mathcal{P}_{c,k}^{int}$. The underlying reason is that, in the latter both $A_1$ and $A_2$ nearly reach one, hence deploying more microcells significantly increases interference, which deteriorates link reliability. Nevertheless, this performance degradation can be effectively mitigated by setting a larger access threshold, since in this way more BSs remain idle, alleviating the network interference.

Property 4.4 implies that as $P_1$ increases, $\mathcal{P}_{c,1}^{int}$ first increases and then decreases, and eventually levels off. Increasing transmit power is not always beneficial to connection performance, since the growth of signal power is counter balanced by the growth of interference power. The same is true for $\mathcal{P}_{c,j}^{int}$, $\forall j \neq 1$. The underlying reason is that, as $P_1$ gets larger, $A_1$ increases while $A_j$ decreases, which increases

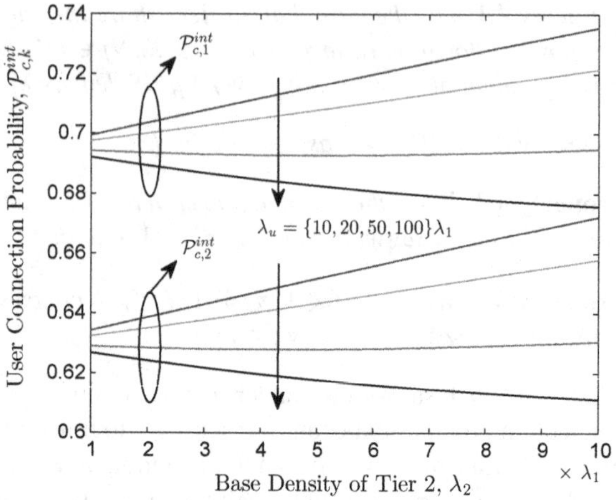


**Fig. 4.4** Connection probability in a 2-tier HCN versus $\lambda_2$ for different $\lambda_u$'s, with $\alpha = 4$, $\{P_1, P_2\} = \{30, 10\}$ dBm, $\{M_1, M_2\} = \{6, 4\}$, $\lambda_1 = \frac{1}{\pi 400^2 \mathrm{m}^2}$, $\tau = -90$ dBm, $\beta_t = 5$, and $\{\phi_1, \phi_2\} = \{1, 0.5\}$. @[2016] IEEE. Reprinted, with permission, from Ref. [1]

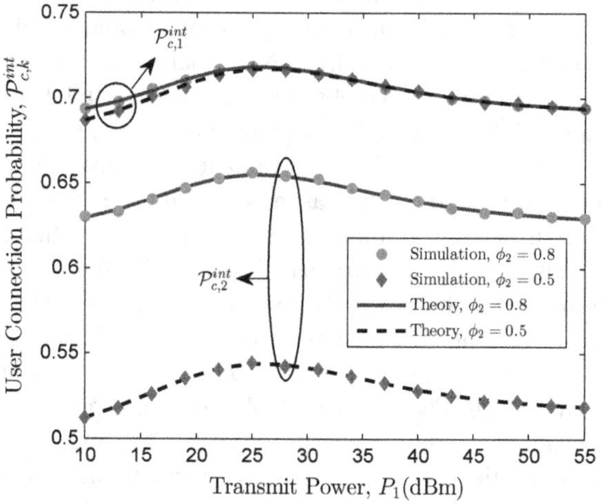


**Fig. 4.5** Connection probability in a 2-tier HCN versus $P_1$, with $\alpha = 4$, $P_2 = 10$ dBm, $\{M_1, M_2\} = \{6, 4\}$, $\lambda_1 = \frac{1}{\pi 400^2 \mathrm{m}^2}$, $\{\lambda_2, \lambda_u\} = \{2\lambda_1, 5\lambda_1\}$, $\tau = -90$ dBm, $\beta_t = 5$, and $\phi_1 = 1$. @[2016] IEEE. Reprinted, with permission, from Ref. [1]

interference from tier 1 while decreases that from the other $K-1$ tiers. When $P_1$ is relatively small, the decrement of interference from the other $K-1$ tiers dominates the increment of interference from tier 1, so the aggregate interference actually reduces; the opposite occurs as $P_1$ further increases. This property is confirmed in Fig. 4.5. We also find that, for a given $P_1$, $\mathcal{P}_{c,2}^{int}$ increases significantly with $\phi_2$, while $\mathcal{P}_{c,1}^{int}$ experiences negligible impact since the inference in tier 1 varies little. Even though, we still observe a slight improvement in $\mathcal{P}_{c,1}^{int}$ in the small $P_1$ region as $\phi_2$ increases. This occurs because focusing more power on the desired UE in tier 2 to some degree decreases the residual interference (artificial noise and leaked signal) to the UE associated with tier 1. However, the reduced interference becomes negligible as $P_1$ increases, and $\mathcal{P}_{c,1}^{int}$ becomes insensitive to $\phi_2$.

### 4.3.2 User Secrecy Probability

This section analyzes the secrecy probability of a randomly located UE, which corresponds to the probability that a secret message is not decoded by any Eve.

We consider a worst-case wiretap scenario in which Eves have the capability of multiuser decoding (e.g., successive interference cancelation), thus the interference created by concurrent signal transmissions from other BS can be completely resolved and canceled [7]. Thereby, Eves are only corrupted by the AN from BSs. The received signal at the Eve located at $e$ is given by

$$y_e = \underbrace{\frac{\sqrt{\phi_k P_k}\boldsymbol{h}_{be}^{\mathrm{T}}\boldsymbol{w}_b s_b}{r_{be}^{\alpha/2}}}_{\text{information signal}} + \underbrace{\frac{\sqrt{(1-\phi_k)P_k}\boldsymbol{h}_{be}^{\mathrm{T}}\mathbf{W}_b\boldsymbol{v}_b}{r_{be}^{\alpha/2}}}_{\text{serving-BS AN}} + \underbrace{\sum_{j\in\mathcal{K}}\sum_{z\in\Phi_j^o\setminus b}\frac{\sqrt{(1-\phi_j)P_j}\boldsymbol{h}_{ze}^{\mathrm{T}}\mathbf{W}_z\boldsymbol{v}_z}{r_{ze}^{\alpha/2}}}_{\text{intra- and cross-tier AN}} + n_e. \tag{4.17}$$

We also consider the non-colluding wiretap scenario, where transmission is secure only if secrecy is achieved against all Eves. Accordingly, the secrecy probability of tier $k$ is defined as the probability of the event that the instantaneous SIR of an arbitrary Eve is below a target SIR $\beta_e \triangleq 2^{R_e} - 1$ with $R_e$ the redundant rate, i.e.,

$$\mathcal{P}_{s,k}^{int} \triangleq \mathbb{E}_{\Phi_1}\cdots\mathbb{E}_{\Phi_K}\mathbb{E}_{\Phi_e}\left[\prod_{e\in\Phi_e}\mathbb{P}\left\{\boldsymbol{SIR}_{e,k} < \beta_e|\Phi_e,\Phi_1,\cdots,\Phi_K\right\}\right], \tag{4.18}$$

where $\boldsymbol{SIR}_{e,k}$ is given by

$$\boldsymbol{SIR}_{e,k} = \frac{\phi_k P_k|\boldsymbol{h}_{be}^{\mathrm{T}}\boldsymbol{w}_b|^2 r_{be}^{-\alpha}}{I_{be} + \sum_{j\in\mathcal{K}} I_{je}}, \ \forall e\in\Phi_e, \tag{4.19}$$

with $I_{be} \triangleq \frac{(1-\phi_k)P_k|\boldsymbol{h}_{be}^{\mathrm{T}}\mathbf{W}_b|^2}{(M_k-1)r_{be}^{\alpha}}$ and $I_{je} \triangleq \sum_{z\in\Phi_j^o\setminus b}\frac{(1-\phi_j)P_j\|\boldsymbol{h}_{ze}^{\mathrm{T}}\mathbf{W}_z\|^2}{(M_j-1)r_{ze}^{\alpha}}$. Unfortunately, it is intractable to derive an accurate analytical expression of $\mathcal{P}_{s,k}^{int}$ from Eq. (4.18). Instead, we provide both upper and lower bounds for it in the following theorem.

**Theorem 4.2** *Let* $\psi_k \triangleq \sum_{j\in\mathcal{K}} A_j\lambda_j C_{\alpha,M_j}\left(\xi_j\phi_{j,k}P_{j,k}\right)^{\delta}$, *and* $\mathcal{P}_{s,k}^{int}$ *in Eq.* (4.18) *satisfies*

$$\mathcal{P}_{s,k}^{int,L} \le \mathcal{P}_{s,k}^{int} \le \mathcal{P}_{s,k}^{int,U}, \tag{4.20}$$

*where*

$$\mathcal{P}_{s,k}^{int,L} = \exp\left(-\lambda_e\psi_k^{-1}\beta_e^{-\delta}(1+\xi_k\beta_e)^{1-M_k}\right), \tag{4.21}$$

$$\mathcal{P}_{s,k}^{int,U} = 1 - \frac{\lambda_e}{\lambda_e + \psi_k\beta_e^{\delta}}(1+\xi_k\beta_e)^{1-M_k}. \tag{4.22}$$

*Proof* Please see Appendix A.3.

Interestingly, when $\lambda_e \ll 1$, the above two bounds merge, i.e.,

$$\mathscr{P}_{s,k}^{int,L} \approx \mathscr{P}_{s,k}^{int,o} \triangleq 1 - \lambda_e \psi_k^{-1} \beta_e^{-\delta} (1 + \xi_k \beta_e)^{1-M_k} \approx \mathscr{P}_{s,k}^{int,U}, \tag{4.23}$$

and $\mathscr{P}_{s,k}^{int,o} \to 1$ as $\lambda_e \to 0$. It implies that as $\mathscr{P}_{s,k}^{int} \to 1$, both the upper and lower bounds approach the exact value. In other words, $\mathscr{P}_{s,k}^{int}$ can be approximated by $\mathscr{P}_{s,k}^{int,o}$ in the high secrecy probability region. Next we establish some properties on $\mathscr{P}_{s,k}^{int,o}$, with the corresponding proof relegated to Appendix A.2.

**Property 4.5** *$\mathscr{P}_{s,k}^{int,o}$ decreases in $\lambda_e$, $\tau$, and $\phi_j$, $\forall j \in \mathscr{K}$, and it increases in $\lambda_u$.*

**Property 4.6** *If $M_{j,k} \ll 1$, $\forall j \in \mathscr{K} \backslash k$, $\mathscr{P}_{s,k}^{int,o}$ increases in $M_k$, and decreases in $\lambda_k$.*

**Property 4.7** *In the high $P_k$ region, $\mathscr{P}_{s,j}^{int,o}$, $\forall j \in \mathscr{K}$, increases in $P_k$; $\mathscr{P}_{s,k}^{int,o}$ converges to a constant value as $P_k \to \infty$ and $\lim_{P_k \to \infty} \mathscr{P}_{s,l}^{int,o} = 1$, $\forall l \neq k$.*

Properties 4.5–4.7 provide some insights into the secrecy probability that differ from those obtained about the connection probability. For example, deploying more pico/femto BSs may increase the connection probability while being harmful to the secrecy probability, which implies that proper BS densities should be designed to balance link quality and secrecy.

Figure 4.6 depicts secrecy probability versus $P_1$ for different values of $\tau$. We see that, the lower bound accurately approximates to the simulated value, while the upper bound becomes asymptotically tight in the high secrecy probability region. As $P_1$ increases, $\mathscr{P}_{s,1}^{int}$ first decreases and then slowly rises to a constant value which is independent of $P_1$. $\mathscr{P}_{s,2}^{int}$ reaches one as $P_k$ becomes large enough, which verifies Property 4.7. We observe that, the secrecy probabilities of both tiers increase as $\tau$ decreases, while Table 4.1 shows that connection probabilities decrease as $\tau$

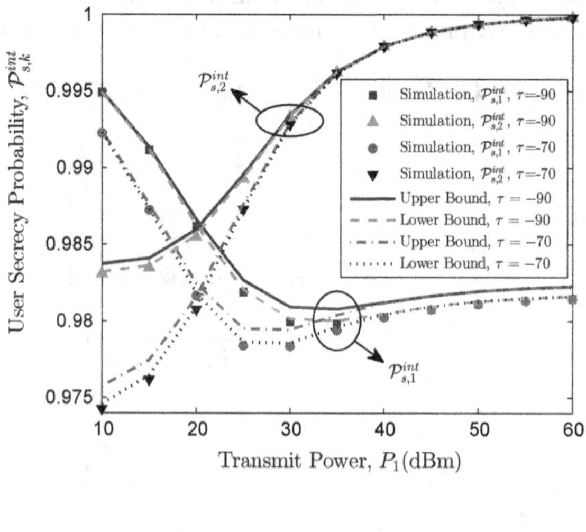


**Fig. 4.6** Secrecy probability in a 2-tier HCN versus $P_1$, with $P_2 = 20$ dBm, $\{M_1, M_2\} = \{6, 4\}$, $\{\lambda_2, \lambda_u, \lambda_e\} = \{2, 2, 0.05\}\lambda_1$, $\beta_e = 1$, and $\{\phi_1, \phi_2\} = \{0.5, 0.5\}$. @[2016] IEEE. Reprinted, with permission, from Ref. [1]

**Table 4.1** Connection probability versus secrecy probability

| Probabilities | $\mathcal{P}_{c,1}^{int}$ | $\mathcal{P}_{c,2}^{int}$ | $\mathcal{P}_{s,1}^{int}$ | $\mathcal{P}_{s,2}^{int}$ |
|---|---|---|---|---|
| $\tau = -70$ dBm | 0.9571 | 0.9477 | 0.9786 | 0.9930 |
| $\tau = -90$ dBm | 0.9186 | 0.9073 | 0.9799 | 0.9936 |

decreases, as indicated in Property 4.1. The access threshold $\tau$ displays a tradeoff between the connection and secrecy probabilities. This is because a smaller $\tau$ results in more interference, which simultaneously degrades the legitimate and wiretap channels. In other words, network interference is a double-edged sword that promotes the secrecy transmission but in turn restrains the legitimate communication.

In Fig. 4.7, we see that as $\phi_2$ increases, i.e., more power is allocated to the information signal, $\mathcal{P}_{c,2}^{int}$ increases and $\mathcal{P}_{s,2}^{int}$ decreases. We should design the power allocation to strike a better balance between reliability and secrecy. Besides, although a smaller $\phi_1$ rarely affects $\mathcal{P}_{c,2}^{int}$, it significantly increases $\mathcal{P}_{s,2}^{int}$, which highlights the validity of the artificial noise method.

### *4.3.3 Network Secrecy Throughput*

In this section, we investigate the network-wide secrecy throughput performance of the HCN. As introduced in Sect. 2.5.3, the network-wide secrecy throughput, with a connection probability constraint $\mathcal{P}_{c,k}(\beta_{t,k}) = \rho$ and a secrecy probability constraint $\mathcal{P}_{s,k}(\beta_{e,k}) = \varepsilon$ for $k \in \mathcal{K}$, is given by

$$\mathcal{T}_s = \sum_{k\in\mathcal{K}} \lambda_k A_k \rho R_{s,k}^* = \sum_{k\in\mathcal{K}} \lambda_k A_k \rho \left[R_{t,k}^* - R_{e,k}^*\right]^+ = \sum_{k\in\mathcal{K}} \lambda_k A_k \rho \left[\log_2\left(\frac{1+\beta_{t,k}^*}{1+\beta_{e,k}^*}\right)\right]^+, \tag{4.24}$$

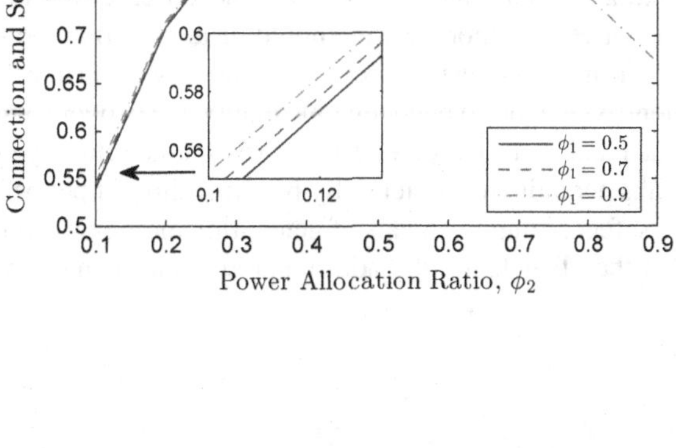

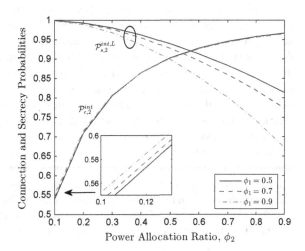

**Fig. 4.7** Connection probability and secrecy probability in a 2-tier HCN versus $\phi_2$, with $\{P_1, P_2\} = \{30, 20\}$ dBm, $\{M_1, M_2\} = \{6, 4\}$, $\{\lambda_2, \lambda_u, \lambda_e\} = \{2, 4, 0.5\}\lambda_1$, $\beta_t = 2$, $\beta_e = 1$, and $\tau = -90$ dBm. @[2016] IEEE. Reprinted, with permission, from Ref. [1]

where $R^*_{s,k} = \left[R^*_{t,k} - R^*_{e,k}\right]^+$, $R^*_{t,k} = \log_2(1+\beta^*_{t,k})$ and $R^*_{e,k} = \log_2(1+\beta^*_{e,k})$ are the confidential information rate, transmission rate and redundant rate for tier $k$, with $\beta^*_{t,k}$ and $\beta^*_{e,k}$ satisfying the equations $\mathcal{P}^{int}_{c,k}(\beta_{t,k}) = \rho$ and $\mathcal{P}^{int}_{s,k}(\beta_{e,k}) = \varepsilon$, respectively. Note that, if $\mathcal{R}^*_{t,k} - \mathcal{R}^*_{e,k}$ is negative, the connection and secrecy probability constraints can not be satisfied simultaneously, and transmissions should be suspended. In the following, we are going to calculate $\beta^*_{t,k}$ and $\beta^*_{e,k}$ from $\mathcal{P}^{int}_{c,k}(\beta_{t,k}) = \rho$ and $\mathcal{P}^{int}_{s,k}(\beta_{e,k}) = \varepsilon$, respectively.

Due to the complicated expression of $\mathcal{P}^{int}_{c,k}$ in Eq. (4.14), we can hardly derive an analytical result of $\beta^*_{t,k}$ from $\mathcal{P}^{int}_{c,k}(\beta_{t,k}) = \rho$. However, since $\mathcal{P}^{int}_{c,k}(\beta_{t,k})$ is obviously a monotonically decreasing function of $\beta_{t,k}$, we can efficiently calculate $\beta^*_{t,k}$ that satisfies $\mathcal{P}^{int}_{c,k}(\beta_{t,k}) = \rho$ using the bisection method.

To guarantee a high level of secrecy, the secrecy probability $\varepsilon$ must be large, which allows us to use Eq. (4.23) to calculate $\beta^*_{e,k}$. For the case $M_k \geq 3$, we can only numerically calculate $\beta^*_{e,k}$ that satisfies $\mathcal{P}^{int}_{s,k}(\beta_{e,k}) = \varepsilon$ using the bisection method. Fortunately, when $M_k = 2$ or $M_k \gg 1$, we can provide closed-form expressions of $\beta^*_{e,k}$, with corresponding proof relegated to Appendix A.4.

**Proposition 4.1** *In the large $\varepsilon$ regime with $\alpha = 4$ and $M_k = 2$, the root of $\mathcal{P}^{int}_{s,k}(\beta_{e,k}) = \varepsilon$ is given by $\beta^o_{e,k} = \left(\frac{3\zeta^{2/3}-1}{3\sqrt{\xi_k}\zeta^{1/3}}\right)^2$, with $\zeta \triangleq \frac{\sqrt{\xi_k}\lambda_e}{2(1-\varepsilon)\psi_k} + \sqrt{\frac{\xi_k\lambda_e^2}{4(1-\varepsilon)^2\psi_k^2} + \frac{1}{27}}$.*

**Proposition 4.2** *In the large $\varepsilon$ regime, as $M_k \to \infty$, the root of $\mathcal{P}^{int}_{s,k}(\beta_{e,k}) = \varepsilon$ is given by $\beta^\star_{e,k} = \delta\frac{\phi_k}{1-\phi_k}\ln\frac{\vartheta}{\mathcal{W}(\vartheta)}$, with $\vartheta \triangleq \frac{\alpha}{2}\frac{1-\phi_k}{\phi_k}\left(\frac{\psi_k(1-\varepsilon)}{\lambda_e}\right)^{-\frac{\alpha}{2}}$, and $\mathcal{W}(x)$ is the Lambert-W function [8].*

To demonstrate the accuracy of $R^\star_{e,k} \triangleq \log_2(1+\beta^\star_{e,k})$ on $R^*_{e,k}$, we define $\Delta R_{e,k} \triangleq \frac{|R^\star_{e,k}-R^*_{e,k}|}{R^*_{e,k}}$. Numerically, we obtain $\Delta R_{e,1} = 0.0462$ when $M_1 = 4$, and $\Delta R_{e,1} = 0.0062$ when $M_1 = 20$. This suggests that $R^\star_{e,k}$ becomes very close to $R^*_{e,k}$ for a large enough $M_k$ (e.g., $M_k \geq 20$).

Substituting $\beta^*_{t,k}$ and $\beta^*_{e,k}$ into Eq. (4.24), we obtain the expression of $\mathcal{T}_s$. Figure 4.8 illustrates the network-wide secrecy throughput $\mathcal{T}_s$ versus $\phi_2$ for different values of $\lambda_e$ and $M_2$. As expected, using more transmit antennas always increases $\mathcal{T}$. We observe that, for a small $\lambda_e$, allocating more power to the information signal (increasing $\phi_2$) improves $\mathcal{T}_s$. However, for a larger $\lambda_e$, $\mathcal{T}_s$ first increases and then decreases as $\phi_2$ increases, and even vanishes for too large a $\phi_2$ (e.g., $\lambda_e = \lambda_1$, and $\phi_2 = 0.8$). There exists an optimal $\phi_2$ that maximizes $\mathcal{T}_s$, which can be numerically calculated by taking the maximum of $\mathcal{T}_s$. We also observe that the optimal $\phi_2$ decreases as $\lambda_e$ increases, i.e., more power should be allocated to the AN to increase $\mathcal{T}_s$.

From the analysis in previous sections, we find that the access threshold $\tau$ triggers a nontrivial tradeoff between link quality and network-wide secrecy throughput. On the one hand, setting a small $\tau$ improves spatial reuse by enabling more communication links per unit area, potentially boosting throughput performance; it is also beneficial to safeguarding by means of generating more powerful AN to impair eavesdroppers. On the other hand, the additional amount of interference caused by the increased

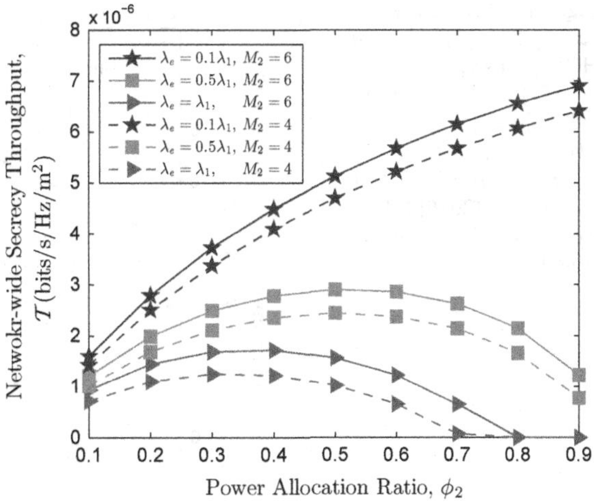


**Fig. 4.8** Secrecy throughput in a 2-tier HCN versus $\phi_2$ for different $\lambda_e$'s and $M_2$'s, $\{P_1, P_2\} = \{30, 10\}$ dBm, $M_1 = 6, \phi_1 = 0.8$, $\{\lambda_2, \lambda_u\} = \{2, 4\}\lambda_1$, $\tau = -90$ dBm, $\rho = 0.9$, and $\varepsilon = 0.95$. @[2016] IEEE. Reprinted, with permission, from Ref. [1]

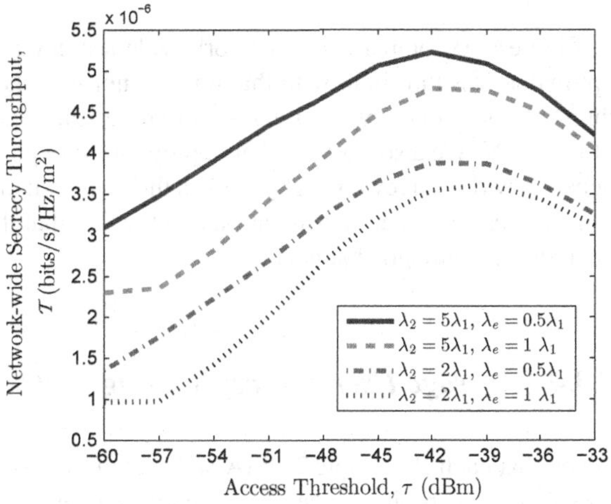


**Fig. 4.9** Network-wide secrecy throughput in a 2-tier HCN versus $\tau$, with $\{P_1, P_2\} = \{30, 10\}$ dBm, $\{M_1, M_2\} = \{4, 4\}$, $\{\phi_1, \phi_2\} = \{0.5, 0.5\}$, $\lambda_u = 10\lambda_1$, $\rho = 0.95$, and $\varepsilon = 0.95$. @[2016] IEEE. Reprinted, with permission, from Ref. [1]

concurrent transmissions (a small value of $\tau$) besets ongoing receptions of UEs, decreasing the probability of successfully connecting the BS-UE pairs. In this regard, neither too large nor too small a $\tau$ can yield a high secrecy throughput. Just as shown in Fig. 4.9, $\mathcal{T}_s$ first increases and then decreases as $\tau$ increases. Only by a proper choice of $\tau$, can we achieve a high network-wide secrecy throughput.

In view of the quasi-concavity of $\mathcal{T}_s$ w.r.t. $\tau$ indicated in Fig. 4.9, we can seek out the optimal $\tau$ that maximizes $\mathcal{T}_s$ using the gold section method. Furthermore, combined with the asymptotic analysis on $\mathcal{P}_{c,k}^{int}$ in Sect. 4.3.1.2 and the expression of $\mathcal{P}_{s,k}^{int}$ in Eq. (4.23), we directly provide asymptotic behaviors of $\mathcal{T}_s$ when $\tau$ goes to zero and goes to infinity: (1) *When all tiers share the same values of $M$ and $\phi$, and $\lambda_u \gg \lambda_j$, $\forall j \in \mathcal{K}$, $\mathcal{T}_s$ converges to a constant value as $\tau \to 0$;* (2) *$\mathcal{T}_s \to 0$ as $\tau \to \infty$.*

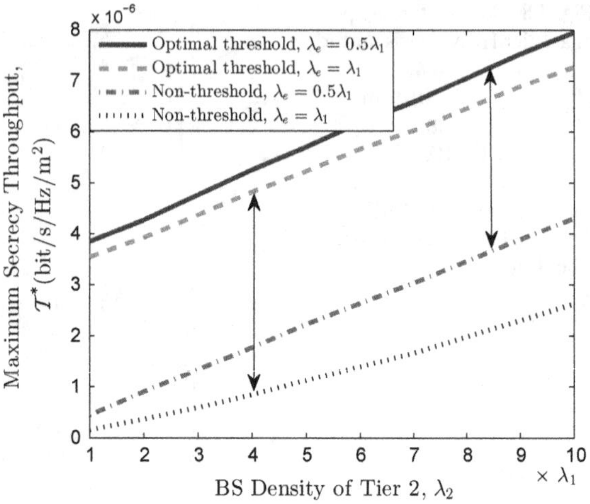


**Fig. 4.10** Network-wide secrecy throughput in a 2-tier HCN versus $\tau$, with $\{P_1, P_2\} = \{30, 10\}$ dBm, $\{M_1, M_2\} = \{6, 4\}$, $\{\phi_1, \phi_2\} = \{0.5, 0.5\}$, $\lambda_u = 10\lambda_1$, $\rho = 0.95$, and $\varepsilon = 0.95$. @[2016] IEEE. Reprinted, with permission, from Ref. [1]

Figure 4.10 compares the network-wide secrecy throughput obtained under the optimal access threshold with that under a non-threshold policy [6]. Obviously, our threshold-based policy significantly improves the secrecy throughput performance of the HCN. We also observe that deploying more picocells is still beneficial to the network-wide secrecy throughput, even throughput it increases network interference. This is because of cell densification and the fact that the increased interference also degrades the wiretap channels.

### 4.3.4 Average User Secrecy Throughput

Given that each BS adopts TDMA with equal time slots allocated to the associated UEs in a round-robin manner, here we investigate the average user secrecy throughput, which is defined as

$$\mathcal{T}_{u,k} \triangleq \frac{\mathcal{T}_k}{N_k}, \tag{4.25}$$

where $\mathcal{T}_k \triangleq A_k \rho \left[R^*_{t,k} - R^*_{e,k}\right]^+$ denotes the secrecy transmission capacity of a cell in tier $k$, and $N_k = \frac{\lambda_u}{\lambda_k} S_k$ denotes the corresponding cell load. From the perspective of a UE, the network-wide secrecy throughput can be alternatively expressed as

$$\mathcal{T}_u = \sum_{k \in \mathcal{K}} \lambda_u \mathcal{T}_{u,k} S_k. \tag{4.26}$$

By substituting Eq. (4.25) into Eq. (4.26), we see that $\mathcal{T}_u = \mathcal{T}_s$, which is also as expected.

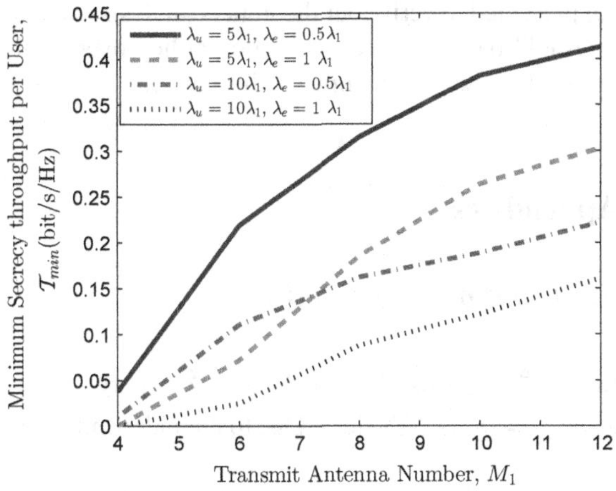


**Fig. 4.11** Minimum secrecy throughput per user in a 2-tier HCN versus $M_1$ for different $\lambda_u$'s and $\lambda_e$'s, with $\alpha = 4$, $\{P_1, P_2\} = \{30, 10\}$ dBm, $M_2 = 4$, $\lambda_1 = \frac{1}{\pi 400^2 \mathrm{m}^2}$, $\lambda_2 = 2\lambda_1$, $\{\phi_1, \phi_2\} = \{0.5, 0.5\}$, $\tau = -60$ dBm, $\rho = 0.95$, and $\varepsilon = 0.95$. @[2016] IEEE. Reprinted, with permission, from Ref. [1]

A UE may be interested in the minimum level of secrecy throughput it can achieve. To this end, we evaluate the minimum average secrecy throughput over all tiers, which is defined as

$$\mathcal{T}_{min} \triangleq \min_{k \in \mathcal{K}} \mathcal{T}_{u,k}. \tag{4.27}$$

Figure 4.11 shows how $\mathcal{T}_{min}$ depends on $M_1$, $\lambda_u$, and $\lambda_e$, respectively. Obviously, average user secrecy throughput deteriorates as the density of Eves increases. This is ameliorated by adding more transmit antennas at BSs. In addition, as $\lambda_u$ increases, the number of UEs sharing limited resources increases, which results in a decrease in per user secrecy throughput.

## 4.4 Conclusions

This chapter comprehensively studies the physical layer security of HCNs where the locations of all BSs, UEs and Eves are modeled as independent homogeneous PPPs. We first propose a mobile association policy based on the truncated ARSP and derive the tier association and BS activation probabilities. We then analyze the connection and secrecy probabilities of the artificial-noise-aided secure transmission. For connection probability, we provide a new tractable expression for the interference-limited case. For secrecy probability, we obtain closed-form expressions for both upper and lower bounds, which are approximate to the exact values at the high secrecy probability regime. We prove that the access threshold, BS density and power allocation ratio each displays a tradeoff between the connection and secrecy probabilities; these parameters should be carefully designed to balance link quality and secrecy. Constrained by the connection and secrecy probabilities, we evaluate the network-wide secrecy throughput, and the minimum secrecy throughput per user. Numerical results are presented to verify our theoretical analysis and to highlight the superiority of our threshold-based mobile association policy over traditional non-threshold policy in terms of secrecy throughput performance.

## Appendices

### A.1 Proof of Theorem 4.1

Let $x_m \triangleq \frac{(-1)^m s^m}{m!}\mathcal{L}_{I_o}^{(m)}(s)$ and $\boldsymbol{x}_{M_k-1} \triangleq [x_1, x_2, \cdots, x_{M_k-1}]^{\mathrm{T}}$. $\mathcal{P}_{c,k}^{int}$ can be rewritten as $\mathcal{P}_{c,k}^{int} = \sum_{m=0}^{M_k-1} \mathbb{E}_{R_k}\left[x_p\right]$. Due to the independence of $I_{io}$ and $I_{jo}$ for $i \neq j$, we have

$$\mathcal{L}_{I_o}(s) = \mathbb{E}_{I_o}\left[e^{-sI_o}\right] = \prod_{j\in\mathcal{K}} \mathcal{L}_{I_{jo}}(s). \tag{4.28}$$

Let $r_{jo} \triangleq \left(P_{j,k}M_{j,k}\right)^{\frac{1}{\alpha}} R_k$ and $P_{jz} \triangleq \phi_j P_j\left(|\boldsymbol{h}_{zo}^{\mathrm{T}}\boldsymbol{w}_z|^2 + \xi_j\|\boldsymbol{h}_{zo}^{\mathrm{T}}\boldsymbol{W}_z\|^2\right)$. Using Eq. [9, (8)], $\mathcal{L}_{I_o}(s)$ can be calculated as

$$\mathcal{L}_{I_o}(s) = \prod_{j\in\mathcal{K}} \mathbb{E}_{\Phi_j}\left[e^{-\sum_{z\in\Phi_j^o\setminus\mathcal{B}(o,r_{jo})} sP_{jz}r_{zo}^{-\alpha}}\right] = \exp\left(-\pi\sum_{j\in\mathcal{K}}\lambda_j^o\int_{r_{jo}^2}^{\infty}\left(1-\varpi\left(P_{jz}\right)\right)dr\right),$$

where $\varpi\left(P_{jz}\right) = \int_0^\infty e^{-sxr^{-\alpha}} f_{P_{jz}}(x)dx$ is given via invoking $f_{P_{jz}}(x)$ in Lemma [7, 1]

$$\varpi\left(P_{jz}\right) = \begin{cases} \left(1+\omega r^{-\frac{\alpha}{2}}\right)^{-M_j}, & \xi_j = 1, \\ \frac{\left(1-\xi_j\right)^{1-M_j}}{1+\omega r^{-\frac{\alpha}{2}}} - \sum\limits_{n=0}^{M_j-2} \frac{\xi_j\left(1-\xi_j\right)^{1-M_j+n}}{\left(1+\xi_j\omega r^{-\frac{\alpha}{2}}\right)^{n+1}}, & \xi_j \neq 1. \end{cases} \tag{4.29}$$

with $\omega \triangleq \phi_j P_j s$. Next, we calculate $\mathcal{L}_{I_o}^{(p)}(s)$. Consider $\phi_j \neq \frac{1}{M_j}$, and the case $\phi_j = \frac{1}{M_j}$ can be obtained in a similar way. We present $\mathcal{L}_{I_o}^{(p)}(s)$ in the following recursive form

$$\mathcal{L}_{I_o}^{(p)}(s) = \pi\sum_{j\in\mathcal{K}}\lambda_j^o\sum_{i=0}^{p-1}\binom{p-1}{i}\frac{(-1)^{p-i}}{(1-\xi_j)^{M_j-1}}\mathcal{L}_{I_o}^{(i)}(s)\times$$
$$\int_{r_{jo}^2}^{\infty}\left(\frac{(p-i)!\left(\phi_j P_j r^{-\frac{\alpha}{2}}\right)^{p-i}}{\left(1+\omega r^{-\frac{\alpha}{2}}\right)^{p-i+1}} - \sum_{n=0}^{M_j-2}\frac{\xi_j(n+p-i)!\left(\xi_j\phi_j P_j r^{-\frac{\alpha}{2}}\right)^{p-i}}{n!(1-\xi_j)^{-n}\left(1+\xi_j\omega r^{-\frac{\alpha}{2}}\right)^{n+p-i+1}}\right)dr.$$

Using transformation $r^{-\frac{\alpha}{2}} \to v$ and plugging $\mathscr{L}_{I_o}^{(p)}(s)$ into $x_p$, we have for $p \geq 1$

$$x_p = \sum_{i=0}^{p-1}\Bigg\{\frac{p-i}{p}\sum_{j\in\mathscr{K}}\frac{\pi\delta\lambda_j^o\omega^{p-i}}{(1-\xi_j)^{M_j-1}}\int_0^{r_{jo}^{-\alpha}}\Bigg(\frac{v^{p-i-\delta-1}}{(1+\omega v)^{p-i+1}} - \sum_{n=0}^{M_j-2}\binom{n+p-i}{n}\frac{\xi_j^{p-i+1}(1-\xi_j)^n v^{p-i-\delta-1}}{(1+\xi_j\omega v)^{n+p-i+1}}\Bigg)dv\Bigg\}x_i. \tag{4.30}$$

Calculating Eq. (4.30) with Eq. [10, (3.194.1)], $x_p$ can be given as

$$x_p = R_k^2\sum_{i=0}^{p-1}\frac{p-i}{p}g_{p-i}x_i, \tag{4.31}$$

where $x_0$ in Eq. (4.31) is calculated as

$$x_0 = \mathscr{L}_{I_o}(s) = \exp\Bigg(-\pi\sum_{j\in\mathscr{K}}\lambda_j^o \times \Bigg(\underbrace{\int_0^{\infty}(1-\varpi(P_{jz}))\,dr}_{\mathscr{I}_{j1}(s)} - \underbrace{\int_0^{r_{jo}^2}(1-\varpi(P_{jz}))\,dr}_{\mathscr{I}_{j2}(s)}\Bigg)\Bigg).$$

$\mathscr{I}_{j1}(s)$ can be directly obtained from Eq. [9, (8)], i.e.,

$$\mathscr{I}_{j1}(s) = \begin{cases} \omega^\delta C_{\alpha,M_j+1}, & \xi_j = 1, \\ \frac{\omega^\delta C_{\alpha,2}}{(1-\xi_j)^{M_j-1}} - \sum_{n=0}^{M_j-2}\frac{\omega^\delta\xi_j^{1+\delta}C_{\alpha,n+2}}{(1-\xi_j)^{M_j-1-n}}, & \xi_j \neq 1. \end{cases} \tag{4.32}$$

$\mathscr{I}_{j2}(s)$ can be derived by invoking $\varpi(P_{jz})$ in Eq. (4.29). Specifically, when $\xi_j = 1$,

$$\mathscr{I}_{j2}(s) = r_{jo}^2 - \delta r_{jo}^2\frac{{}_2F_1\left(M_j, M_j+\delta; M_j+\delta+1; -\frac{r_{jo}^\alpha}{\omega}\right)}{\left(M_j+\delta\right)(\omega r_{jo}^{-\alpha})^{M_j}}, \tag{4.33}$$

and when $\xi_j \neq 1$,

$$\mathscr{I}_{j2}(s) = r_{jo}^2\Bigg[1-\delta\Bigg(\frac{{}_2F_1\left(1,\delta+1;\delta+2;-(\omega r_{jo}^{-\alpha})^{-1}\right)}{(1+\delta)(1-\xi_j)^{M_j-1}(\omega r_{jo}^{-\alpha})^{-1}} - \sum_{n=0}^{M_j-2}\frac{{}_2F_1\left(n+1,n+1+\delta;n+2+\delta;-(\xi_j\omega r_{jo}^{-\alpha})^{-1}\right)}{(n+1+\delta)(1-\xi_j)^{M_j-1-n}\left(\xi_j\omega r_{jo}^{-\alpha}\right)^n}\Bigg)\Bigg]. \tag{4.34}$$

Having obtained a linear recurrence form for $x_p$ in Eq. (4.31), $\boldsymbol{x}_{M_k}$ can be given by

$$\boldsymbol{x}_{M_k-1} = \sum_{i=1}^{M_k-1} R_k^{2i} x_0 \boldsymbol{G}_{M_k-1}^{i-1} \boldsymbol{g}_{M_k-1}, \tag{4.35}$$

where $\boldsymbol{g}_{M_k}$ and $\boldsymbol{G}_{M_k}$ can be found in [11]. From Eq. [11, (39)], we have $\boldsymbol{G}_{M_k-1}^{i-1}\boldsymbol{g}_{M_k-1} = \frac{1}{i!}\boldsymbol{Q}_{M_k}^{i}(2 : M_k, 1)$, with $\boldsymbol{Q}_{M_k}^{i}(2 : M_k, 1)$ the entries from the second to the $M_k$th row in the first column of $\boldsymbol{Q}_{M_k}^{i}$, with $\boldsymbol{Q}_{M_k}$ shown in Eq. (4.16). Then $x_p$ can be expressed as

$$x_p = \sum_{i=0}^{M_k-1} R_k^{2i} x_0 \frac{1}{i!} \boldsymbol{Q}_{M_k}^{i}(p+1, 1), \tag{4.36}$$

and consequently, $\mathscr{P}_{c,k}^{int}$ can be given by

$$\mathscr{P}_{c,k}^{int} = \sum_{m=0}^{M_k-1} \sum_{i=0}^{M_k-1} \mathbb{E}_{R_k}\left[\frac{1}{i!} x_0 R_k^{2i} \boldsymbol{Q}_{M_k}^{i}(m+1, 1)\right], \tag{4.37}$$

which can be alternatively expressed as follows using the $L_1$ induced matrix norm

$$\mathscr{P}_{c,k}^{int} = \sum_{i=0}^{M_k-1} \mathbb{E}_{R_k}\left[\left\|\frac{1}{i!} x_0 R_k^{2i} \boldsymbol{Q}_{M_k}^{i}\right\|_1\right]. \tag{4.38}$$

To calculate the above expectation, we give the PDF of $R_k$ in the following lemma.

**Lemma 4.3** ([6, Lemma 3]) *The PDF of $R_k$ is given by*

$$f_{R_k}(x) = \begin{cases} \frac{2\pi\lambda_k}{S_k} x \exp\left(-\pi \Xi (P_k M_k)^{-\delta} x^2\right), & x \le D_k, \\ 0, & x > D_k. \end{cases} \tag{4.39}$$

Averaging over $R_k$ using Eq. (4.39) completes the proof.

## *A.2 Proof of Properties 4.1–4.7*

*i. Property* 4.1: For the case $\{M_j\} = M$, $\{\phi_j\} = \phi$ and $\lambda_u \gg \lambda_j$, $\forall j \in \mathscr{K}$, $A_j \to 1$ as $\tau \to 0$; $\Upsilon_k$ and $\boldsymbol{Q}_{M_k}$ can be reexpressed as $\Upsilon_k = \frac{\Xi}{(P_k M)^{\delta}} \tilde{\Upsilon}_0$, and $\boldsymbol{Q}_{M_k} = \frac{\Xi}{(P_k M)^{\delta}} \tilde{\boldsymbol{Q}}_M$, where both $\tilde{\Upsilon}_0$ and $\tilde{\boldsymbol{Q}}_M$ are independent of $P_j$, $\lambda_j$ and $k$. Since $D_k \to \infty$ as $\tau \to 0$, by omitting the term $\sum_{l=0}^{m} \frac{\pi^l e^{-\pi \Upsilon_k D_k^2}}{l! D_k^{-2l} \Upsilon_k^{-l}}$ from Eq. (4.14) and substituting in $\Upsilon_k$, $\boldsymbol{Q}_{M_k}$ along with $S_k^{\varepsilon=0} = \frac{\lambda_k (P_k M)^{\delta}}{\Xi}$, we obtain

$$\mathscr{P}_{c,k}^{int,\varepsilon=0} = \sum_{m=0}^{M-1} \frac{1}{\pi^m \tilde{\Upsilon}_0^{m+1}} \left\| \tilde{Q}_M^m \right\|_1, \quad \forall k \in \mathscr{K} \tag{4.40}$$

which is obviously independent of $P_j$, $\lambda_j$ and $k$.

*ii. Property* 4.2: To complete the proof, we first give the following lemma.

**Lemma 4.4** *The connection probability of a UE associated with tier k satisfies*

$$\mathscr{P}_{c,k}^{int,B}(\beta_t) \leq \mathscr{P}_{c,k}^{int} \leq \mathscr{P}_{c,k}^{int,B}(\varphi_k \beta_t), \tag{4.41}$$

$$\mathscr{P}_{c,k}^{int,B}(\beta) = \frac{\lambda_k}{S_k} \sum_{m=1}^{M_k} \binom{M_k}{m} \frac{(-1)^{m+1}}{\hat{\Upsilon}_{k,m\beta}} \left(1 - e^{-\pi \hat{\Upsilon}_{k,m\beta} D_k^2}\right). \tag{4.42}$$

*where* $\varphi_k \triangleq (M_k!)^{-\frac{1}{M_k}}$ *and the value of* $\hat{\Upsilon}_{k,m\beta}$ *equal to that of* $\Upsilon_k$ *at* $\beta_t = m\beta$.

*Proof* Recalling Eq. (4.13), since $\|\boldsymbol{h}_b\|^2 \sim \Gamma(M_k, 1)$, we have $\mathbb{P}\left\{\|\boldsymbol{h}_b\|^2 \geq x\right\} = 1 - \int_0^x \frac{e^{-v} v^{M_k-1}}{(M_k-1)!} dv$, which equals to $1 - \frac{1}{\Gamma(1+1/t)} \int_0^z e^{-v^t} dv$ with $t = 1/M_k$ and $z = x^{M_k}$. Then according to Alzer's inequality [12], we obtain the following relationship

$$1 - \left(1 - e^{-x}\right)^{M_k} \leq \mathbb{P}\left\{\|\boldsymbol{h}_b\|^2 \geq x\right\} \leq 1 - \left(1 - e^{-\varphi_k x}\right)^{M_k}. \tag{4.43}$$

Substituting Eq. (4.43) into $\mathscr{P}_{c,k}^{int} = \mathbb{E}_{R_k} \mathbb{E}_{I_o} \left[\mathbb{P}\left\{\|\boldsymbol{h}_b\|^2 \geq sI_o\right\}\right]$ yields Eq. (4.41). ■

As $\tau \to \infty$, we have $A_k \to 0$ for $k \in \mathscr{K}$. Accordingly, we obtain $\Upsilon_k = \frac{\Xi}{(P_k M_k)^\delta}$, which becomes independent of $\beta_t$, and so does $\hat{\Upsilon}_{k,m\beta}$. This implies $\mathscr{P}_{c,k}^{int,B}(\beta_t) = \mathscr{P}_{c,k}^{int,B}(\varphi_k \beta_t) = \mathscr{P}_{c,k}^{int}$. Substituting Eq. (4.5) into Eq. (4.42), $\mathscr{P}_{c,k}^{int}$ can be finally reduced to $\sum_{m=1}^{M_k} \binom{M_k}{m} (-1)^{m+1} = 1$, which completes the proof.

*iii. Property* 4.3: Considering $P_{j,1} \to 0$, $\forall j \neq 1$, we have $S_j \to 0$ and $A_j \to 0$, and accordingly $\Upsilon_1 \propto \lambda_1 A_1$, $\Upsilon_j \propto \lambda_1 A_1 P_{1,j}^\delta$, and $\left\|\boldsymbol{Q}_{M_1}^m\right\|_1 \propto (\lambda_1 A_1)^m$, $\left\|\boldsymbol{Q}_{M_j}^m\right\|_1 \propto (\lambda_1 A_1 P_{1,j}^\delta)^m$. We see that, both $D_1$ and $\Upsilon_j$ goes to infinite as $P_{j,1} \to 0$, then by omitting the exponential term from Eq. (4.14), and combined with the above observations, we obtain $\mathscr{P}_{c,1}^{int} \propto \eta_1 \triangleq \frac{1}{S_1 A_1}$ and $\mathscr{P}_{c,j}^{int} \propto \eta_j \triangleq \frac{\lambda_{j,1} P_{j,1}^{2/\alpha}}{S_j A_1}$. From Eqs. (4.5) and (4.9), we can readily see that both $\frac{1}{S_1 A_1}$ and $\frac{\lambda_{j,1}}{S_j A_1}$ monotonically increase on $\tau$ and $\lambda_l$, $\forall l \neq 1$, while decrease on $\lambda_u$, which completes the proof.

*iv. Property* 4.4: Similar to the proof for Property 4.2, we have $\mathscr{P}_{c,1}^{int} \propto \eta_1$ and $\mathscr{P}_{c,j}^{int} \propto \eta_j$ as $P_{j,1} \ll 1$. Since $P_1$ increases $S_1, A_1$ and $P_1 S_j$, we see that both $\eta_1$ and $\eta_j$ decrease on $P_1$. As $P_1 \to \infty$, we obtain $S_1 \to 1, A_1 \to 1 - e^{-\frac{\lambda_u}{\lambda_1}}$ and $\eta_j \to \frac{\lambda_1}{A_1} M_{j,1}^{-2/\alpha}$, and it is clear that $\mathscr{P}_{c,k}^{int}$, $\forall k \in \mathscr{K}$, is independent of $P_1$, which completes the proof.

*v. Property* 4.5: We obtain the monotonicity of $\xi_k$ and $\psi_k$ on $\lambda_e$, $\tau$, and $\phi_k$ from Eq. (4.23): (1) Both $\xi_k$ and $\psi_k$ are independent of $\lambda_e$; (2) $\psi_k$ monotonically decreases on $\tau$ and $\phi_l$, $\forall l \in \mathcal{K}\backslash k$, while $\xi_k$ is independent of $\tau$ and $\phi_l$; (3) Both $\xi_k$ and $\psi_k$ monotonically decrease on $\phi_k$; (4) $\psi_k$ monotonically increases on $\lambda_u$, while $\xi_k$ is independent of $\lambda_u$. Combining these results directly completes the proof.

*vi. Property* 4.6: Considering $M_{j,k} \to 0$, we have $(1+\xi_k\beta_e)^{1-M_k} \approx e^{-(\phi_k^{-1}-1)\beta_e}$ and $A_j \to 0$, then we obtain $1-\mathcal{P}_{s,k}^{int,o} \propto \frac{\lambda_e(M_k-1)}{\lambda_k A_k C_{\alpha,M_k}}$. We can prove that $\frac{M_k-1}{\lambda_k A_k C_{\alpha,M_k}}$ monotonically decreases on $M_k$ while increases on $\lambda_k$, which completes the proof.

*vii. Property* 4.7: For an extremely large $P_k$, we have $1-\mathcal{P}_{s,k}^{int,o} \propto \chi_k \triangleq \frac{\lambda_e}{\lambda_k A_k}$ and $1-\mathcal{P}_{s,j}^{int,o} \propto \chi_j \triangleq \frac{\lambda_e P_{j,k}^{2/\alpha}}{\lambda_j A_k}$, $\forall j \neq k$. We can prove both $\chi_k$ and $\chi_j$ decrease on $P_k$, i.e., $\mathcal{P}_{s,j}^{int,o}$ increases on $P_k$. As $P_k \to \infty$, we have $A_k \to 1-e^{-\frac{\lambda_u}{\lambda_k}}$, such that $\mathcal{P}_{s,k}^{int,o}$ tends to be constant. Besides, we have $\lim_{P_k\to\infty}\chi_j = 0$, which yields $\lim_{P_k\to\infty}\mathcal{P}_{s,j}^{int,o} = 1$.

## A.3 Proof of Theorem 4.2

Applying the PGFL over PPP along with the Jensen's inequality yields

$$\begin{aligned}\mathcal{P}_{s,k}^{int} &= \mathbb{E}_{\Phi_1}\cdots\mathbb{E}_{\Phi_K}\Big[\exp\Big(-2\pi\lambda_e\int_0^\infty \mathbb{P}\left\{\boldsymbol{SIR}_{e,k} \geq \beta_e|\Phi_1,\cdots,\Phi_K\right\} rdr\Big)\Big]\\ &\geq \exp\left(-2\pi\lambda_e\int_0^\infty \mathbb{P}\left\{\boldsymbol{SIR}_{e,k} \geq \beta_e\right\} rdr\right). \end{aligned} \tag{4.44}$$

Let $I_e = I_{be} + \sum_{j\in\mathcal{K}} I_{je}$ and $\kappa = \frac{r_{be}^{\alpha}\beta_e}{\phi_k P_k}$, and we calculate $\mathbb{P}\{\boldsymbol{SIR}_{e,k} > \beta_e\}$ as follows

$$\mathbb{P}\{\boldsymbol{SIR}_{e,k} > \beta_e\} = \mathbb{P}\left\{\left|\boldsymbol{h}_{be}^{\mathrm{T}}\boldsymbol{w}_b\right|^2 > \kappa I_e\right\} \overset{(h)}{=} \mathbb{E}_{I_e}\left[e^{-\kappa I_e}\right] = \mathcal{L}_{I_e}(\kappa), \tag{4.45}$$

where Eq. ($h$) holds because $U \triangleq \left|\boldsymbol{h}_{be}^{\mathrm{T}}\boldsymbol{w}_b\right|^2 \sim \mathrm{Exp}(1)$ is independent of $I_e$. Note that, $U$ is also independent of $V \triangleq \|\boldsymbol{h}_{be}^{\mathrm{T}}\boldsymbol{W}_b\|^2 \sim \Gamma(M_k-1,1)$ due to the orthogonality of $\boldsymbol{w}_b$ and $\boldsymbol{W}_b$. Similar to Eq. (4.28), the Laplace transform of $I_e$ can be expressed as

$$\mathcal{L}_{I_e}(\kappa) = \mathcal{L}_{I_{be}}(\kappa)\prod_{j\in\mathcal{K}}\mathcal{L}_{I_{je}}(\kappa). \tag{4.46}$$

We first calculate $\mathcal{L}_{I_{be}}(\kappa)$ as

$$\mathcal{L}_{I_{be}}(\kappa) = \mathbb{E}_{I_{be}}\left[e^{-\kappa I_{be}}\right] = \int_0^\infty e^{-\xi_k\phi_k P_k r_{be}^{-\alpha}\kappa v} f_V(v)dv = \left(1+\xi_k\phi_k P_k r_{be}^{-\alpha}\kappa\right)^{1-M_k},$$

where the last equality is obtained by invoking $f_V(v) = \frac{v^{M_k-2}e^{-v}}{\Gamma(M_k-1)}$ and using Eq. [10, (3.326.2)]. We then obtain $\mathcal{L}_{I_{je}}(\kappa)$ from Eq. [9, (8)], which is given by

$$\mathscr{L}_{I_{je}}(\kappa) = \exp\left(-\pi \lambda_j^o C_{\alpha,M_j}(\xi_j \phi_j P_j \kappa)^\delta\right). \tag{4.47}$$

Substituting $\mathscr{L}_{I_{be}}(\kappa)$ and Eq. (4.47) into Eq. (4.45) yields

$$\mathbb{P}\{\boldsymbol{SIR}_{e,k} \geq \beta_e\} = \frac{e^{-\kappa N_0} e^{-\pi \sum_{j\in\mathcal{K}} A_j \lambda_j C_{\alpha,M_j}(\xi_j\phi_j P_j \kappa)^\delta}}{(1+\xi_k\beta_e)^{M_k-1}}. \tag{4.48}$$

Plugging Eq. (4.48) with $\kappa = \frac{r_{be}^\alpha \beta_e}{\phi_k P_k}$ into Eq. (4.44), we obtain the lower bound $\mathcal{P}_{s,k}^{int,L}$.

Next, we derive the upper bound $\mathcal{P}_{s,k}^{int,U}$ by only considering the nearest Eve to the serving BS. Given a serving BS located at $b$ in tier $k$ and the nearest Eve located at $e$, we have

$$\mathcal{P}_{s,k}^{int,U} = \int_0^\infty \mathbb{P}\{\boldsymbol{SIR}_{e,k} < \beta_e\} f_{r_{be}}(r) dr, \tag{4.49}$$

where $f_{r_{be}}(r) = 2\pi\lambda_e r e^{-\pi\lambda_e r^2}$ and $\mathbb{P}\{\boldsymbol{SIR}_{e,k} < \beta_e\} = 1 - \mathbb{P}\{\boldsymbol{SIR}_{e,k} \geq \beta_e\}$ can be directly obtained from Eq. (4.48). Calculating the integral completes the proof.

## A.4 Proof of Propositions 4.1 and 4.2

*i. Proposition* 4.1: Substituting $\alpha = 4$ and $M_k = 2$ into Eq. (4.23) yields $\mathcal{P}_{s,k}^{int,o}(\beta_{e,k}) = 1 - \frac{\lambda_e(\xi_k\beta_{e,k})^{-1/2}}{\psi_k(1+\xi_k\beta_{e,k})}$. Let $x \triangleq (\xi_k \beta_{r,k})^{\frac{1}{2}}$. We obtain a cubic equation $x^3 + x - \frac{\lambda_e}{\psi_k(1-\varepsilon)} = 0$ from $\mathcal{P}_{s,k}^{int,o}(\beta_{e,k}) = \varepsilon$. Solving it with Cardano's formula [13] completes the proof.

*ii. Proposition* 4.2: As $\lim_{M\to\infty}\left(1+\frac{x}{M}\right)^{-M} = e^{-x}$, we have $\mathcal{P}_{s,k}^{int,o}(\beta_{e,k}) = 1 - \frac{\lambda_e e^{-(\phi_k^{-1}-1)\beta_{e,k}}}{\psi_k \beta_{e,k}^\delta}$. Let $\frac{1-\phi_k}{\phi_k}\beta_{e,k} \to x$ and $e^{\frac{\alpha}{2}x} \to y$. We obtain $y^y = e^\theta$ from $\mathcal{P}_{s,k}^{int,o}(\beta_{e,k}) = \varepsilon$ with $\theta \triangleq \frac{\alpha}{2}\frac{1-\phi_k}{\phi_k}\left(\frac{(1-\varepsilon)\psi_k}{\lambda_e}\right)^{-\frac{\alpha}{2}}$. The solution is $y = \frac{\theta}{\mathcal{W}(\theta)}$, which yields $\beta_{e,k}^\star$.

## References


1. H.-M. Wang, T.-X. Zheng, J. Yuan, D. Towsley, M.H. Lee, Physical layer security in heterogeneous cellular networks. IEEE Trans. Commun. **64**(3), 1204–1219 (2016)
2. M. Haenggi, On distances in uniformly random networks. IEEE Trans. Inf. Theory **51**(10), 3584–3586 (2005)
3. J.G. Andrews, F. Baccelli, R.K. Ganti, A tractable approach to coverage and rate in cellular networks. IEEE Trans. Commun. **59**(11), 3122–3134 (2011)
4. A.M. Hunter, J.G. Andrews, S. Weber, Transmission capacity of ad hoc networks with spatial diversity. IEEE Trans. Wirel. Commun. **7**(12), 5058–5071 (2008)

5. H.S. Dhillon, R.K. Ganti, F. Baccelli, J.G. Andrews, Modeling and analysis of K-tier downlink heterogeneous cellular networks. IEEE J. Sel. Areas Commun. **30**(3), 550–560 (2012)
6. H.-S. Jo, Y.J. Sang, P. Xia, J.G. Andrews, Heterogeneous cellular networks with flexible cell association: a comprehensive downlink SINR analysis. IEEE Trans. Wirel. Commun. **11**(10), 3484–3495 (2012)
7. X. Zhang, X. Zhou, M.R. McKay, Enhancing secrecy with multi-antenna transmission in wireless ad hoc networks. IEEE Trans. Inf. Forensics Secur. **8**(11), 1802–1814 (2013)
8. F.W.J. Olver, D.W. Lozier, R.F. Boisvert, C.W. Clark, *NIST Handbook of Mathematical Functions* (Cambrige Univ. Press, Cambrige, 2010)
9. M. Haenggi, J. Andrews, F. Baccelli, O. Dousse, M. Franceschetti, Stochastic geometry and random graphs for the analysis and design of wireless networks. IEEE J. Sel. Areas Commun. **27**(7), 1029–1046 (2009)
10. I.S. Gradshteyn, I.M. Ryzhik, A. Jeffrey, D. Zwillinger, S. Technica, *Table of Integrals, Series, and Products*, 7th edn. (Academic Press, New York, 2007)
11. C. Li, J. Zhang, K.B. Letaief, Throughput and energy efficiency analysis of small cell networks with multi-antenna base stations. IEEE Trans. Wirel. Commun. **13**(5), 2505–2517 (2014)
12. H. Alzer, On some inequalities for the incomplete gamma function. Math. Comput. **66**(218), 771–778 (1997)
13. W. Dunham, Cardano and the solution of the cubic, Ch. 6 in *Journey Through Genius: The Great Theorems of Mathematics* (Wiley, London, 1990), pp. 133–154

# Chapter 5
# Physical Layer Security in Heterogeneous Ad hoc Networks with Full-Duplex Receivers

**Abstract** In this chapter, we study the benefits of full-duplex (FD) receiver jamming. It enhances the physical layer security of a two-tier heterogeneous wireless ad hoc network, in which each tier is deployed with a large number of pairs of a single-antenna transmitter and a multiple-antenna receiver. The receivers in the underlying tier work in the half-duplex (HD) mode and those in the overlaid tier work in the FD mode. We provide a comprehensive performance analysis and network design under a stochastic geometry framework. Specifically, we consider the scenarios where each FD receiver uses single- and multiple-antenna jamming, and analyze the connection probability and the secrecy outage probability of a typical FD receiver with accurate expressions and more tractable approximations provided. We further determine the optimal density of the FD tier that maximizes network-wide secrecy throughput subject to constraints including the given dual probabilities and the network-wide throughput of the HD tier. Numerical results are demonstrated to verify our theoretical findings, and show that network-wide secrecy throughput is significantly improved by properly deploying the FD tier.

## 5.1 Introduction

In the previous two chapters, we see that to improve transmission secrecy, AN aided signaling is an efficient way to degrade eavesdroppers' wiretapping ability. However, this scheme relies on the multiple antennas equipped at the transmitters. In many applications, such as in an uplink transmission, or in ad hoc networks, a mobile terminal/sensor is usually equipped with only one single antenna, subject to the physical size of the terminal and the sensors' cost. In these scenarios, it is still challenging to protect information from eavesdropping.

Fortunately, as we have already indicated in Sect. 1.4.3, the recent progress of developing in-band FD radios raises the possibility of enhancing network security in the aforementioned scenarios. using a more powerful FD data collection station provides extra degrees of freedom to protect information delivery, e.g., radiating jamming signals to degrade eavesdroppers while receiving desired signals simultaneously. In particular, when the FD receiver is equipped with multiple antennas, it



H.-M. Wang and T.-X. Zheng, *Physical Layer Security in Random Cellular Networks*, SpringerBriefs in Computer Science,
DOI 10.1007/978-981-10-1575-5_5

provides us with potential benefits not only in alleviating SI but also in designing jamming signals. However, the works we mentioned in Sect. 1.4.3 are confined to a point-to-point scenario. When considering a random wireless network, analyzing the influence of FD radios on network security becomes much more sophisticated due to the presence of not only the mutual interference between nodes but also the self-interference.

In this chapter, we investigate the FD receiver jamming scheme in enhancing the physical layer security of a two-tier heterogeneous wireless ad hoc network, where in each tier deployed a large number of pairs of a single-antenna transmitter and a multiple-antenna receiver. In the underlying tier, the transmitter sends unclassified information, and each receiver works in the HD mode receiving the desired signal. In the overlaid tier, the transmitter deliveries confidential information in the presence of randomly located eavesdroppers, and the receiver works in the FD mode radiating jamming signals to confuse eavesdroppers and receiving the desired signal simultaneously. For convenience, we name the two tiers the HD tier and the FD tier in this chapter. The reasons why we consider this model are

- This model characterizes a practical communication scenario where a security-oriented network is newly deployed over an existing network that has no security requirement, e.g., an unlicensed security secondary tier in an underlay cognitive radio network should make its interference to the primary tier under control to guarantee smooth communications for the latter.
- This is a more general ad hoc model that incorporates communications with and without security requirements. The secure decentralized ad hoc network models discussed in [1, 2] are just special cases of our model when we simply put aside the HD tier.
- In addition, investigating the achievable performances in such a two-tier heterogeneous network facilitates us to gain a better understanding of the interplay between the classified and unclassified networks, and to evaluate the impact of FD jamming to an existing communication network without security constraint.

In the following sections, we will first analyze the connection probability and the secrecy outage probability of a typical FD receiver, and provide accurate integral expressions as well as analytical approximations for the given metrics; then we will optimize the deployment density of the FD tier to maximize network-wide secrecy throughput subject to constraints including the connection probability, the SOP, and the HD tier throughput.

## 5.2 System Model

### 5.2.1 Heterogeneous Ad hoc Networks

Consider a two-tier heterogeneous wireless ad hoc network in which an existing tier that provides unclassified services is overlaid with another deployed tier that has classified services. In either tier, each data source (Tx) has only a single antenna due to hardware cost, and reports data up to its paired data collection station (Rx); each Rx is equipped with multiple antennas for signal enhancement, interference suppression, information protection, etc. In the underlying tier, the Tx sends an unclassified message to the Rx, and the latter works in the HD mode, using all its antennas to receive the desired signal. In the overlaid tier, the Tx deliveries a confidential message to its Rx in the presence of randomly located eavesdroppers, and the Rx works in the FD mode, simultaneously using part of its antennas to receive the desired signal and using the remaining to radiate jamming signals to confuse eavesdroppers. An illustration of a network snapshot is depicted in Fig. 5.1.

We model the locations of HD Rxs, FD Rxs, and eavesdroppers according to independent homogeneous PPPs $\Phi_h$ with density $\lambda_h$, $\Phi_f$ with density $\lambda_f$, and $\Phi_e$ with density $\lambda_e$, respectively. We further use $\hat{\Phi}_h$ and $\hat{\Phi}_f$ to denote the sets of locations of the Txs in the HD and FD tiers, which also obey independent PPPs with densities

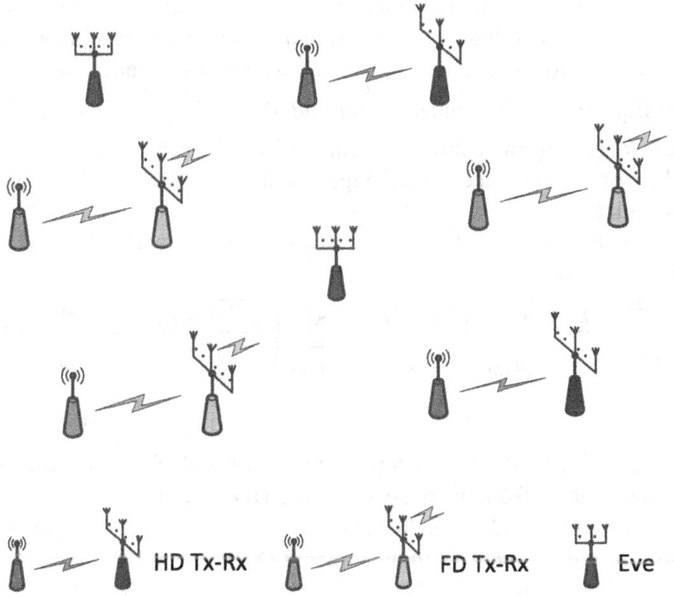


**Fig. 5.1** An illustration of a two-tier heterogeneous Ad hoc network consisting of both HD and FD tiers. Each HD (FD) Rx receives data from an intended Tx. The ongoing transmission between the FD Tx-Rx pair is overheard by randomly located eavesdroppers (Eves)

$\lambda_h$ and $\lambda_f$ according to the displacement theorem [3, p. 35]. Wireless channels are assumed to undergo a large-scale path loss governed by the exponent $\alpha > 2$ along with flat Rayleigh fading with fading coefficients independent and identically distributed (i.i.d.) obeying $\mathcal{CN}(0, 1)$. We assume that in both tiers each Rx knows the ICSI of its paired Tx as well as the SCSI of eavesdroppers.

### 5.2.2 Signal Model

Consider a typical Tx-Rx pair in the FD tier and place the Rx at the origin $o$ of the coordinate system. The received signal of the typical FD Rx is given by

$$y_f = \underbrace{\frac{\sqrt{P_f}\boldsymbol{f}_{\hat{o}o}s_{f,\hat{o}}}{D_f^{\alpha/2}}}_{\text{desired signal}} + \underbrace{\sqrt{P_t}\boldsymbol{F}_{oo}\boldsymbol{v}_o}_{\text{SI}} + \underbrace{\sum_{\hat{z}\in\hat{\Phi}_h}\frac{\sqrt{P_h}\boldsymbol{f}_{\hat{z}o}s_{h,\hat{z}}}{D_{\hat{z}o}^{\alpha/2}}}_{\text{HD tier undesired}} + \underbrace{\sum_{\hat{z}\in\hat{\Phi}_f\setminus\hat{o}}\left(\frac{\sqrt{P_f}\boldsymbol{f}_{\hat{z}o}s_{f,\hat{z}}}{D_{\hat{z}o}^{\alpha/2}} + \frac{\sqrt{P_t}\boldsymbol{F}_{zo}\boldsymbol{v}_z}{D_{zo}^{\alpha/2}}\right)}_{\text{FD tier undesired and jamming signals}} + \boldsymbol{n}_f, \tag{5.1}$$

where $s_{f,\hat{z}}$ ($s_{h,\hat{z}}$) denotes the signal from the Tx at $\hat{z}$ in the FD (HD) tier with $\mathbb{E}[|s_{f,\hat{z}}|^2] = 1$ ($\mathbb{E}[|s_{h,\hat{z}}|^2] = 1$); $\boldsymbol{v}_z \in \mathbb{C}^{N_t\times 1}$ denotes a jamming signal vector from the FD Rx at $z$ with $\mathbb{E}[\|\boldsymbol{v}_z\|^2] = 1$; $\boldsymbol{n}$ denotes thermal noise; $P_f$ ($P_h$) and $P_t$ denote the transmit powers of the Tx in the FD (HD) tier and of an FD Rx, respectively; $\boldsymbol{f}_{xy} \in \mathbb{C}^{(N_f-N_t)\times 1}$ ($\boldsymbol{F}_{xy} \in \mathbb{C}^{(N_f-N_t)\times N_t}$) denotes the small-scale fading coefficient vector (matrix) of the channel from the node at $x$ to the FD Rx at $y$ ($\boldsymbol{F}_{oo}$ denotes the self-interference (SI) channel related to the residual SI after passive SI suppression like antenna isolation). Note that, due to the fixed Tx-Rx pair separation distance $D_f$, $D_{\hat{z}o}$ and $D_{zo}$ in Eq. (5.1) are not independent and $D_{\hat{z}o} = \sqrt{D_{zo}^2 + D_f^2 - 2D_{zo}D_f\cos\theta_z}$, where angle $\theta_z$ is uniformly distributed in $[0, 2\pi]$. As can be seen in subsequent analysis, this correlation makes it challenging to derive tractable results for involved performance metrics.

As to an HD Rx located at $b$, since it suffers no SI, the received signal is

$$y_h = \frac{\sqrt{P_h}\boldsymbol{h}_{\hat{b}b}s_{h,\hat{b}}}{D_h^{\alpha/2}} + \sum_{\hat{z}\in\hat{\Phi}_h\setminus\hat{b}}\frac{\sqrt{P_h}\boldsymbol{h}_{\hat{z}b}s_{h,\hat{z}}}{D_{\hat{z}b}^{\alpha/2}} + \sum_{\hat{z}\in\hat{\Phi}_f}\left(\frac{\sqrt{P_f}\boldsymbol{h}_{\hat{z}b}s_{f,\hat{z}}}{D_{\hat{z}b}^{\alpha/2}} + \frac{\sqrt{P_t}\boldsymbol{H}_{zb}\boldsymbol{v}_z}{D_{zb}^{\alpha/2}}\right) + \boldsymbol{n}_h, \tag{5.2}$$

where $\boldsymbol{h}_{xy} \in \mathbb{C}^{N_h\times 1}$ ($\boldsymbol{H}_{xy} \in \mathbb{C}^{N_h\times N_t}$) denotes the small-scale fading coefficient vector (matrix) of the channel from the node at $x$ to the HD Rx at $y$.

Similarly, for an eavesdropper located at $e$ that is intended to wiretap the data transmission from the typical Tx to the typical FD Rx, the received signal is

$$y_e = \frac{\sqrt{P_f}\boldsymbol{g}_{\hat{o}e}s_{f,\hat{o}}}{D_{\hat{o}e}^{\alpha/2}} + \frac{\sqrt{P_t}\boldsymbol{G}_{oe}\boldsymbol{v}_o}{D_{oe}^{\alpha/2}} + \sum_{\hat{z}\in\hat{\Phi}_h}\frac{\sqrt{P_h}\boldsymbol{g}_{\hat{z}e}s_{h,\hat{z}}}{D_{\hat{z}e}^{\alpha/2}} + \sum_{\hat{z}\in\hat{\Phi}_f\setminus\hat{o}}\left(\frac{\sqrt{P_f}\boldsymbol{g}_{\hat{z}e}s_{f,\hat{z}}}{D_{\hat{z}e}^{\alpha/2}} + \frac{\sqrt{P_t}\boldsymbol{G}_{ze}\boldsymbol{v}_z}{D_{ze}^{\alpha/2}}\right) + \boldsymbol{n}_e, \tag{5.3}$$

with $\boldsymbol{g}_{xe} \in \mathbb{C}^{N_e \times 1}$ ($\boldsymbol{G}_{xe} \in \mathbb{C}^{N_e \times N_t}$) the fading coefficient vector (matrix) of the link from the node at $x$ to the eavesdropper at $e$.

### 5.2.3 Performance Metrics

As presented in previous chapters, we consider a non-colluding wiretap scenario and use the Wyner's wiretap codes. The connection probability of a typical FD Rx is defined as the probability that the SINR of the FD Rx lies above an SINR threshold $\beta_t \triangleq 2^{R_t} - 1$ with $R_t$ the transmission rate, i.e.,

$$\mathcal{P}_t \triangleq \mathbb{P}\{\boldsymbol{SINR}_f > \beta_t\}. \tag{5.4}$$

Similarly, the connection probability of an HD Rx is defined by $\mathcal{P}_c \triangleq \mathbb{P}\{\boldsymbol{SINR}_h > \beta_c\}$, where $\beta_c \triangleq 2^{R_c} - 1$ with $R_c$ the corresponding transmission rate.

The SOP is defined as the complement of the probability that the SINR of an arbitrary eavesdropper at $e$, denoted by $\boldsymbol{SINR}_e$, lies below an SINR threshold $\beta_e \triangleq 2^{R_e} - 1$ with $R_e$ the redundant rate, i.e.,

$$\mathcal{P}_{so} \triangleq 1 - \mathbb{E}_{\Phi_e}\left[\prod_{e\in\Phi_e} \mathbb{P}\{\boldsymbol{SINR}_e < \beta_e|\Phi_e\}\right]. \tag{5.5}$$

In this chapter, we focus on the *network-wide secrecy throughput* under a connection probability $\mathcal{P}_t(\beta_t) = \sigma$ and a secrecy outage probability $\mathcal{P}_{so}(\beta_e) = \epsilon$, i.e.,

$$\mathcal{T}_s \triangleq \lambda_f \sigma R_s^* = \lambda_f \sigma \left[R_t^* - R_e^*\right]^+ = \lambda_f \sigma \left[\log_2\left(1 + \beta_t^*\right) - \log_2\left(1 + \beta_e^*\right)\right]^+, \tag{5.6}$$

where $R_t^* \triangleq \log_2(1 + \beta_t^*)$, $R_e^* \triangleq \log_2(1 + \beta_e^*)$ and $R_s^* = R_t^* - R_e^*$ denote the transmission rate, redundant rate, and confidential information rate at a Tx in the FD tier, with $\beta_t^*$ and $\beta_e^*$ satisfying $\mathcal{P}_t(\beta_t^*) = \sigma$ and $\mathcal{P}_{so}(\beta_e^*) = \epsilon$, respectively.

Likewise, the network-wide throughput of the HD tier under a connection probability $\mathcal{P}_c(\beta_c) = \sigma_c$ is defined by $\mathcal{T}_c \triangleq \lambda_h \sigma_c R_c^*$, where $R_c^* \triangleq \log_2(1 + \beta_c^*)$ with $\beta_c^*$ satisfying $\mathcal{P}_c(\beta_c) = \sigma_c$.

We emphasize that the FD tier density strikes a nontrivial tradeoff between spatial reuse, reliable connection, and safeguarding. On one hand, increasing the density of the FD tier establishes more communication links per unit area, potentially increasing throughput; meanwhile, the increased jamming signals introduced by newly deployed FD Rxs greatly degrade the wiretap channels. On the other hand, the additional amount of interference caused by adding new devices deteriorates ongoing receptions, decreasing the probability of successfully connecting Tx-Rx pairs. The overall balance of such opposite effects on secrecy throughput needs to be carefully addressed.

Therefore, in this chapter, we aim to determine the deployment of the FD tier to achieve its maximum network-wide secrecy throughput while guaranteeing a certain level of network-wide throughput for the HD tier. In the following sections, we deal with network design by considering the scenarios of each FD Rx using single-antenna jamming ($N_t = 1$) and multiple-antenna jamming ($N_t > 1$), respectively. For tractability, we consider the *interference-limited* case by ignoring thermal noise, as we have done in Chap. 4. For ease of notation, we define $\delta \triangleq 2/\alpha$, and $P_{ab} \triangleq P_a/P_b$ for $a, b \in \{h, f, t\}$.

## 5.3 Single-Antenna-Jamming FD Receiver

This section considers the scenario where each FD Rx uses single-antenna jamming, i.e., $N_t = 1$. Thereby, matrices $\boldsymbol{F}, \boldsymbol{H}$ and $\boldsymbol{G}$ given in Eqs. (5.1)–(5.3) reduce to vectors $\boldsymbol{f}, \boldsymbol{h}$, and $\boldsymbol{g}$, respectively, and vector $\boldsymbol{v}$ reduces to scalar $v$. Without loss of generality, we consider a typical FD Tx-Rx pair $(\hat{o}, o)$.

To counteract SI and meanwhile strengthen the desired signal, the weight vector $\boldsymbol{w}_f$ at the FD Rx's input can be chosen according to a hybrid zero forcing and maximal ratio combining (ZF-MRC) criterion,

$$\boldsymbol{w}_f = \frac{\boldsymbol{f}_{\hat{o}o}^{\mathrm{H}} \boldsymbol{U}\boldsymbol{U}^{\mathrm{H}}}{\|\boldsymbol{f}_{\hat{o}o}^{\mathrm{H}} \boldsymbol{U}\|}, \tag{5.7}$$

where $\boldsymbol{U} \in \mathbb{C}^{(N_f-1)\times(N_f-2)}$ is the projection matrix onto the null space of vector $\boldsymbol{f}_{oo}^{\mathrm{H}}$ and the columns of $\left[\frac{\boldsymbol{f}_{oo}^{\mathrm{H}}}{\|\boldsymbol{f}_{oo}\|}, \boldsymbol{U}\right]$ constitute an orthogonal basis, such that $\boldsymbol{w}_f \boldsymbol{f}_{oo} = 0$.

We first analyze the connection probability and the secrecy outage probability of the typical FD Rx in Sects. 5.3.1 and 5.3.2, respectively, and then maximize network-wide secrecy throughput by optimizing the density of the FD tier in Sect. 5.3.3.

### 5.3.1 *Connection Probability*

In this subsection, we investigate the connection probability of the typical FD Rx. From Eqs. (5.1) and (5.7), the SIR of the typical FD Rx is given by

$$\boldsymbol{SIR}_f = \frac{P_f \|\boldsymbol{f}_{\hat{o}o}^{\mathrm{H}} \boldsymbol{U}\|^2 D_f^{-\alpha}}{I_h + I_f}, \tag{5.8}$$

where $I_h \triangleq \sum_{\hat{z}\in\hat{\Phi}_h} \frac{P_h |\boldsymbol{w}_f \boldsymbol{f}_{\hat{z}o}|^2}{D_{\hat{z}o}^{\alpha}}$ and $I_f \triangleq \sum_{\hat{z}\in\hat{\Phi}_f\setminus\hat{o}} \left(\frac{P_f |\boldsymbol{w}_f \boldsymbol{f}_{\hat{z}o}|^2}{D_{\hat{z}o}^{\alpha}} + \frac{P_t |\boldsymbol{w}_f \boldsymbol{f}_{zo}|^2}{D_{zo}^{\alpha}}\right)$ are the aggregate interferences from the HD tier and FD tier, respectively. The following theorem provides a general expression of the connection probability.

**Theorem 5.1** *The connection probability of a typical FD Rx defined in Eq.* (5.4) *is*

$$\mathscr{P}_t = \sum_{m=0}^{N_f-3} \frac{(-1)^m}{m!} \left(\frac{D_f^\alpha \beta_t}{P_f}\right)^m \left(e^{-\lambda_h C_{\alpha,2}(P_h s)^\delta} \mathscr{L}_{I_f}\left(D_f^\alpha \beta_t / P_f\right)\right)^{(m)}, \qquad (5.9)$$

*where* $\mathscr{L}_{I_f}(s)$ *denotes the Laplace transform of* $I_f$, *i.e.,*

$$\mathscr{L}_{I_f}(s) = \exp\left(-\lambda_f \int_0^\infty \left(2\pi - \int_o^{2\pi} \frac{(1+P_f s r^{-\alpha})^{-1} d\theta}{1+P_t s\left(r^2+D_f^2-2rD_f\cos\theta\right)^{-\alpha/2}}\right) r dr\right).$$

*Proof* Please see Appendix A.1. ∎

Theorem 5.1 provides an exact connection probability without requiring time-consuming Monte Carlo simulations. A special case is that when $N_f = 3$, $\mathscr{P}_t$ simplifies to $e^{-\lambda_h C_{\alpha,2}(P_h s)^\delta} \mathscr{L}_{I_f}\left(D_f^\alpha \beta_t / P_f\right)$. However, for the more general case, the double integral term in $\mathscr{L}_{I_f}(s)$ makes computing $\mathscr{L}_{I_f}^{(m)}(s)$ quite difficult, thus making Eq. (5.9) rather unwieldy to analyze. This motivates the need for more compact forms, and in the following theorem we provide closed-form lower and upper bounds for $\mathscr{P}_t$.

**Theorem 5.2** *The connection probability* $\mathscr{P}_t$ *of a typical FD Rx is lower bounded by* $\mathscr{P}_t^L$ *and upper bounded by* $\mathscr{P}_t^U$; *which share the same closed form given below,*

$$\mathscr{P}_t^S = e^{-\Lambda_f^S \beta_t^\delta} + e^{-\Lambda_f^S \beta_t^\delta} \sum_{m=1}^{N_f-3} \frac{1}{m!} \sum_{n=1}^{m} \left(\delta \Lambda_f^S \beta_t^\delta\right)^n \Upsilon_{m,n}, \ \forall S \in \{L, U\} \qquad (5.10)$$

$\Lambda_f^L \triangleq C_{\alpha,2}\left(P_{hf}^\delta \lambda_h + \left(1 + P_{tf}^\delta\right)\lambda_f\right) D_f^2$, $\quad \Lambda_f^U \triangleq C_{\alpha,2}\left(P_{hf}^\delta \lambda_h + \frac{1+\delta}{2}\left(1 + P_{tf}^\delta\right)\lambda_f\right) D_f^2$ *and* $\Upsilon_{m,n} = \sum_{\psi_j \in \text{comb}\binom{m-1}{m-n}} \prod_{\substack{l_{ij}\in\psi_j \\ i=1,\ldots,m-n}} \left(l_{ij} - \delta(l_{ij} - i + 1)\right)$. *Here* $\text{comb}\binom{m-1}{m-n}$ *denotes the set of all distinct subsets of the natural numbers* $\{1, 2, \ldots, m-1\}$ *with cardinality* $m - n$. *The elements in each subset are arranged in an increasing order with* $l_{ij}$ *the* $i$*th element of* $\psi_j$. *For* $m \geq 1$, *we have* $\Upsilon_{m,m} = 1$.

*Proof* Please see Appendix A.2. ∎

Considering a practical need of a high level of reliability, we focus on the large probability region in which $\mathscr{P}_t^S \to 1$ for $S \in \{L, U\}$, and provide a much simpler approximation for $\mathscr{P}_t^S$ in the following corollary.

**Corollary 5.1** *In the large probability region, i.e.,* $\mathscr{P}_t \to 1$, $\mathscr{P}_t^S$ *approximates to*

$$\mathscr{P}_t^S \approx 1 - \Lambda_f^S \beta_t^\delta K_{\alpha,N_f-2}, \ \forall S \in \{L, U\} \qquad (5.11)$$

*where* $K_{\alpha,N} = 1 + \sum_{m=1}^{N-1} \frac{1}{m!} \prod_{l=0}^{m-1}(l - \delta)$.

*Proof* We see from Eq. (5.10) that $\mathscr{P}_t^S \to 1$ as $\Lambda_f^S \to 0$. Here, $\Lambda_f^S \to 0$ reflects all cases of system parameters such as $D_f$, $\lambda_f$ and $\lambda_h$ that may lead to a large $\mathscr{P}_t^S$. A reasonable case of $\Lambda_f^S \to 0$ is but is not limited to that the Tx-Rx pair distance is much less than the average distance between any two Txs (or between two Rxs), i.e., $D_f^2\lambda_f, D_f^2\lambda_h \ll 1$. Using the first-order Taylor expansion with Eq. (5.10) around $\Lambda_f^S = 0$ and discarding the high order terms $\Theta\left(\left(\Lambda_f^S\right)^2\right)$, we complete the proof. ■

The given bound results are shown in Fig. 5.2, where we see in the large probability region lower bound $\mathscr{P}_t^L$ is tight to the exact $\mathscr{P}_t$ from Monte Carlo simulations. Therefore in subsequent analysis, we focus on the lower bound $\mathscr{P}_t^L$ instead of $\mathscr{P}_t$.

Likewise, since the connection probability $\mathscr{P}_c$ of a typical HD Rx shares a similar form as $\mathscr{P}_t$, we can obtain an approximation for $\mathscr{P}_c$ in the large probability region, which is provided by the following corollary.

**Corollary 5.2** *Define* $\Lambda_h \triangleq C_{\alpha,2}\left(\lambda_h + \left(P_{fh}^\delta + P_{th}^\delta\right)\lambda_f\right)D_h^2$. *In the large probability region, the connection probability* $\mathscr{P}_c$ *of a typical HD Rx is approximated by*

$$\mathscr{P}_c \approx 1 - \Lambda_h \beta_c^\delta K_{\alpha,N_h}. \tag{5.12}$$

### 5.3.2 *Secrecy Outage Probability*

This subsection investigates the secrecy outage probability Eq. (5.5) which corresponds to the probability that a secret message is decoded by *at least* one eavesdropper.

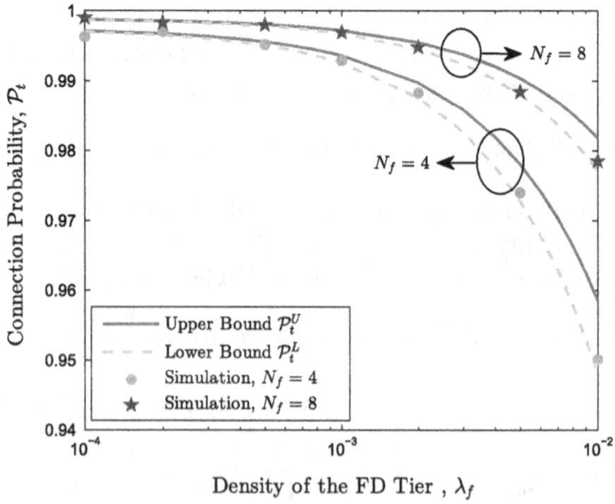


**Fig. 5.2** Connection probability versus $\lambda_f$, with $P_t = 0\,\text{dBm}$, $N_t = 1$, and $\beta_t = 1$. Unless specified otherwise, we set $\alpha = 3.5$, $P_f = P_h = 0\,\text{dBm}$, $N_h = 4$, $\lambda_h = 10^{-3}$ and $D_f = D_h = 1$

We consider a worst-case wiretap scenario where each eavesdropper has multiuser decoding ability and adopts a successive interference cancellation minimum mean square error (SIC-MMSE) receiver [4]. The eavesdropper located at $e$ is able to decode and cancel undesired information signals and uses the MMSE detector

$$\boldsymbol{w}_e = \boldsymbol{R}_e^{-1}\boldsymbol{g}_{\hat{o}e}, \tag{5.13}$$

where $\boldsymbol{R}_e \triangleq P_t\boldsymbol{g}_{oe}\boldsymbol{g}_{oe}^{\mathrm{H}}D_{oe}^{-\alpha} + \sum_{z\in\Phi_f\setminus o} P_t\boldsymbol{g}_{ze}\boldsymbol{g}_{ze}^{\mathrm{H}}D_{ze}^{-\alpha}$, to aggregate the desired confidential signal. The resulting SIR is given by

$$\boldsymbol{SIR}_e = P_f\boldsymbol{g}_{\hat{o}e}^{\mathrm{H}}\boldsymbol{R}_e^{-1}\boldsymbol{g}_{\hat{o}e}D_{\hat{o}e}^{-\alpha}. \tag{5.14}$$

**Theorem 5.3** *The secrecy outage probability $\mathscr{P}_{so}$ of a typical FD Rx is*

$$\mathscr{P}_{so} = 1 - \exp\left(-\lambda_e \sum_{n=0}^{N_e-1}\sum_{i=0}^{\min(n,1)} \frac{B^{n-i}}{(n-i)!}\int_0^\infty Q_i(r) r^{2(n-i)} e^{-Br^2} r dr\right), \tag{5.15}$$

*where* $B \triangleq C_{\alpha,2}\lambda_f\left(P_{tf}\beta_e\right)^{\delta}$, *and* $Q_i(r) = \int_0^{2\pi} \frac{\left(P_{tf}\beta_e\left(r/\sqrt{r^2+D_f^2-2rD_f\cos\theta}\right)^{\alpha}\right)^i}{1+P_{tf}\beta_e\left(r/\sqrt{r^2+D_f^2-2rD_f\cos\theta}\right)^{\alpha}} d\theta.$

*Proof* Please see Appendix A.3. ■

In a wireless ad hoc network, a Tx is generally a simple low-power node and has very short coverage, e.g., a sensor. To guarantee a reliable communication, the distance $D_f$ is usually set small. In view of this, we resort to an asymptotic analysis by considering $D_f \to 0$, and give a simple approximation for $\mathscr{P}_{so}$ in Corollary 5.3. Nevertheless, as can be seen in Fig. 5.3, Corollary 5.3 applies more generally, and

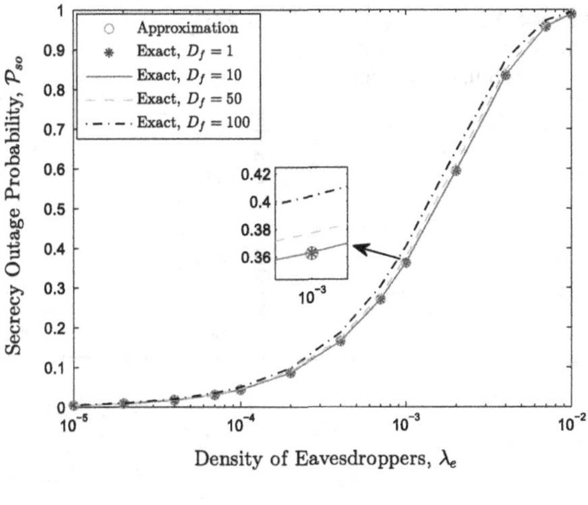


**Fig. 5.3** Secrecy outage probability versus $\lambda_e$, with $P_t = 10\,\mathrm{dBm}$, $N_e = 4$, $\lambda_f = 10^{-3}$ and $\beta_e = 1$

Eq. (5.16) is accurately approximate for quite a wide range of $D_f$. This illustrates the rationality of the given hypothesis. Hereafter, we focus on the case $D_f \to 0$ for $\mathscr{P}_{so}$.

**Corollary 5.3** *In the small $D_f$ regime, i.e., $D_f \to 0$, $\mathscr{P}_{so}$ in Eq. (5.15) approximates*

$$\mathscr{P}_{so}^{\circ} = 1 - e^{-\pi\lambda_e\left(N_e - 1 + \frac{1}{1+P_{tf}\beta_e}\right)/(C_{\alpha,2}\lambda_f P_{tf}^{\delta}\beta_e^{\delta})}. \tag{5.16}$$

*Proof* As $D_f \to 0$, $Q_i(r) = \frac{2\pi(P_{tf}\beta_e)^i}{1+P_{tf}\beta_e}$. Substituting $Q_i(r)$ into Eq. (5.15) and using formula $\int_0^{\infty} r^{2(n-i)} e^{-Ar} r dr = \frac{(n-i)!}{A^{n-i+1}}$, we complete the proof. ■

Figure 5.4 shows that $\mathscr{P}_{so}^{\circ}$ is quite close to the exact results of Monte Carlo simulations. Secrecy outage probability increases as either the number of eavesdropper's antennas or the density of eavesdroppers increases. To reduce it, we should better deploy more FD jammers to confuse eavesdroppers.

If the eavesdroppers are equipped with a large number of antennas, i.e., $N_e \to \infty$, $\mathscr{P}_{so}^{\circ}$ reduces to

$$\mathscr{P}_{so} = 1 - e^{-(\pi\lambda_e N_e)/(C_{\alpha,2}\lambda_f P_{tf}^{\delta}\beta_e^{\delta})}. \tag{5.17}$$

We see that $\mathscr{P}_{so}$ increases as $\alpha$ increases, since for more severe path loss, jamming signals have undergone stronger attenuation before they arrive at eavesdroppers.

### 5.3.3 Network-Wide Secrecy Throughput

In this subsection, we aim to maximize $\mathscr{T}_s$ by optimizing $\lambda_f$ under a guarantee that $\mathscr{T}_c$ lies above a target throughput $T_c$. This optimization problem is formulated as

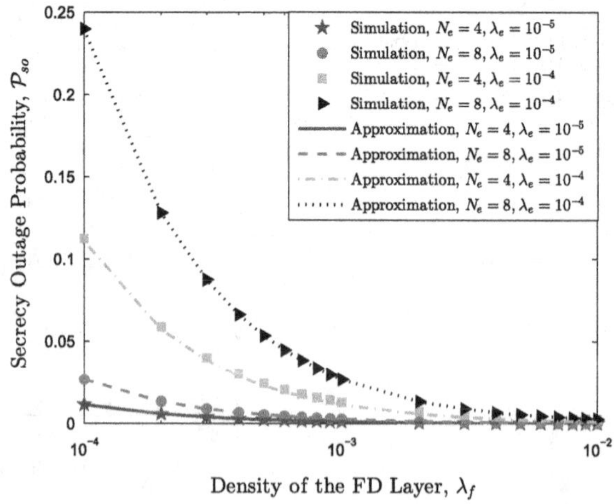


**Fig. 5.4** Secrecy outage probability versus $\lambda_f$, with $P_t = 20\,\text{dBm}$, $N_t = 1$ and $\beta_e = 1$

$$\max_{\lambda_f} \mathcal{T}_s, \quad \text{s.t. } \mathcal{T}_c \geq T_c. \tag{5.18}$$

According to the definition in Eq. (5.6), we should first calculate $\beta_t^*$ and $\beta_e^*$ from $\mathcal{P}_t(\beta_t) = \sigma$ and $\mathcal{P}_{so}(\beta_e) = \varepsilon$, respectively. In general, the analytical expressions of the exact $\beta_t^*$ and $\beta_e^*$ are unavailable due to the complexity of Eqs. (5.9) and (5.15); we can only numerically calculate $\beta_t^*$ and $\beta_e^*$, which makes solving problem (5.18) extremely difficult. To facilitate the analysis and provide useful insights into network design, we resort to some approximate results of the connection and secrecy outage probabilities.

First, to ensure a high level of reliability, the connection probability $\sigma$ is expected to be large, which allow us to use Eq. (5.11) to calculate $\beta_t^*$.

**Lemma 5.1** *In the large $\sigma$ regime, i.e., $\sigma \to 1$, $\beta_t$ that satisfies $\mathcal{P}_t(\beta_t) = \sigma$ is*

$$\beta_t^* = \left( \frac{1-\sigma}{C_{\alpha,2} D_f^2 K_{\alpha,N_f-2} \left( P_{hf}^\delta \lambda_h + (1 + P_{tf}^\delta)\lambda_f \right)} \right)^{\frac{\alpha}{2}}. \tag{5.19}$$

*Proof* From Corollary 5.1, we obtain Eq. (5.19) by solving $1 - \Lambda_f^L \beta_t^\delta K_{\alpha,N_f-2} = \sigma$. ∎

Second, considering the scenario of large-antenna eavesdroppers, i.e., $N_e \gg 1$, we have the following lemma to calculate $\beta_e^*$.

**Lemma 5.2** *In the large $N_e$ regime, $\beta_e$ that satisfies $\mathcal{P}_{so}(\beta_e) = \varepsilon$ is given by*

$$\beta_e^* = \frac{1}{P_{tf}} \left( \frac{\pi \lambda_e N_e}{C_{\alpha,2} \lambda_f \ln \frac{1}{1-\varepsilon}} \right)^{\frac{\alpha}{2}}. \tag{5.20}$$

*Proof* From Eq. (5.17), we obtain Eq. (5.20) by solving $1 - e^{-\pi \lambda_e N_e / \left( C_{\alpha,2} \lambda_f P_{tf}^\delta \beta_e^\delta \right)} = \varepsilon$. ∎

Having obtained $\beta_t^*$ and $\beta_e^*$, we reform problem (5.18) as follows

$$\max_{\lambda_f} \mathcal{T}_s = \frac{\sigma}{\ln 2} \left[ F(\lambda_f) \right]^+, \quad \text{s.t. } 0 < \lambda_f \leq \lambda_f^U, \tag{5.21}$$

where $F(\lambda_f) = \lambda_f \ln \frac{1+X(1+Y\lambda_f)^{-\alpha/2}}{1+Z\lambda_f^{-\alpha/2}}$, $\lambda_f^U \triangleq \frac{(1-\sigma_c)/\left(C_{\alpha,2} D_h^2 K_{\alpha,N_h}\right)\left(2^{T_c/(\lambda_h \sigma_c)}-1\right)^{-\delta} - \lambda_h}{P_{th}^\delta + P_{fh}^\delta}$ is given from $\mathcal{T}_c = \lambda_h \sigma_c \log_2(1 + \beta_c^*) = T_c$ in Eq. (5.18), and $X \triangleq \left( \frac{1-\sigma}{C_{\alpha,2} D_f^2 K_{\alpha,N_f-2} P_{hf}^\delta \lambda_h} \right)^{\frac{\alpha}{2}}$, $Y \triangleq \frac{1+P_{tf}^\delta}{P_{hf}^\delta \lambda_h}$ and $Z \triangleq \frac{1}{P_{tf}} \left( \frac{\pi \lambda_e N_e}{C_{\alpha,2} \ln \frac{1}{1-\varepsilon}} \right)^{\frac{\alpha}{2}}$. To achieve a positive $\mathcal{T}_s$ in Eq. (5.21), $F(\lambda_f) > 0$, i.e., $X(1 + Y\lambda_f)^{-\alpha/2} > Z\lambda_f^{-\alpha/2}$ must be guaranteed, and thus we have $\lambda_f > \lambda_f^L \triangleq 1/\left((X/Z)^\delta - Y\right)$ and $(X/Z) > Y^{\frac{\alpha}{2}}$, which further yields

$$(1-\sigma)\ln\frac{1}{1-\varepsilon} > \pi\lambda_e N_e D_f^2 K_{\alpha,N_f-2}\left(1+P_{tf}^{-\delta}\right), \tag{5.22}$$

i.e., a large $\sigma$ and a small $\varepsilon$ might not be simultaneously promised. Consider the case that a positive $\mathcal{T}_s$ exists, i.e., $\lambda_f > \lambda_f^L$, problem (5.21) is then equivalent to

$$\max_{\lambda_f} F(\lambda_f), \quad \text{s.t. } \lambda_f^L < \lambda_f \le \lambda_f^U. \tag{5.23}$$

In the following theorem, we prove the *quasi-concavity* [5, Sect. 3.4.2] of $F(\lambda_f)$ on $\lambda_f$ in the range $(\lambda_f^L, \infty)$, and derive the optimal $\lambda_f$ that maximizes $F(\lambda_f)$ (or $\mathcal{T}_s$).

**Theorem 5.4** *The optimal $\lambda_f$ that maximizes $\mathcal{T}_s$ is*

$$\lambda_f^* = \begin{cases} \min(\lambda^\star, \lambda_f^U), & (X/Z) > Y^{\frac{\alpha}{2}} \text{ and } \lambda_f^L \le \lambda_f^U, \\ \varnothing, & \text{otherwise}, \end{cases} \tag{5.24}$$

*where $\lambda^\star$ is the unique root of the following equation,*

$$\ln\frac{f_1(\lambda)}{f_2(\lambda)} + \frac{\frac{\alpha}{2}f_1(\lambda)[f_2(\lambda)-1] - \frac{\alpha}{2}\lambda[f_1(\lambda)-f_2(\lambda)]Y}{f_1(\lambda)f_2(\lambda)(1+\lambda Y)} = 0, \tag{5.25}$$

*with $f_1(\lambda) = 1 + X(1+Y\lambda)^{-\frac{\alpha}{2}}$ and $f_2(\lambda) = 1 + Z\lambda^{-\frac{\alpha}{2}}$. The left-hand side (LHS) of Eq. (5.25) is first positive and then negative; thus, the value of $\lambda^\star$ can be efficiently calculated using the bisection method. Here, $\lambda_f^* = \varnothing$ means no $\lambda_f$ can produce a positive $\mathcal{T}_s$ under a given pair $(\sigma, \varepsilon)$.*

*Proof* Please see Appendix A.4. ■

This theorem solves the network-wide secrecy throughput maximization problem Eq. (5.18). Substituting the optimal $\lambda_f^*$ into Eq. (5.21) yields the maximum $\mathcal{T}_s^*$,

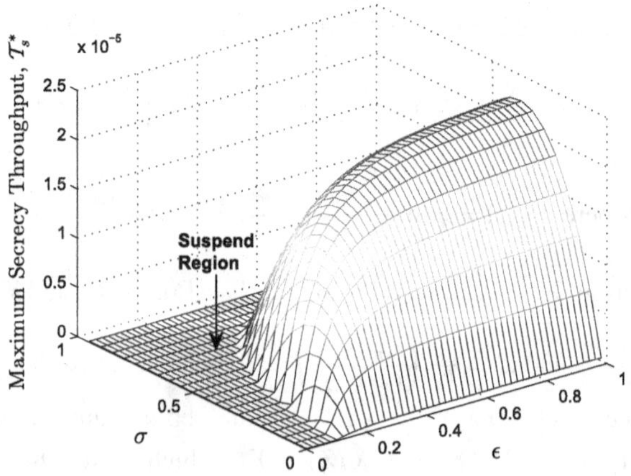


**Fig. 5.5** Relationship between the maximum $\mathcal{T}_s^*$ and $\sigma$ and $\varepsilon$. In the *dark blue areas*, there is no positive $\mathcal{T}_s$ that simultaneously satisfies connection and secrecy outage probabilities

which is shown in Fig. 5.5. Just as analyzed previously, only those $\sigma$ and $\varepsilon$ that satisfy Eq. (5.22) can yield a positive $\mathcal{T}_s^*$. We see that $\mathcal{T}_s^*$ initially increases in $\sigma$ and then decreases in it. The underlying reason is, too small a $\sigma$ corresponds to a small probability of successful transmission, whereas too large a $\sigma$ limits the transmission rate; either aspect results in a small $\mathcal{T}_s^*$, as can be seen from Eq. (5.6).

## 5.4 Multi-antenna Jamming FD Receiver

In this section, we consider the scenario of the FD Rx using multiple-antenna jamming. Thanks to the extra degrees of freedom provided by multiple jamming antennas, each FD Rx is able to inject jamming signals into the null space of the SI channel such that SI will not leak out to the Rx's input, and MRC reception can be simply adopted at the input for the desired signal. This is motivated by the idea of AN scheme investigated in the previous chapters.

Specifically, we first use MRC reception at the input of the typical FD Rx, the weight vector of which can be obtained from Eq. (5.1), i.e., $\tilde{\boldsymbol{w}}_f = \frac{\boldsymbol{f}_{\hat{o}o}^{\mathrm{H}}}{\|\boldsymbol{f}_{\hat{o}o}\|}$. Here we use superscript $\tilde{}$ to distinguish the multiple-antenna jamming case from the single-antenna jamming case. We then design the jamming signal $\boldsymbol{v}_o$ as $\boldsymbol{v}_o = \tilde{\boldsymbol{F}}_o \tilde{\boldsymbol{v}}_o$, where $\tilde{\boldsymbol{v}}_o \in \mathbb{C}^{N_j \times 1}$ is an $N_j$-stream jamming signal vector with i.i.d. entries $\tilde{v}_i \sim CN\left(0, 1/N_j\right)$ and $N_j \leq N_t - 1$, $\tilde{\boldsymbol{F}}_o \in \mathbb{C}^{N_t \times N_j}$ is the projection matrix onto the null space of vector $\left(\tilde{\boldsymbol{w}}_f \boldsymbol{F}_{oo}\right)^{\mathrm{H}}$ such that the columns of $\left[\frac{(\tilde{\boldsymbol{w}}_f \boldsymbol{F}_{oo})^{\mathrm{H}}}{\|\tilde{\boldsymbol{w}}_f \boldsymbol{F}_{oo}\|}, \tilde{\boldsymbol{F}}_o\right]$ constitute an orthogonal basis, i.e., $\tilde{\boldsymbol{w}}_f \boldsymbol{F}_{oo} \boldsymbol{v}_o = 0$. In this way, SI is completely eliminated in the spatial domain. Note that, $\tilde{\boldsymbol{v}}_o$ includes but is not limited to an $N_t - 1$-stream signal vector. Although $N_t - 1$-dimension null space should better be injected with jamming signals to confuse eavesdroppers in a point-to-point transmission [6], there is no general conclusion from the network perspective, since jamming signals impair not only eavesdroppers but also legitimate users.

### 5.4.1 Connection Probability

From the above discussion, the SIR of the typical FD Rx can be obtained from Eq. (5.1),

$$\widetilde{SIR}_f = \frac{P_f \|\boldsymbol{f}_{\hat{o}o}\|^2 D_f^{-\alpha}}{\tilde{I}_h + \tilde{I}_f}, \tag{5.26}$$

where $\tilde{I}_h \triangleq \sum_{\hat{z} \in \hat{\Phi}_h} \frac{P_h |\tilde{\boldsymbol{w}}_f \boldsymbol{f}_{\hat{z}o}|^2}{D_{\hat{z}o}^{\alpha}}$ and $\tilde{I}_f \triangleq \sum_{\hat{z} \in \hat{\Phi}_f \setminus \hat{o}} \left(\frac{P_f |\tilde{\boldsymbol{w}}_f \boldsymbol{f}_{\hat{z}o}|^2}{D_{\hat{z}o}^{\alpha}} + \frac{P_t \|\tilde{\boldsymbol{w}}_f \boldsymbol{F}_{zo} \tilde{\boldsymbol{F}}_z\|^2}{N_j D_{zo}^{\alpha}}\right)$ are the aggregate interferences from the HD and FD tiers, respectively. Substituting Eq. (5.26) into Eq. (5.4) produces the connection probability of the typical FD Rx, denoted by $\tilde{\mathscr{P}}_t$. In the following theorem, we provide a tight and more tractable lower bound for $\tilde{\mathscr{P}}_t$.

**Theorem 5.5** *The connection probability $\tilde{\mathscr{P}}_t$ of an FD Rx is lower bounded by*

$$\tilde{\mathscr{P}}_t^L = e^{-\tilde{\Lambda}_f^L \beta_t^\delta}\left(1+\sum_{m=1}^{N_f-N_t-1}\frac{1}{m!}\sum_{n=1}^{m}\left(\delta\tilde{\Lambda}_f^L\beta_t^\delta\right)^n \Upsilon_{m,n}\right), \tag{5.27}$$

*where* $\tilde{\Lambda}_f^L \triangleq C_{\alpha,2}D_f^2\lambda_f\left(P_{hf}^\delta\frac{\lambda_h}{\lambda_f}+1+\frac{C_{\alpha,N_j+1}}{C_{\alpha,2}}\left(\frac{P_{tf}}{N_j}\right)^\delta\right)$ *and* $\Upsilon_{m,n}$ *is defined in Eq.* (5.10).

*Proof* The proof simply follows from Appendix A.2; the only difference lies in computing $\mathscr{L}_{I_f}(s)$ by realizing that $\|\tilde{\boldsymbol{w}}_f\boldsymbol{F}_{zo}\tilde{\boldsymbol{F}}_z\|^2 \sim \Gamma(N_j, 1)$. ■

To further facilitate the analysis, an approximation for $\tilde{\mathscr{P}}_t$ is provided by the following corollary.

**Corollary 5.4** *In the large connection probability region, i.e.,* $\tilde{\mathscr{P}}_t \rightarrow 1$, $\tilde{\mathscr{P}}_t$ *is approximated by*

$$\tilde{\mathscr{P}}_t \approx 1 - \tilde{\Lambda}_f\beta_t^\delta K_{\alpha,N_f-N_t}, \tag{5.28}$$

*where* $\tilde{\Lambda}_f = \tilde{\Lambda}_f^L$ *and* $K_{\alpha,N}$ *has been defined in Corollary 5.1.*

Figure 5.6 shows that the result in Eq. (5.28) approximates to the exact connection probability $\tilde{\mathscr{P}}_t$ provided by Monte Carlo simulations. We see that $\tilde{\mathscr{P}}_t$ greatly reduces as the number $N_t$ of jamming antennas increases. In addition, $\tilde{\mathscr{P}}_t$ suffers a slight decrease when the number $N_j$ of jamming signal streams increases. This implies when the value of $N_t$ is fixed, $\tilde{\mathscr{P}}_t$ is less insensitive to the value of $N_j$.

**Fig. 5.6** Connection probability versus $N_t$, with $P_t = 20\,\text{dBm}$, $N_f = 8$, $\lambda_f = 10^{-3}$ and $\beta_t = 1$

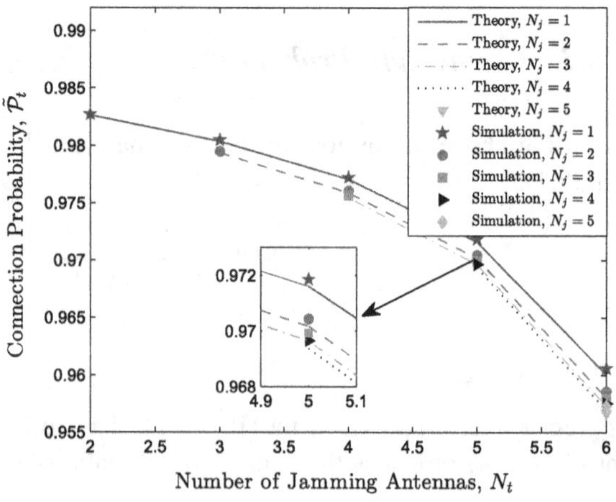

Following similar steps in Corollary 5.4, an approximation for the connection probability $\tilde{\mathscr{P}}_c$ of an HD Rx in the large connection probability region can be obtained.

**Corollary 5.5** *Let $\tilde{\Lambda}_h = C_{\alpha,2}\lambda_h D_h^2 + C_{\alpha,2}P_{fh}^{\delta}\lambda_f D_h^2 + C_{\alpha,N_j+1}\left(P_{th}/N_j\right)^{\delta}\lambda_f D_h^2$. In the large probability region, i.e., $\tilde{\mathscr{P}}_c \to 1$, connection probability $\tilde{\mathscr{P}}_c$ approximates to*

$$\tilde{\mathscr{P}}_c \approx 1 - \tilde{\Lambda}_h \beta_c^{\delta} K_{\alpha,N_h}. \tag{5.29}$$

## 5.4.2 Secrecy Outage Probability

Similar to Eq. (5.13), the weight vector of the eavesdropper located at $e$ is given by

$$\tilde{\boldsymbol{w}}_e = \tilde{\boldsymbol{R}}_e^{-1}\boldsymbol{g}_{\hat{o}e}, \tag{5.30}$$

where $\tilde{\boldsymbol{R}}_e \triangleq \frac{P_t \boldsymbol{G}_{oe}\tilde{\boldsymbol{F}}_o\tilde{\boldsymbol{F}}_o^{\mathrm{H}}\boldsymbol{G}_{oe}^{\mathrm{H}}}{N_j D_{oe}^{\alpha}} + \sum_{z\in\Phi_f\setminus o}\frac{P_t \boldsymbol{G}_{ze}\tilde{\boldsymbol{F}}_z\tilde{\boldsymbol{F}}_z^{\mathrm{H}}\boldsymbol{G}_{ze}^{\mathrm{H}}}{N_j D_{ze}^{\alpha}}$; the resulting SIR is

$$\widetilde{\boldsymbol{SIR}}_e = P_f \boldsymbol{g}_{\hat{o}e}^{\mathrm{H}}\tilde{\boldsymbol{R}}_e^{-1}\boldsymbol{g}_{\hat{o}e}D_{\hat{o}e}^{-\alpha}. \tag{5.31}$$

Due to the presence of multiple-stream jamming signals, deriving SOP requires using the integer partition theory [7]. We describe the integer partitions of a positive integer $k$ via an integer partition matrix $\boldsymbol{P}_k$. For example, $\boldsymbol{P}_4$ is given by

$$\boldsymbol{P}_4 = \begin{bmatrix} 4 & & & \\ 3 & 1 & & \\ 2 & 2 & & \\ 2 & 1 & 1 & \\ 1 & 1 & 1 & 1 \end{bmatrix}. \tag{5.32}$$

In the following, we denote $|\xi_k|$ as the number of rows of $\boldsymbol{P}_k$, and $\xi_{i,j,k}$, $|\xi_{j,k}|$, $\phi_{i,j,k}$ and $|\phi_{j,k}|$ as the $i$th entry, the number of entries, the number of the $i$th largest entry and the number of non-repeated entries in the $j$th row of $\boldsymbol{P}_k$, respectively. Recalling Eq. (5.5), we provide a closed-form expression for $\tilde{\mathscr{P}}_{so}$ in the following theorem.

**Theorem 5.6** *The SOP of a multiple-antenna jamming FD Rx is*

$$\tilde{\mathscr{P}}_{so} = 1 - \exp\left(-\frac{\pi\lambda_e}{C_{\alpha,N_j+1}\lambda_f}\sum_{n=0}^{N_e-1}\sum_{i=0}^{\min(n,N_j)}\binom{N_j}{i}\frac{\left(P_{tf}\beta_e/N_j\right)^{i-\delta}}{\left(1+P_{tf}\beta_e/N_j\right)^{N_j}}\sum_{j=1}^{|\xi_{n-i}|}(-1)^{|\xi_{j,n-i}|}|\xi_{j,n-i}|!\,\Xi_{j,n-i}\right), \tag{5.33}$$

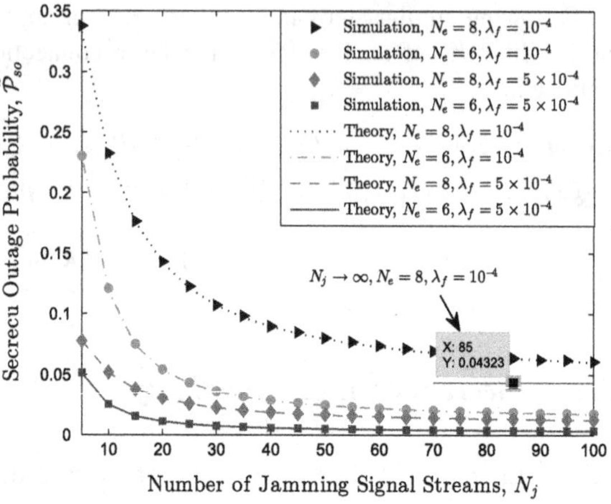


**Fig. 5.7** Secrecy outage probability versus $N_j$, with $P_t = 10\,\text{dBm}$, $\lambda_e = 10^{-4}$ and $\beta_e = 1$

*where* $\Xi_{j,n} = \frac{\prod_{m=1}^{|\xi_{j,n}|} \prod_{k=1}^{\xi_{m,j,n}} \frac{(N_j+1-k)(k-1-\delta)}{k(N_j-k+\delta)}}{\prod_{i=1}^{|\phi_{j,n}|} \phi_{i,j,n}!}$. *Here, we let* $|\xi_0| = 1$, $|\xi_{j,0}| = 0$ *and* $\Xi_{j,0} = 1$.

*Proof* Please see Appendix A.5. ■

We see that $\tilde{\mathcal{P}}_{so}$ is affected by the number $N_j$ of jamming signal streams rather than the number $N_t$ of jamming antennas. The result in Eq. (5.33) is well verified by Monte Carlo simulations, in Fig. 5.7. To better understand the effect of $N_j$ on $\tilde{\mathcal{P}}_{so}$, we investigate the asymptotic behavior of $\tilde{\mathcal{P}}_{so}$ w.r.t. $N_j$ by considering the cases $N_j = 1$ and $N_j \to \infty$, respectively.

**Corollary 5.6** *When* $N_j = 1$, $\tilde{\mathcal{P}}_{so}$ *equals to as the one given in Eq.* (5.16).

*Proof* Substituting $N_j = 1$ into $\Xi_{j,n-i}$, we have $\Xi_{j,n-i} = 0$ for $j < |\xi_{n-i}|$. Since the $|\xi_{n-i}|$th integer partition of $n - i$ (i.e., the last row of $\mathbf{P}_{n-i}$) must be $n - i$ ones, we have $|\phi_{|\xi_{n-i}|,n-i}| = 1$ and $|\xi_{|\xi_{n-i}|,n-i}| = \phi_{1,|\xi_{n-i}|,n-i}$. Therefore, the term $\sum_{j=1}^{|\xi_{n-i}|} (-1)^{|\xi_{j,n-i}|} |\xi_{j,n-i}|! \Xi_{j,n-i}$ reduces to $(-1)^{|\xi_{|\xi_{n-i}|,n-i}|} |\xi_{|\xi_{n-i}|,n-i}|! \Xi_{|\xi_{n-i}|,n-i} = 1$, substituting which into Eq. (5.33) completes the proof. ■

Corollary 5.6 implies emitting a single-stream jamming signal via multiple antennas has the same effect as single-antenna jamming in confusing eavesdroppers.

**Corollary 5.7** *As* $N_j \to \infty$, $\tilde{\mathcal{P}}_{so}$ *in Eq.* (5.33) *tends to the following constant value*

$$1 - \exp\left( -\frac{\lambda_e}{\Gamma(1-\delta)\lambda_f} \sum_{n=0}^{N_e-1} \sum_{i=0}^{n} \frac{e^{-P_{tf}\beta_e}}{i!(P_{tf}\beta_e)^{\delta-i}} \sum_{j=1}^{|\xi_{n-i}|} \frac{|\xi_{j,n-i}|! \prod_{m=1}^{|\xi_{j,n-i}|} \prod_{k=1}^{\xi_{m,j,n-i}} \frac{k-1-\delta}{k}}{(-1)^{|\xi_{j,n-i}|} \prod_{i=1}^{|\phi_{j,n-i}|} \phi_{i,j,n-i}!} \right). \quad (5.34)$$

*Proof* Invoking $\lim_{N\to\infty} \frac{\Gamma(N+\delta)}{\Gamma(N)N^{\delta}} = 1$ and $\lim_{N\to\infty} \left(1 + \frac{x}{N}\right)^N = e^x$ in Eq. (5.33) yields Eq. (5.34). ■

Corollary 5.7 implies increasing jamming signal streams can not arbitrarily reduce secrecy outage probability, as validated in Fig. 5.7. This is because the total power $P_t$ of jamming signals is limited. Conversely, if $P_t \to \infty$, $\tilde{\mathscr{P}}_{so}$ reduces to zero.

### 5.4.3 Network-Wide Secrecy Throughput

The network-wide secrecy throughput $\tilde{\mathscr{T}}_s$ in multiple-antenna jamming scenario under a connection probability $\tilde{\mathscr{P}}_t(\beta_t) = \sigma$ and an SOP $\tilde{\mathscr{P}}_{so}(\beta_e) = \varepsilon$ has the same form as Eq. (5.6). We aim to optimize $\lambda_f$ to maximize $\tilde{\mathscr{T}}_s$ while guaranteeing a certain level of the HD tier throughput, i.e., $\tilde{\mathscr{T}}_c \geq T_c$. Similarly to the derivations in Sect. 5.3.3, we should first compute $\beta_t^*$ and $\beta_e^*$ from the equations $\tilde{\mathscr{P}}_t(\beta_t) = \sigma$ and $\tilde{\mathscr{P}}_{so}(\beta_e) = \varepsilon$, respectively.

Parallel to Lemmas 5.1 and 5.2, we have the following two propositions.

**Proposition 5.1** *In the large connection probability region, i.e.,* $\sigma \to 1$, *we have*

$$\beta_t^* = \frac{(1-\sigma)^{\alpha/2}}{D_f^{\alpha} K_{\alpha,N_f-N_t}^{\alpha/2} \left( C_{\alpha,2} P_{hf}^{\delta} \lambda_h + C_{\alpha,2}\lambda_f + C_{\alpha,N_j+1} \left(\frac{P_{tf}}{N_j}\right)^{\delta} \lambda_f) \right)^{\alpha/2}}. \tag{5.35}$$

*Proof* From Eq. (5.28), Eq. (5.35) is obtained by solving $1 - \tilde{\Lambda}_f \beta_t^{\delta} K_{\alpha,N_f-N_t} = \sigma$. ■

**Proposition 5.2** *When* $N_e \gg 1$ *and* $N_j = 1$, $\beta_e$ *that satisfies* $\tilde{\mathscr{P}}_{so}(\beta_e) = \varepsilon$ *has the same expression as the one given in Eq.* (5.20).

For the more general case $N_j \geq 2$, the value of $\beta_e^*$ can be obtained via numerical calculation, i.e., $\beta_e^* = \tilde{\mathscr{P}}_{so}^{-1}(\varepsilon)$, where $\tilde{\mathscr{P}}_{so}^{-1}(\varepsilon)$ is the inverse function of $\tilde{\mathscr{P}}_{so}(\beta_e)$.

In Fig. 5.8, we illustrate some numerical examples of network-wide secrecy throughput $\tilde{\mathscr{T}}_s$. We see that $\tilde{\mathscr{T}}_s$ first increases and then decreases as the FD tier density $\lambda_f$ increases. The value of $\lambda_f$ should be properly chosen in order to maximize $\tilde{\mathscr{T}}_s$. We also find that, $\tilde{\mathscr{T}}_s$ improves as the number $N_j$ of jamming signal streams increases on the premise of a fixed number $N_t$ of jamming antennas.

Next, we formulate the problem of maximizing $\tilde{\mathscr{T}}_s$ as follows,

$$\max_{\lambda_f} \ \tilde{\mathscr{T}}_s = \frac{\lambda_f \sigma}{\ln 2} \left[ \ln \frac{1 + \tilde{X}(1+\tilde{Y}\lambda_f)^{-\alpha/2}}{1 + \tilde{\mathscr{P}}_{so}^{-1}(\varepsilon)} \right]^{+}, \quad \text{s.t. } 0 < \lambda_f \leq \tilde{\lambda}_f^U, \tag{5.36}$$

where $\tilde{\lambda}_f^U \triangleq \frac{(1-\sigma_c)/(D_h^2 K_{\alpha,N_h})\left(2^{T_c/(\lambda_h \sigma_c)}-1\right)^{-\delta} - C_{\alpha,2}\lambda_h}{C_{\alpha,2}P_{fh}^{\delta} + C_{\alpha,N_j+1}\left(P_{th}/N_j\right)^{\delta}}$ is obtained from $\tilde{\mathscr{T}}_c = T_c$, $\tilde{X} \triangleq \left(\frac{(1-\sigma)/(K_{\alpha,N_f-N_t})}{C_{\alpha,2}D_f^2 P_{hf}^{\delta}\lambda_h}\right)^{\alpha/2}$ and $\tilde{Y} \triangleq \frac{C_{\alpha,2} + C_{\alpha,N_j+1}(P_{tf}/N_j)^{\delta}}{C_{\alpha,2}P_{hf}^{\delta}\lambda_h}$.

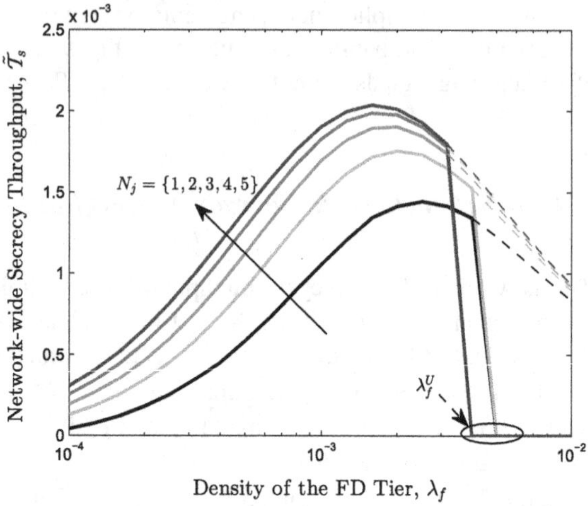


**Fig. 5.8** Network-wide secrecy throughput versus $\lambda_f$ for different values of $N_j$, with $P_t = 20\,\text{dBm}$, $N_f = N_e = 8$, $N_t = 6$, $\lambda_e = 10^{-4}$, $\sigma = \sigma_c = 0.9$, $\varepsilon = 0.02$ and $T_c = 10^{-3}$. The *dashed lines* show the values of $\tilde{\mathcal{T}}_s$ without an HD tier throughput constraint, i.e., $T_c = 0$

For the single jamming signal stream case $N_j = 1$, $\tilde{\mathcal{P}}_{so}^{-1}(\varepsilon)$ has a closed-form expression given in Eq. (5.20), i.e., $\tilde{\mathcal{P}}_{so}^{-1}(\varepsilon) = \beta_e^* = \tilde{Z}\lambda_f^{-\frac{\alpha}{2}}$ with $\tilde{Z} \triangleq \frac{1}{P_{tf}} \left(\frac{\pi\lambda_e N_e}{C_{\alpha,2}\ln\frac{1}{1-\varepsilon}}\right)^{\frac{\alpha}{2}}$. Accordingly, Eq. (5.36) has the same form as Eq. (5.23). As a consequence, the optimal $\lambda_f$ that maximizes $\tilde{\mathcal{T}}_s$ also shares the same form as Eq. (5.24), simply with $X$, $Y$, $Z$ and $\lambda_f^U$ replaced by $\tilde{X}$, $\tilde{Y}$, $\tilde{Z}$ and $\tilde{\lambda}_f^U$, respectively.

For the more general case $N_j \geq 2$, we can only solve problem (5.36) using one-dimension exhaustive search in the range $(0, \tilde{\lambda}_f^U]$. Since increasing the number $N_j$ of jamming signal streams always benefits network-wide secrecy throughput, we should set $N_j = N_t - 1$. Thus, $N_t - 1$-dimension null space is fully injected with jamming signals. In Figs. 5.9 and 5.10, we illustrate the optimal density $\lambda_f^*$ and the corresponding maximum network-wide secrecy throughput $\tilde{\mathcal{T}}_s^*$, respectively.

From Fig. 5.9, we observe a general trend that the value of $\lambda_f^*$ decreases as $N_t$ increases on the premise of the existence of a positive $\tilde{\mathcal{T}}_s^*$. The reason behind is twofold: on one hand, adding jamming antennas provides relief to deploying more FD jammers to degrade the wiretap channels; on the other hand, reducing the number of FD Tx-Rx pairs reduces network interference, thus improving the main channels. How the value of $\lambda_f^*$ is influenced by $N_e$ depends on the specific values of $\lambda_e$ and $N_t$. For example, if each eavesdropper adds receive antennas, more FD jammers are needed for a relatively small $N_t$ or a small $\lambda_e$ (see Fig. 5.9a, b, c), whereas fewer FD jammers might be better as $N_t$ or $\lambda_e$ goes large (see $N_t = 7$ in Fig. 5.9c and $N_t = 5$ in Fig. 5.9d). This is because, if we continue to add FD jammers, we can scarcely achieve a positive secrecy throughput.

In Fig. 5.10, we see that $\tilde{\mathcal{T}}_s^*$ always decreases as $\lambda_e$ or $N_e$ increases. How the value of $\tilde{\mathcal{T}}_s^*$ is affected by $N_t$ depends on the specific values of $\lambda_e$ and $N_e$. Specifically, for relatively small values of $\lambda_e$ and $N_e$, $\tilde{\mathcal{T}}_s^*$ decreases as $N_t$ increases (see Fig. 5.10a).

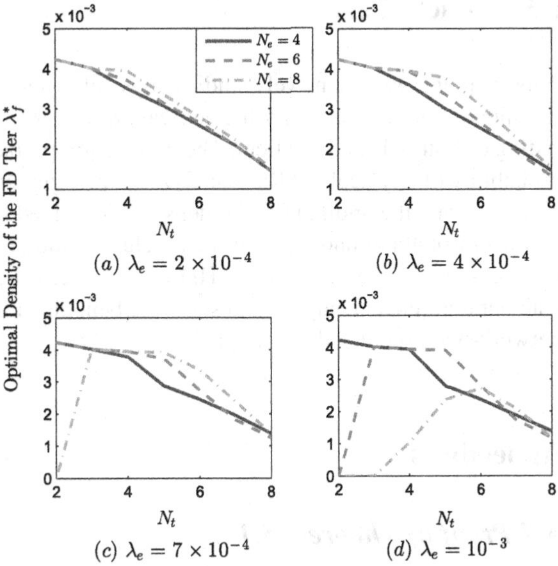


**Fig. 5.9** Optimal density of the FD tier versus $N_t$, with $P_t = 20\,\text{dBm}$, $N_f = 8$, $N_j = N_t - 1$, $\lambda_f = 2 \times 10^{-3}$, $\sigma = \sigma_c = 0.9$, $\varepsilon = 0.02$ and $T_c = 10^{-3}$. Note that $\lambda_f^* = 0$ when $N_t = 2$ in Fig. 5.9c and $N_t = 2, 3$ in Fig. 5.9d. This means a positive secrecy throughput that simultaneously satisfies the connection and secrecy outage probability constraints cannot be achieved, regardless of the value of $\lambda_f$

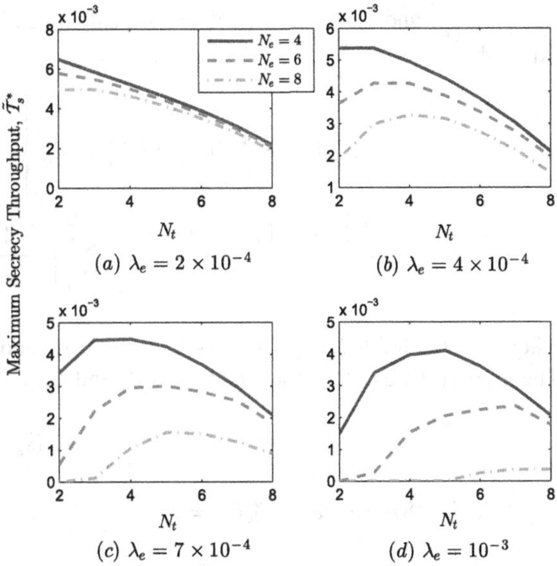


**Fig. 5.10** Maximum network-wide secrecy throughput versus $N_t$, with $P_t = 20\,\text{dBm}$, $N_f = 8$, $N_j = N_t - 1$, $\lambda_f = 2 \times 10^{-3}$, $\sigma = \sigma_c = 0.9$, $\varepsilon = 0.02$ and $T_c = 10^{-3}$

This means we should use as few jamming antennas as possible. However, as $\lambda_e$ or $N_e$ increases, $\tilde{\mathcal{T}}_s^*$ first increases and then decreases as $N_t$ increases (see Fig. 5.10b, c and d). This implies that a modest value of $N_t$ is required to balance improving the main channels with degrading the wiretap channels.

## 5.5 Conclusions

This chapter comprehensively studies physical layer security using FD Rx jamming techniques against randomly located eavesdropper in a heterogeneous DWN consisting of both HD and FD tiers. The connection probability and the secrecy outage probability of a typical FD Rx is analyzed for single- and multiple-antenna jamming scenarios, and the optimal FD tier density is provided for maximizing network-wide secrecy throughput under constraints including the given dual probabilities and the network-wide throughput of the HD tier. Numerical results are presented to validate our theoretical analysis, and show the benefits of FD Rx jamming in improving network-wide secrecy throughput.

## Appendices

### *A.1 Proof of Theorem 5.1*

Let $s \triangleq \frac{D_f^\alpha \beta_t}{P_f}$ and $I_o = I_h + I_f$. $\mathscr{P}_t$ can be calculated by substituting Eq. (5.8) into Eq. (5.4)

$$\mathscr{P}_t = \mathbb{E}_{I_o}\left[\mathbb{P}\left\{\|\boldsymbol{f}_{\hat{o}o}^{\mathrm{H}}\boldsymbol{U}\|^2 \geq sI_o\right\}\right] \overset{(a)}{=} \mathbb{E}_{I_o}\left[e^{-sI_o}\sum_{m=0}^{N_f-3}\frac{s^m I_o^m}{m!}\right]$$
$$= \sum_{m=0}^{N_f-3}\mathbb{E}_{I_o}\left[\frac{s^m e^{-sI_o}}{m!}I_o^m\right] \overset{(b)}{=} \sum_{m=0}^{N_f-3}\left[\frac{(-1)^m s^m}{m!}\mathscr{L}_{I_o}^{(m)}(s)\right], \tag{5.37}$$

where Eq. $(a)$ holds for $\|\boldsymbol{f}_{\hat{o}o}^{\mathrm{H}}\boldsymbol{U}\|^2 \sim \Gamma(N_f-2, 1)$, and Eq. $(b)$ is obtained from [8, Theorem 1]. Due to the independence of $I_h$ and $I_f$, $\mathscr{L}_{I_o}(s)$ is given by

$$\mathscr{L}_{I_o}(s) = \mathbb{E}_{I_o}\left[e^{-sI_o}\right] = \mathscr{L}_{I_h}(s)\mathscr{L}_{I_f}(s). \tag{5.38}$$

From Eq. [9, (8)], we have $\mathscr{L}_{I_h}(s) = e^{-\lambda_h C_{\alpha,2}(P_h s)^\delta}$. $\mathscr{L}_{I_f}(s)$ can be computed as

$$\mathscr{L}_{I_f}(s) = \mathbb{E}_{I_f}\left[e^{-sI_f}\right] = \mathbb{E}_{\hat{\Phi}_f}\left[\prod_{\hat{z}\in\hat{\Phi}_f\setminus\hat{o}} e^{-s\left(P_f|\boldsymbol{w}_f\boldsymbol{f}_{\hat{z}o}|^2 D_{\hat{z}o}^{-\alpha}+P_t|\boldsymbol{w}_f\boldsymbol{f}_{zo}|^2 D_{zo}^{-\alpha}\right)}\right] \tag{5.39}$$

$$\overset{(c)}{=} \mathbb{E}_{\hat{\Phi}_f}\left[\prod_{\hat{z}\in\hat{\Phi}_f\setminus\hat{o}}\frac{1}{1+P_f s D_{\hat{z}o}^{-\alpha}}\frac{1}{1+P_t s D_{zo}^{-\alpha}}\right] \tag{5.40}$$

where Eq. ($c$) holds for $|\mathbf{w}_{f}\mathbf{f}_{\hat{z}o}|^2$, $|\mathbf{w}_{f}\mathbf{f}_{zo}|^2 \sim \mathrm{Exp}(1)$. Using PGFL over a PPP [10] and substituting the result along with $\mathscr{L}_{I_h}(s)$ into Eq. (5.38) completes the proof.

## A.2 Proof of Theorem 5.2

To provide a lower bound for $\mathscr{P}_t$, we need only provide a lower bound for $\mathscr{L}_{I_f}(s)$. This is because, a lower bound for $\mathscr{L}_{I_f}(s)$ actually overestimates the aggregate interference $I_f$, which leads to a lower bound for $\mathscr{P}_t$. From Eq. (5.39), we have

$$\begin{aligned}
\mathscr{L}_{I_f}(s) &= \mathbb{E}\left[\prod_{\hat{z}\in\hat{\Phi}_f\backslash\hat{o}} e^{-s\left(P_f|\mathbf{w}_f\mathbf{f}_{\hat{z}o}|^2 D_{\hat{z}o}^{-\alpha}+P_t|\mathbf{w}_f\mathbf{f}_{zo}|^2 D_{zo}^{-\alpha}\right)}\right]\\
&\overset{(d)}{\geq} \mathbb{E}\left[\prod_{\hat{z}\in\hat{\Phi}_f\backslash\hat{o}} e^{-sP_f|\mathbf{w}_f\mathbf{f}_{\hat{z}o}|^2 D_{\hat{z}o}^{-\alpha}}\right]\mathbb{E}\left[\prod_{z\in\Phi_f\backslash o} e^{-sP_t|\mathbf{w}_f\mathbf{f}_{zo}|^2 D_{zo}^{-\alpha}}\right]\\
&\overset{(e)}{=} e^{-\lambda_f C_{\alpha,2}(P_f s)^{\delta}} e^{-\lambda_f C_{\alpha,2}(P_t s)^{\delta}},
\end{aligned} \tag{5.41}$$

where Eq. ($d$) follows from the FKG inequality [3], since both $\prod_{\hat{z}\in\hat{\Phi}_f\backslash\hat{o}} e^{-sP_f|\mathbf{w}_f\mathbf{f}_{\hat{z}o}|^2 D_{\hat{z}o}^{-\alpha}}$ and $\prod_{\in\Phi_f\backslash o} e^{-sP_t|\mathbf{w}_f\mathbf{f}_{zo}|^2 D_{zo}^{-\alpha}}$ are decreasing random variables as the number of terms increases; Eq. ($e$) holds for invoking Eq. [10, (8)]. Substituting $\mathscr{L}_{I_h}(s)$ and Eq. (5.41) into Eq. (5.9) and invoking [8, Theorem 1], we obtain the lower bound $\mathscr{P}_t^L$.

An upper bound for $\mathscr{P}_t$ is obtained from an upper bound for $\mathscr{L}_{I_f}(s)$. From Eq. (5.40),

$$\begin{aligned}
\mathscr{L}_{I_f}(s) &= \mathbb{E}\left[\prod_{\hat{z}\in\hat{\Phi}_f\backslash\hat{o}} \frac{1}{1+P_f s D_{\hat{z}o}^{-\alpha}}\frac{1}{1+P_t s D_{zo}^{-\alpha}}\right]\\
&\overset{(f)}{\leq} \mathbb{E}\left[\prod_{\hat{z}\in\hat{\Phi}_f\backslash\hat{o}} \frac{1}{\left(1+P_f s D_{\hat{z}o}^{-\alpha}\right)^2}\right]\mathbb{E}\left[\prod_{z\in\Phi_f\backslash o} \frac{1}{\left(1+P_t s D_{zo}^{-\alpha}\right)^2}\right]\\
&\overset{(g)}{=} e^{-\lambda_f C_{\alpha,2}\frac{1+\delta}{2}(P_f s)^{\delta}(1+P_{tf}^{\delta})},
\end{aligned} \tag{5.42}$$

where Eq. ($f$) follows from the Cauchy–Schwarz inequality and Eq. ($g$) holds for the PGFL over a PPP. Substituting $\mathscr{L}_{I_h}(s)$ and Eq. (5.42) into Eq. (5.9) yields the upper bound $\mathscr{P}_t^U$.

## A.3 Proof of Theorem 5.3

Let $r \triangleq D_{\hat{o}e}$. Substituting Eq. (5.14) into Eq. (5.5) and applying the PGFL over a PPP yield

$$\mathcal{P}_{so} = 1 - \exp\left(-\lambda_e \int_0^\infty \int_0^{2\pi} \mathbb{P}\left\{\boldsymbol{SIR}_e \geq \beta_e\right\} rd\theta dr\right). \tag{5.43}$$

Define $v \triangleq r^\alpha \beta_e / P_f$, $\mathbb{P}\left\{\boldsymbol{SIR}_e \geq \beta_e\right\}$ can be calculated by invoking Eq. [4, (11)], i.e.,

$$\mathbb{P}\left\{\boldsymbol{SIR}_e \geq \beta_e\right\} = \mathbb{E}_{\Phi_f}\left[\frac{1}{W}\sum_{n=0}^{N_e-1} w_n v^n\right], \tag{5.44}$$

with $W = \left(1 + P_t D_{oe}^{-\alpha} v\right) \prod_{z \in \Phi_f \backslash o} \left(1 + P_t D_{ze}^{-\alpha} v\right)$ and $w_n$ the coefficient of $v^n$ in $W$,

$$w_n = \sum_{i=0}^{\min(n,1)} \frac{\left(P_t D_{\hat{o}e}^{-\alpha}\right)^i}{(n-i)!} \sum_{z_k \in \Phi_f \backslash o}^{k \in [1, n-i]} \prod_{j=1}^{n-i} \frac{P_t}{D_{z_j e}^\alpha}. \tag{5.45}$$

Substituting $W$ and $w_n$ into Eq. (5.44), $\mathbb{P}\left\{\boldsymbol{SIR}_e \geq \beta_e\right\}$ equals to

$$\begin{aligned} &\mathbb{E}\left[\sum_{n=0}^{N_e-1}\sum_{i=0}^{\min(n,1)} \frac{\left(P_t D_{oe}^{-\alpha} v\right)^i}{\left(1 + P_t D_{oe}^{-\alpha} v\right)(n-i)!} \sum_{z_k \in \Phi_f \backslash o}^{k \in [1, n-i]} \frac{P_t^{n-i} v^{n-i} \prod_{j=1}^{n-i} D_{z_j e}^{-\alpha}}{\prod_{z \in \Phi_f \backslash o}\left(1 + P_t D_{ze}^{-\alpha} v\right)}\right] = \\ &\sum_{n=0}^{N_e-1}\sum_{i=0}^{\min(n,1)} \frac{\left(P_t D_{oe}^{-\alpha} v\right)^i}{\left(1 + P_t D_{oe}^{-\alpha} v\right)(n-i)!} \mathbb{E}_{\Phi_f}\left[\sum_{z_k \in \Phi_f \backslash o}^{k \in [1, n-i]} \frac{P_t^{n-i} v^{n-i} \prod_{j=1}^{n-i} D_{z_j e}^{-\alpha}}{\prod_{z \in \Phi_f \backslash o}\left(1 + P_t D_{ze}^{-\alpha} v\right)}\right]. \end{aligned} \tag{5.46}$$

Using Campbell–Mecke theorem [9, Theorem 4.2] yields

$$\begin{aligned} &\mathbb{E}_{\Phi_f}\left[\sum_{z_k \in \Phi_f \backslash o}^{k \in [1, n-i]} \frac{P_t^{n-i} v^{n-i} \prod_{j=1}^{n-i} D_{z_j e}^{-\alpha}}{\prod_{z \in \Phi_f \backslash o}\left(1 + P_t D_{ze}^{-\alpha} v\right)}\right] \\ &= \left(2\pi\lambda_f \int_0^\infty \frac{P_t v r^{-\alpha}}{1 + P_t v r^{-\alpha}} rdr\right)^{n-i} \exp\left(-2\pi\lambda_f \int_0^\infty \frac{P_t v r^{-\alpha}}{1 + P_t v r^{-\alpha}} rdr\right) \\ &\overset{(h)}{=} \left(C_{\alpha,2}\lambda_f P_t^\delta v^\delta\right)^{n-i} e^{-C_{\alpha,2}\lambda_f P_t^\delta v^\delta}, \end{aligned} \tag{5.47}$$

where Eq. $(h)$ is obtained by transforming $P_t v r^{-\alpha} \to \mu$ and invoking formula Eq. [11, (3.241.2)]. Substituting Eqs. (5.46) and (5.47) into Eq. (5.43), we complete the proof.

## A.4 Proof of Theorem 5.4

To complete the proof, we need only derive the optimal $\lambda_f$, denoted by $\lambda_f^\star$, that maximizes $F(\lambda_f)$ in the range $[\lambda_f^L, \infty)$. Apparently, if $0 < \lambda_f^L \le \lambda_f^U$, the solution to problem (5.23) is $\lambda_f^* = \min(\lambda_f^\star, \lambda_f^U)$; otherwise, there is no feasible solution. For convenience, we omit subscript $f$ from $\lambda_f$. Define $f_1(\lambda) = 1 + X(1 + Y\lambda)^{-\frac{\alpha}{2}} > 1$, $f_2(\lambda) = 1 + Z\lambda^{-\frac{\alpha}{2}} > 1$ and $f(\lambda) = \ln\frac{f_1(\lambda)}{f_2(\lambda)}$, then the objective function in Eq. (5.23) changes into $F(\lambda) = \lambda f(\lambda)$. We give the first-order derivative of $F(\lambda)$ on $\lambda$

$$F^{(1)}(\lambda) = f(\lambda) + \lambda f^{(1)}(\lambda) = f(\lambda)G(\lambda). \tag{5.48}$$

The introduced auxiliary function $G(\lambda)$ is defined as $G(\lambda) = 1 + \frac{\lambda f^{(1)}(\lambda)}{f(\lambda)}$, where

$$f^{(1)}(\lambda) = \frac{f_1^{(1)}(\lambda)}{f_1(\lambda)} - \frac{f_2^{(1)}(\lambda)}{f_2(\lambda)}, \tag{5.49}$$

with $f_1^{(1)}(\lambda) = -\frac{\alpha(f_1(\lambda)-1)Y}{2(1+\lambda Y)}$ and $f_2^{(1)}(\lambda) = -\frac{\alpha(f_2(\lambda)-1)}{2\lambda}$. Note that $f(\lambda)$ in Eq. (5.48) is positive, such that the sign of $F^{(1)}(\lambda)$ remains consistent with that of $G(\lambda)$. First, we investigate the sign of $F^{(1)}(\lambda)$ at the boundaries of $[\lambda_f^L, \infty)$. A complete expression of $F^{(1)}(\lambda)$ is given by substituting Eq. (5.49) into Eq. (5.48)

$$F^{(1)}(\lambda) = \ln\frac{f_1(\lambda)}{f_2(\lambda)} + \frac{f_1(\lambda)[f_2(\lambda) - 1] - \lambda[f_1(\lambda) - f_2(\lambda)]Y}{\delta f_1(\lambda)f_2(\lambda)(1 + \lambda Y)}. \tag{5.50}$$

Case $\lambda = \lambda_f^L$: We have $f_1(\lambda^L) = f_2(\lambda^L)$, thus $F^{(1)}(\lambda^L) = \frac{f_1(\lambda^L)[f_1(\lambda^L)-1]}{\delta f_1^2(\lambda^L)(1+\lambda^L Y)} > 0$.

Case $\lambda \to \infty$: We have $\lim_{\lambda\to\infty} f_1(\lambda) = 1$ and $\lim_{\lambda\to\infty} f_2(\lambda) = 1$, such that $\lim_{\lambda\to\infty} F^{(1)}(\lambda) = \frac{[f_2(\lambda)-1]-\lambda[f_1(\lambda)-f_2(\lambda)]Y}{\delta(1+\lambda Y)}$. Substituting in $f_1(\lambda)$ and $f_2(\lambda)$ yields

$$\lim_{\lambda\to\infty} F^{(1)}(\lambda) = \lim_{\lambda\to\infty} Z\lambda^{-\alpha/2}\left(1 - \frac{X}{Z}Y^{-\alpha/2}\right) < 0, \tag{5.51}$$

where the inequality holds for $\lambda_f^L = 1/\left((X/Z)^\delta - Y\right) > 0 \Rightarrow \left(XY^{-\alpha/2}\right)/Z > 1$.

The above two cases also indicate that $G(\lambda^L) > 0$ and $\lim_{\lambda\to\infty} G(\lambda) < 0$.

Supposing $G(\lambda)$ monotonically decreases with $\lambda$, there obviously exists a unique $\lambda^\star$ that makes $F^{(1)}(\lambda)$ first positive and then negative after $\lambda$ exceeds $\lambda^\star$. That is, $F(\lambda)$ is a first-increasing-then-decreasing function of $\lambda$, and the given $\lambda^\star$ is the optimal solution that maximizes $F(\lambda)$, which is obtained at $F^{(1)}(\lambda) = 0$. Based on the above discussion, in what follows we focus on proving the monotonicity of $G(\lambda)$ w.r.t. $\lambda$. We first compute the first-order derivative of $G(\lambda)$ on $\lambda$

$$G^{(1)}(\lambda) = \frac{1}{f^2(\lambda)}\left(f^{(1)}(\lambda)f(\lambda) + \lambda f^{(2)}(\lambda)f(\lambda) - \lambda\left(f^{(1)}(\lambda)\right)^2\right). \tag{5.52}$$

Computing $G^{(1)}(\lambda)$ requires computing $f^{(2)}(\lambda)$, which can be obtained from Eq. (5.49)

$$f^{(2)}(\lambda) = \frac{f_1^{(2)}(\lambda)f_1(\lambda) - (f_1^{(1)}(\lambda))^2}{f_1^2(\lambda)} - \frac{f_2^{(2)}(\lambda)f_2(\lambda) - (f_2^{(1)}(\lambda))^2}{f_2^2(\lambda)}, \tag{5.53}$$

where $f_1^{(2)}(\lambda) = \frac{\frac{\alpha}{2}(\frac{\alpha}{2}+1)(f_1(\lambda)-1)Y^2}{(1+\lambda Y)^2}$ and $f_2^{(2)}(\lambda) = \frac{\frac{\alpha}{2}(\frac{\alpha}{2}+1)(f_2(\lambda)-1)}{\lambda^2}$ are the second-order derivatives of $f_1(\lambda)$ and $f_2(\lambda)$, substituting which into Eq. (5.53) further yields

$$f^{(2)}(\lambda) = \frac{\frac{\alpha}{2}(f_1(\lambda) - 1)(f_1(\lambda) + \frac{\alpha}{2})Y}{(f_1(\lambda))^2(1 + \lambda Y)^2} - \frac{\frac{\alpha}{2}(f_2(\lambda) - 1)(f_2(\lambda) + \frac{\alpha}{2})}{\lambda^2(f_2(\lambda))^2}. \tag{5.54}$$

Substituting Eqs. (5.49) and (5.54) into Eq. (5.52) and using $\ln \frac{f_1(\lambda)}{f_2(\lambda)} \le \frac{f_1(\lambda)}{f_2(\lambda)} - 1$ yield

$$\begin{aligned} G^{(1)}(\lambda) \le &-\frac{\alpha\lambda f_1(\lambda)}{2f(\lambda)}\Big(f_2(\lambda)[f_1(\lambda) - 1] + \alpha[f_2(\lambda) - 1][f_1(\lambda) - f_2(\lambda)]\Big)Y \\ &- \frac{\alpha^2\lambda^2 f_2(\lambda)}{4f(\lambda)}[f_2(\lambda) - 1][f_1(\lambda) - f_2(\lambda)]^2Y^2 - \frac{\alpha^2 f_1^2(\lambda)}{4f(\lambda)}[f_2(\lambda) - 1]. \end{aligned} \tag{5.55}$$

Since $f_1(\lambda) > f_2(\lambda) > 1$, all the coefficients of $Y^i$ for $i = 0, 1, 2$ in the right-hand side of Eq. (5.55) are negative, such that $G^{(1)}(\lambda) < 0$. This means $G(\lambda)$ is a monotonically decreasing function of $\lambda$ in the range $[\lambda_f^L, \infty)$. By now, we have completed the proof.

## A.5 Proof of Theorem 5.6

Following Eq. (5.43), we first compute $\mathbb{P}\{\widetilde{\boldsymbol{SIR}}_e \ge \beta_e\}$. Recalling Eq. (5.31), each term in $\tilde{\boldsymbol{R}}_e$, e.g., $\boldsymbol{G}_{ze}\tilde{\boldsymbol{F}}_z\tilde{\boldsymbol{F}}_z^{\mathrm{H}}\boldsymbol{G}_{ze}^{\mathrm{H}}$, is a superposition of single-stream signals with $N_j$ colocated interferers. Denote the $n$th column of $\boldsymbol{G}_{ze}\tilde{\boldsymbol{F}}_z$ by $\tilde{\boldsymbol{g}}_{ze,n}$, then $\boldsymbol{R}_{e,N_t,N_j}$ is reformed as

$$\tilde{\boldsymbol{R}}_e = \frac{P_t}{N_j}\sum_{n=1}^{N_j}\tilde{\boldsymbol{g}}_{oe,n}\tilde{\boldsymbol{g}}_{oe,n}^{\mathrm{H}}D_{oe}^{-\alpha} + \sum_{z\in\Phi_f\backslash o}\frac{P_t}{N_j}\sum_{n=1}^{N_j}\tilde{\boldsymbol{g}}_{ze,n}\tilde{\boldsymbol{g}}_{ze,n}^{\mathrm{H}}D_{ze}^{-\alpha}. \tag{5.56}$$

Let $r \triangleq D_{oe}$ and $z \triangleq r^\alpha\beta_e P_f$. Invoking Eq. [4, (11)] yields

$$\mathbb{P}\{\widetilde{\boldsymbol{SIR}}_e \ge \beta_e\} = \mathbb{E}_{\Phi_f}\left[\frac{1}{W_{N_j}}\sum_{n=0}^{N_e-1}y_n z^n\right], \tag{5.57}$$

where $W_{N_j} = \left(1 + \frac{P_t}{N_j}r^{-\alpha}z\right)^{N_j}\prod_{z\in\Phi_f\backslash o}\left(1 + \frac{P_t}{N_j}D_{ze}^{-\alpha}z\right)^{N_j}$ and $y_n$ is the coefficient of $z^n$ in the polynomial expansion of $W_{N_j}$. Define $\tilde{A} \triangleq C_{\alpha,N_j+1}\lambda_f\left(\frac{P_{tf}\beta_e}{N_j}\right)^\delta$, and we have

$$\mathbb{P}\left\{\widetilde{\boldsymbol{SIR}}_e \geq \beta_e\right\} = \sum_{n=0}^{N_e-1} \sum_{i=0}^{\min(n,N_j)} \binom{N_j}{i} \left(\frac{P_{tf}\beta_e}{N_j}\right)^i \sum_{j=1}^{|\xi_{n-i}|} \frac{\Xi_{j,n-i}(-\tilde{A}r^2)^{|\xi_{j,n-i}|} e^{-\tilde{A}r^2}}{\left(1+P_{tf}\beta_e/(N_j)\right)^{N_j}},$$

Substituting which into Eq. (5.43) completes the proof.

## References


1. X. Zhou, R. Ganti, J. Andrews, A. Hjørungnes, On the throughput cost of physical layer security in decentralized wireless networks. IEEE Trans. Wirel. Commun. **10**(8), 2764–2775 (2011)
2. X. Zhang, X. Zhou, M.R. McKay, Enhancing secrecy with multi-antenna transmission in wireless ad hoc networks. IEEE Trans. Inf. Forensics Secur. **8**(11), 1802–1814 (2013)
3. M. Haenggi, *Stochastic Geometry for Wireless Networks* (Cambridge University Press, Cambridge, 2012)
4. H. Gao, P.J. Smith, M.V. Vlark, Theoretical reliability of MMSE linear diversity combining in Rayleigh-fading additive interference channels. IEEE Trans. Commun. **46**(5), 666–672 (1998)
5. S. Boyd, L. Vandenberghe, *Convex Optimization* (Cambridge Univ. Press, Cambridge, 2004)
6. S. Goel, R. Negi, Guaranteeing secrecy using artificial noise. IEEE Trans. Wirel. Commun. **7**(6), 2180–2189 (2008)
7. R.H.Y. Louie, M.R. McKay, N. Jindal, I.B. Collings, Spatial multiplexing with MMSE receivers in ad hoc networks, in *Proceedings of IEEE ICC, Kyoto, Japan* (2011), pp. 1–5
8. A.M. Hunter, J.G. Andrews, S. Weber, Transmission capacity of ad hoc networks with spatial diversity. IEEE Trans. Wirel. Commun. **7**(12), 5058–5071 (2008)
9. D. Stoyan, W. Kendall, J. Mecke, *Stochastic Geometry and Its Applications*, 2nd edn. (Wiley, London, 1996)
10. M. Haenggi, J. Andrews, F. Baccelli, O. Dousse, M. Franceschetti, Stochastic geometry and random graphs for the analysis and design of wireless networks. IEEE J. Sel. Areas Commun. **27**(7), 1029–1046 (2009)
11. I.S. Gradshteyn, I.M. Ryzhik, A. Jeffrey, D. Zwillinger, S. Technica, *Table of Integrals, Series, and Products*, 7th edn. (Academic Press, New York, 2007)

# Chapter 6
# Conclusions and Future Research Directions

**Abstract** This chapter concludes the whole book and also provides some future research directions.

## 6.1 Conclusions

Human society is striding into the era of "Internet of Everything", and people are becoming more and more dependent on wireless networks to send privacy or sensitive information. In the near future, the fifth generation wireless communications network (5G) is not only a cellular network for mobile users but also is able to support the "Internet of Things". It will become the neural system to support the human society in the information age.

Security has become a first priority in designing a wireless network. Unfortunately, the openness of wireless network architecture and the broadcast nature of wireless communications pose a unprecedented challenge to wireless network security, and modern cryptographic approach alone becomes insufficient for achieving a desired communication security in many practical scenarios, e.g., secret key management and distribution being extremely difficult in a decentralized network architecture without infrastructure and low-end wireless devices with limited computational capacity being not able to use complicated cryptographic algorithms.

Physical layer security, or information-theoretic security, is a novel approach that attains secure transmissions at the physical layer by exploiting the randomness inherent to wireless channels, completely abandoning the dependencies of a secret key eavesdroppers computational resource.

The main contributions of this book are summarized as follows:

- Physical layer security in a single-cell cellular under TDMA is investigated, and a joint wiretap encoding and artificial noise scheme is proposed against randomly distributed eavesdroppers. The secrecy outage probability is efficiently reduced by adaptively adjusting the ratio of the power allocation between the desire signal



H.-M. Wang and T.-X. Zheng, *Physical Layer Security in Random Cellular Networks*, SpringerBriefs in Computer Science,
DOI 10.1007/978-981-10-1575-5_6

and the artificial noise to the instantaneous CSI of the legitimate channel. When a certain level of secrecy outage is tolerated, both adaptive and non-adaptive transmission schemes are proposed to improve secrecy throughput. Both schemes have respective advantages. Specifically, the adaptive scheme provides the maximum secrecy throughput, whereas the non-adaptive scheme greatly reduces the computational complexity and provides a near-optimal throughput performance in sparse eavesdropper situations or under moderate secrecy outage constraints.

- Physical layer security in a multi-tier HCN is investigated, and an analytical framework is built to analyze physical layer security from an outage perspective. In this book, a security-oriented mobile association policy based on an access threshold is introduced, associating each user with the BS providing the maximum average received signal powers beyond the access threshold. Due to the randomness of both interference and wiretap channels, both reliable connection and secrecy transmission for a mobile user can only be probabilistically achieved. Under the proposed mobile association policy, the connection and secrecy probabilities are analyzed, and the tradeoff between them is revealed resorting to asymptotic analysis. The network-wide secrecy throughput is further evaluated, which can be maximized by properly choosing the access threshold.
- Physical layer security in a two-tier heterogeneous wireless ad hoc network is investigated, and a joint FD receiver jamming and spatial self-interference cancellation transmission strategy is proposed. A heterogeneous wireless ad hoc network comprising of a classified communication tier and an unclassified communication tier is considered, where in the classified tier all the legitimate receivers work in the FD mode to jam potential eavesdroppers and in the unclassified tier all the legitimate receivers work in the HD mode. Utilizing the abundant degrees of freedom brought by multiple antennas, a FD is able to not only strengthen signal reception and degrade the wiretap channels, but also eliminate the self-interference caused by itself in the spatial domain. Nevertheless, deploying too many FD receivers will introduce great interference to both tiers. The deployment of the classified tier triggers a nontrivial tradeoff between spatial reuse, reliable connection, and secrecy, and the optimal deployment density is provided to maximize the network-wide secrecy throughput while guaranteeing a minimum required network-wide throughput for the unclassified communication tier.

## 6.2 Future Research Directions

With the research of 5G emerging all over the world, there is no doubt that there are still many gaps to fill in on physical layer security in random cellular networks. To further promote the pace of physical layer security toward really practical approaches, future researches can be carried out in the following several aspects:

- Physical layer security under a more realistic wireless network model. Although PPP has been widely adopted to model the positions of nodes randomly distributed in wireless networks, it is still controversial to model BS's positions using a PPP model. In practical scenario, no one can can find two BSs belong to the same service provider arbitrarily close to each other. In addition, picocells and femtocells are often demand-based but appear in the form of clusters. Therefore, a more proper model for charactering practical network topologies might be that using a repulsive HCPP to model the positions of marcocells and using a clustered PCP to model the positions of picocells and femtocells. Using such a "heterogeneous" network model, the mathematical analysis will bear the brunt. How to achieve a good balance between accurately describing network topologies and providing an analytically tractable framework is a topic worthy of in-depth study.

- Physical layer security based on BS cooperation. In cellular networks, BSs can be connected to core-network infrastructure via a high-speed backhaul network, thus making BS cooperation possible. Through sharing users' ICSI among BSs and properly designing transmit precoding matrices, the optimal balance is likely to be achieved among aspects in link quality, neighboring cell interference and information leakage. Nevertheless, cooperation among all BSs in the network requires a large amount of information exchange, which results in severe overhead and network delay. A proper approach to overcome this is the neighboring cell cooperation, e.g., adjacent BSs gather in a cluster and deal with signals in a centralized fashion. Through carefully choosing the scale of a collaborative cluster, network security performance can be maximized under a premise of reliable communications.
- Physical layer security based on massive MIMO and millimeter wave (mmWave) technologies. Heterogeneous networks, massive MIMO, and mmWave are recognized as the "big three" 5G technologies, where the first technology, i.e., heterogeneous networks has been discussed in this book. The combination of physical layer with massive MIMO and mmWave has the potential to further enhance the security of wireless networks. Specifically, the large array gain provided by massive MIMO can be used to greatly improve the quality of the main channel and the directionality can be used to reduce the signal leakage, the short-range but highly directional communication of mmWave efficiently degrades the wiretap channels. Nevertheless, there are some fundamental challenges facing the physical layer security under massive MIMO and mmWave. For example, the severe pilot contamination and antenna correlation increases the complexity of the design of precoding matrices; traditional artificial noise scheme may no longer be practical due to the extremely high computation complexity of the null space for the large-dimensional channel matrix, and low-complexity jamming strategies need to be developed; an mathematical framework for analyzing physical layer security combined with mmWave with both line-of-sight and non-line-of-sight links needs to be established, and the affect of path loss, blocking, permeation, adsorption, etc., on mmWave communications need to be quantitatively characterized.

Printed in the United States
By Bookmasters

Printed in the United States
By Bookmasters